Visual Basic 6

Addison-Wesley
Nitty Gritty

PROGRAMMING SERIES

Visual Basic 6

Jürgen Bayer

ADDISON-WESLEY

An imprint of Pearson Education

Boston • San Francisco • New York • Toronto • Montreal • London • Munich
Paris • Madrid • Cape Town • Sydney • Tokyo • Singapore • Mexico City

PEARSON EDUCATION LIMITED

Head Office
Edinburgh Gate, Harlow, Essex CM20 2JE
Tel: +44 (0)1279 623623 Fax: +44 (0)1279 431059

London Office
128 Long Acre, London WC2E 9AN
Tel: +44 (0)20 7447 2000 Fax: +44 (0)20 7240 5771
Websites:
www.it-minds.com   www.aw.com/cseng

First published in Great Britain 2002
© Pearson Education Limited 2002

First published in 2000 as *Visual Basic 6 Nitty-Gritty* by Addison-Wesley
Verlag, Germany.

The rights of Jürgen Bayer to be identified as Author of this Work have been
asserted by him in accordance with the Copyright, Designs and Patents Act 1988.

Library of Congress Cataloguing Publication Data
Applied for.

British Library Cataloguing in Publication Data
A CIP catalogue record for this book can be obtained from the British Library.

ISBN 0-201-75876-8

10 9 8 7 6 5 4 3 2 1

Translated and typeset by Berlitz GlobalNET (UK) Ltd. of Luton, Bedfordshire.
Printed and bound in Great Britain by Biddles Ltd. of Guildford and King's Lynn.

The publishers' policy is to use paper manufactured from sustainable forests.

Contents

Part II – Take that!
Programming in Visual Basic 55

Part III – Go ahead!
Advanced programming   215

This is my first foreword, which tells you that this is also my first book. I myself have never read a foreword before. Now that I have written one I can see the reason for it: I want to give you an overview of this book and show you what possibilities are open to you when it comes to the Internet.

This book deals only with Visual Basic, my favorite programming language which is increasingly gaining ground in the face of its competitors. This begs the question perhaps as to why Visual Basic has become such a popular programming language in the meantime.

With Visual Basic you can do everything conceivable for Microsoft operating systems. Visual Basic supports the latest Microsoft technologies so that your programs are always up to date. You can usually download state-of-the-art technologies directly from the Microsoft website, install and (with a little know-how) insert them into Visual Basic.

With Visual Basic you can produce not only normal Windows applications but also (with some limitations) do object-oriented programming, access almost any databases and other data sources, develop reusable components and controls, create real multilayer applications, write multithreading components and create multimedia and Internet applications. So just about everything is possible!

OK, so some features are missing in the current Version 6, for example real inheritance, but firstly you will probably get by best with those features available for standard applications and secondly the new Version 7 adds clear finishing touches.

Visual Basic is not all about advantages and I do not wish to keep silent about the disadvantages. One of the most serious of these is that Microsoft with Visual Basic still carries around a lot of *padding* (you could say *garbage*), which was inherited from the original version of (Microsoft-DOS)Basic. Another disadvantage is that programming of the new features for the current VB versions was very 'sloppy' and favors the user with a lot of inconsistencies and bugs. Unfortunately Microsoft to date has set a lot of store by the development of new features and has hardly, if at all removed the bugs in the old ones. VB.NET adds the finishing touches here. Microsoft has committed each developer in the VB team to develop no more new features but firstly to remove errors in the current ones if they receive reports of more than 25 (it begs the question of how development was done previously).

But I do not wish to join in the chorus of other people in making out that Visual Basic is bad. If you know the pitfalls, VB is a wonderful, fast and simple programming language. I have got used to simply ignoring the defective or bad programmed features I know and, where necessary, using other components (bought or as Freeware mostly from the Internet). You will certainly read some criticisms in this book, but you will find rather more that most features are described positively (I have simply not bothered to describe features which are not going to be used). So that you avoid the pitfalls, I do of course describe the problems as well and usually provide a solution.

And to those programmers who believe C program to be considerably faster, suffice it to say that the VB compiler utilizes the Microsoft C compiler at the lowest level[1].

---

1. This is undocumented but nevertheless reliable information. At first I had wondered why VB sometimes reported a linker error during compilation in Main.C (!), now I know why.

As you may have already noticed, this book is a paperback. Therefore space available is terribly limited compared with a "proper" book. The Nitty Gritty series as its name suggests gets down to the nitty-gritty so everything has to be scaled down. I am working on the basis therefore that you understand the basics of programming and have a sound knowledge of Windows. On this assumption you can learn with the help of this book the most important features and components of Visual Basic. Since Visual Basic in the meantime has become a very powerful programming language, I cannot describe everything in approximately 400 pages. The book does not deal with some of the features and components which are in my view less important (unfortunately including OOP).

Information and tips and tricks

The individual sections of the book are usually laid out so that a description telling you how to use a particular feature in practice follows a general introduction. Then there is an overview in table format showing you the most important elements. The conclusion is frequently a section in which I describe tips and tricks for that particular topic.

The contents of the book

So that you get an overall view of the topics included in the book, I am listing them here, chapter by chapter:

Chapter 1 gives you an overview of Visual Basic and VBA, the programming language used in Visual Basic.

Chapter 2 introduces you to programming with Visual Basic (without however explaining the fundamentals of programming) and gives an overview of the possibilities open to you.

Chapter 3 describes in great detail how you program with VBA (variables, loops, branches, functions, etc.).

Chapter 4 explains the functions of the VBA library and describes the few objects predefined in VB.

In **Chapter 5** there is a description of the correct procedure for dealing with standard controls, the most important ActiveX controls and windowless controls using forms and menus. Because of the large number and complexity of some ActiveX controls, not all ActiveX elements are described in this chapter.

Chapter 6 explains, in my view, the most important program development technologies, with some topics, such as graphics and printing, and database programming only being described in later chapters.

Chapter 7 concentrates on the treatment of run-time errors, debugging and testing an application.

Chapter 8 deals with the output of text and graphics on forms or the printer using VB graphics methods and, by way of example, the Windows GDI functions.

Chapter 9 explains how to deal with FileSystemObjects to access the file system and to read and write text files.

Chapter 10 introduces you to working with databases. This chapter emphasizes the fundamentals of data access with ActiveX Data Objects and leaves untouched many "Quick and Dirty" Visual Basic database features.

Finally, **Chapter 11** shows you how to create an installation version out of your VB project that can be installed on other computers.

What the book does not include

Of course you should also know what topics are not described in the book. For this reason I am listing them here.

What is missing in the fundamental functionality area

→ The financial-mathematical VBA functions
   The financial-mathematical VBA functions are very complicated. In addition I have absolutely no idea about financial mathematics (which is probably why my bank account is always empty).

What is missing in database programming

→ The database tools of the development environment
   The development environment contains tools which display the structure and content of a database and even allow you to edit these (amongst other things `data view`, menu `query` and `diagrams`).
→ Database connections to the Data Environment
   The data environment has interesting potential because you can create connections very quickly to databases and generate queries. However I have always avoided the Data Environment up to now because initializing the run-time is difficult and you lose control of your database connection. I have not described the Data Environment in this book.
→ The utilization of binding controls to a database (the book conveys only the fundamental principles)
   I only describe the basics for binding controls to data sources in this book.

→ Designing reports using the Integrated Report Generator or the Crystal Reports components
The Integrated Report Generator, which can do hardly anything really well, is brought to its limits very quickly when it comes to printing reports. Crystal Reports is the considerably better alternative here. Unfortunately Seagate no longer supplies the Crystal Reports Designer component free of charge, which up to Crystal Reports 6 had been free. Nevertheless on the website I describe how you can produce reports using the Integrated Report Generator and the Crystal Reports component.

→ The query language SQL
SQL is described over and over again in many programming books. I think however this extensive language is better described elsewhere to leave room for the actual programming language features. Therefore you will not find SQL described in this book.

What is missing when it comes to special technologies

→ Multimedia programming
You can achieve simple multimedia effects with some VB controls. If you want to write good multimedia programs, you cannot escape DirectX-API.

→ Remote control of Word, Excel and co
Remote control of Word, Excel and co using COM automation is a very interesting process, in which you can borrow the functionality of these applications for your application without the user knowing anything about it. So I can print my invoices in my accountancy program using a Word document template, which I open in Word from my VB program and which I describe in Word.

Object-oriented programming (OOP)

Object-oriented programming, i.e. the production of intrinsic classes and based on this the production of a listing of classes, class hierarchies, COM (component object model) components and ActiveX controls, is omitted from this book. At first I had planned to include some fundamental information, but this had to be removed again because of lack of space. In addition this information would probably have been too incomplete.

Internet programming

Internet programming is omitted from this book. Visual Basic alone is also insufficient to write good Internet applications. I am in the process of writing a book especially about Internet programming with ASP and Visual Basic in the Nitty Gritty series. Along with buying this book I recommend "Microsoft Active Server Pages" by Jörg Krause.

I hope I have made the overview of this book easier for you.

P.2 Typographic conventions

This book uses some typographic conventions which I hope do not deviate too much from the general norm.

Syntax descriptions

Syntax descriptions are shown as in the following example:

```
[Return =] MsgBox(Prompt [, Buttons] [, Title] _
  [, HelpFile] [, HelpContext])
```

Words in italics in syntax descriptions are placeholders for information you provide. For example, in the above using the *Prompt* argument you have to enter a text that the MsgBox will then issue. The elements in square brackets are optional. You cannot, indeed must not, specify them. If you omit the relevant element, then a presetting is automatically used. Incidentally the square brackets are only a part of the syntax description and are not written in the program code.

Curved brackets with vertical dividing lines are far more rarely used: {*this | or that*}. Curved brackets mean that you have the choice between two or more elements. You have to choose one of the elements, unless all the elements are in square brackets anyway. When declaring variables you can, for example, determine the scope and the lifetime of the variables using the keywords Dim, Static, Private or Public

```
{Dim | Static | Private | Public} Name1 [As Data type]
```

In this example you must therefore either identify Dim, Static, Private or Public

Example listings

Example listings are shown in the font style *Courier*:

```
Dim strDate As String
strDate = Format$(Now, "dd.mm.yy")
MsgBox "Today is the " & strDate
```

Since space on the page is limited, I very often have to use word wrap. Because this is not so simple to do in Visual Basic, I always use the correct syntax in the examples. Where word wrap has to be used in a sentence, an underscore is added to the end:

```
Dim strDate As String
strDate = Format$(Now, "dd.mm.yy")
MsgBox "Today is the " & strDate, vbInformation, _
      "Today's date"
```

If a break is made in a character chain, the character chain has to be concluded before the break and has to be linked with the character chain in the following line:

```
MsgBox "This is quite a long text, " & _
      "which unfortunately has to be broken."
```

The whole matter is sometimes rather unclear, but this is inevitable. You can however also omit the line break if you type out the example (instead of downloading it from the Internet).

Typographic conventions in continuous text

In normal text *language-specific keywords* are shown in font type `Courier`. Words in capitals in normal text describe menus, file and order names and Internet addresses (`File | Exit`, VBA.INI, www.it-minds.com etc.). Keyboard keys **F5** stand for keys and key combinations, which you can activate to start certain actions.

P.3 Where you can find help and further information

You can look for information in Visual Basic Help. Unfortunately this is always installed for the complete Visual Basic package, so that you will also find help topics for Visual C, Visual Foxpro etc. Take care therefore that when you look for a particular item in the Help index the help topic you find actually relates to Visual Basic. As Visual Basic Help in any case is only an excerpt from the MSDN (Microsoft Developer Network), it is better in my view to keep a general search to the relevant Microsoft search page (which I describe likewise in this section). In fact my use of Help is still only context-sensitive, i.e. I put the cursor on a keyword in the program code or enable a control and activate **F1**. The context-sensitive Help function is usually very good.

If I have particular questions I always in the first instance use the Microsoft developer search page (Search.Microsoft.com/Search/us/dev/default.asp). Here you can search in the Microsoft *MSDN* and in the *Knowledge Base*. The MSDN contains all documentation on Microsoft products, whole books, articles and a lot more. The Knowledge Base contains a lot of "How to" articles and bug reports. Here you usually strike it lucky – even when it comes to complex problems.

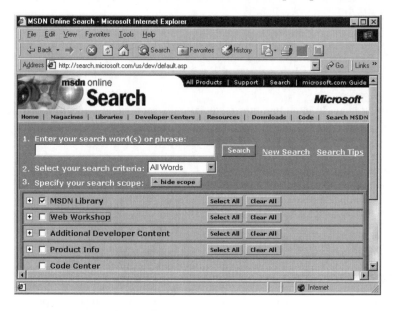

Figure P.1   *Search Microsoft's developer search page*

Figure P.1 shows an example of the search for a solution to the problem of playing `Wav` files in Visual Basic. Ensure that when searching you deactivate the *Web Workshop* and that you always only enter "Visual Basic" in the Search item. Then there is no need to check the individual search areas with the complex secondary options.

If you have no luck with Microsoft, you can still search in newsgroups. http://groups.google.com/advanced_group_search is one of the best addresses.

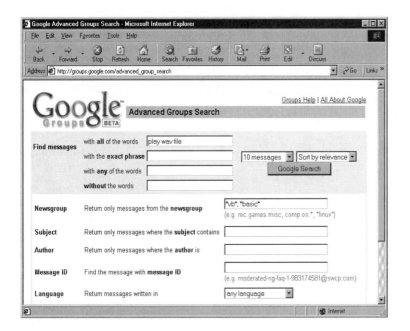

Figure P.2 *Search in Power Search of Google.com*

Enter your search item into the search area at the top of the page. Take care when searching in the NEWSGROUP field that the newsgroups are restricted to those which have at least "vb" in their name. To do this you can simply mask the newsgroup names with "*vb*" and/or "*basic*". You will then only receive results from newsgroups with "vb" and/or "basic" in their name (which is basically all Visual Basic newsgroups). Several newsgroup addresses are simply separated by a comma. Figure P.2 shows an example of this kind of search in Visual Basic newsgroups. You should usually restrict the newsgroups to Visual Basic, otherwise you often find too many contributions from newsgroups which have nothing to do with Visual Basic. However, when you mask the newsgroup with "*vb*, *basic*", you must also take care that the article that you are reading actually belongs to Visual Basic 6. Newsgroups which belong to the new VB.NET likewise have "vb" in their name (e. g. microsoft.public.dotnet.vb).

It is better to identify the search item without "Visual Basic", because you cannot always assume that this name will appear in all contributions. As Figure P.2 shows, you can be quite flexible in your search for all possible combinations of terms. This is an example of the search for a solution to the problem of playing WAV files (sound files) in Visual Basic

If you would like to ask any questions yourself or would like me to answer queries in the newsgroups, I recommend that you use the newsgroups at Microsoft's site. The names of the VB groups always begin with microsoft.public.vb.

So, you are now probably well equipped to deal with the tough everyday life of the programmer. It just remains for me to wish you hours of fun with Visual Basic.

Jürgen Bayer
juergen.bayer@t-online.de

Part I

Start up!

Visual Basic, VBA and VBScript

1.1 What are Visual Basic, VBA and VBScript?

Surely you already know what Visual Basic is (also denoted in this book as *VB*). It is a development system for normal Windows applications, reusable components, database and Internet applications. If you have read the foreword, you will also know why I consider Visual Basic to be a very good programming system.

Visual Basic has its foundations in the Basic language. The fundamental elements of the VB programming language are contained in a version known as *VBA*. *VBA* is an abbreviation of the term *Visual Basic for Applications*, a programming language employed in Microsoft Office as a macro language. However, VBA is now commonly used as the name for the programming language used in Visual Basic, Office and other applications. It is – even in Office – a library of functions, procedures, variables, types and constants. What this means is that VBA can no longer claim to be just the language of Office, even though many books still mean Office programming when they speak of VBA programming. Where I use the term VBA in this book, what I mean is the programming language (independent of Office).

VBScript (Visual Basic Script) has been developed from VBA and is largely identical to it. VBScript is mainly used in HTML and ASP[1] documents for the execution of programs. It is fundamentally comparable with JavaScript, although unfortunately VBScript will only run as a script language within HTML documents in Internet Explorer.

---

1. Active Server Pages (ASP) are HTML documents with integrated programming. Programming is carried out on the server and normally generates pure HTML code on the client for the browser.

1.2 Programming in Visual Basic

Visual Basic is one of the modern programming environments, a group which also includes Delphi. In these environments, you do not have to create the interface for an application in program code, but make use of ready-made forms (windows) and controls. Of course, you will also need to do some programming, but it will be focused on solving the problem and not the shape of the interface. If you soon find yourself running out of controls, you can use VB to program your own controls or other components yourself. Otherwise, you can buy them from other manufacturers (this option often being the better, less stressful alternative) and either incorporate them in your VB project directly (if you have the source code) or include them as ActiveX components. In this way you can keep adding to your "toolbox" over time. You may then reach the stage where you can almost construct an application purely out of ready-made components (although even then you will probably still have to do a little programming of your own).

Another plus point is that VBA, the programming language used in Visual Basic, is very easy to learn and understand. Unlike some programming languages, VBA guards against some errors that in other programming languages, such as C++ or Delphi, can lead to long nights of frustrating searching. It achieves this by applying a simple principle: the programmer has no direct access to the computer's resources. Thus, for example, VBA does not recognize pointers or dynamically allocated memory, it generates a run-time error if an attempt is made to access an as yet uncreated object (instead of causing an access violation, as with Delphi). It also independently manages the release of objects no longer needed (which you have to do yourself with Delphi and C++). Sometimes I feel the lack of some feature or another in VB, but so far I have been able to solve all problems using VBA, even though sometimes I have had to use some special technique or other. The Windows API is always my first resort when looking for a solution. In his book "Hardcore Visual Basic", Bruce McKinney describes how you can go beyond the normal bounds of Visual Basic. If you possess this book, you will even learn how to program threads in VB.

It is well known that VB is the development environment that allows the fastest conversion of ideas into executable programs. And since Visual Basic programs can be extended with classic DLLs and up-to-date COM components, the programming possibilities are really boundless (you only need to know how to go about it).

A further important aspect is the ever closer integration of VB applications and Internet programs. The creation of COM components, which is very simple in VB, and the seamless integration of these components into the Microsoft Transaction Server (MTS) mean that programming web server Internet applications (with ASP) is really straightforward. New components, such as WebClasses in VB6 or the new WebForms and WebServices coming in Version 7, will further simplify the programming of Internet applications.

1.3 What can Visual Basic do?

Visual Basic has developed into a very versatile development environment with which you can create a range of different types of application:

→ **Windows applications**: The traditional use for VB is for creating "normal" windows applications as EXE files. This book is concerned almost exclusively with this type of application.

→ **COM components**: VB can generate components based on the component object model (COM). You can use these components, also known as ActiveX components, in all programs that support the COM model (almost all Windows programs nowadays). ActiveX code components include classes for later generation of objects, while ActiveX controls are objects that also possess an interface. You can reuse COM components in any ActiveX-compatible application, such as Excel or Word, and, of course, in VB projects. You can find a detailed description of how ActiveX components are generated in the article "OOP with Visual Basic" on the Nitty Gritty website.

→ **ActiveX documents**: ActiveX documents are documents that can contain data and program code. ActiveX documents are mainly executed in Internet Explorer. This gives you the possibility to place complete applications in the form of ActiveX documents centrally on a web server and execute them in Internet Explorer. If a user loads a document of this type via the Internet, the ActiveX server belonging to the document is loaded onto his or her computer and installed. This allows the document to be executed. ActiveX documents therefore offer you a very simple possibility for centralized management of applications for any number of clients (assuming the ActiveX concept in question for Internet/intranet use is wanted on an intranet at all). Unfortunately, ActiveX documents only run problem-free under Internet Explorer. Other browsers, such as Netscape Navigator, require plug-ins before they can display ActiveX documents.

→ **DHTML applications**: from Version 6, Visual Basic has an editor for VB-specific DHTML applications. DHTML (Dynamic HTML) is an extension of HTML supported by Microsoft and Netscape (unfortunately differently). DHTML regards all the tags of an HTML document as individual objects. You can react to events that depend on the content of a tag with VBScript or JavaScript and alter these objects dynamically. For example, set the color of a text enclosed within a <B> tag to red when the mouse pointer is moved onto this text and back to black when it moves off again. If you write a DHTML application using VB, it is a simple matter to make it react to the events of a tag, although unfortunately VB does not generate a pure DHTML file but an HTML file, which ties in an ActiveX component created via the project with the <OBJECT> tag. This ActiveX component contains the interface and the program code. Unfortunately, this restricts VB-DHTML applications on Internet Explorer (Netscape Navigator can only handle ActiveX components through a plug-in). In addition, a DHTML application of this type requires that the ActiveX concept which is rightly controversial on the Internet is not switched off in Internet Explorer. You should preferably write pure DHTML applications which – correctly programmed – will also run on Netscape Navigator. You can generate pure DHTML applications with, for example, Visual Interdev.

→ **IIS applications**: IIS applications are ones that are executed in Internet Information Server (Microsoft's standard web server). An IIS application consists of at least one ActiveX code component (contained within the program) and one ASP document. An ASP document is an HTML document extended with program code. The program code is written in VBScript or JavaScript and bound into ASP tokens. An ASP program is executed when the ASP document is loaded in the web server and usually generates pure HTML code for the client. With IIS applications, the ASP document does not contain much program code. The program is accommodated in ActiveX code components that are installed on the server. In principle, the ASP document does nothing other than create an object from these ActiveX code components and use it. What is unique about IIS applications compared with pure ASP documents is that the associated ActiveX code components are written in Visual Basic and can enclose the entire user interface. You therefore do not have to create it in HTML or ASP, both being very laborious processes.

→ **Database applications**: You can take advantage of the highly flexible and homogeneous system of data access using ADO (ActiveX data objects) in all VB applications. This means that, with the same code, you can access a great many database systems from within Windows applications, HTML or ASP applications (with VBScript), in ActiveX components or in IIS applications. Here ADO offers a unified object model and some excellent features (though also some problematic aspects, such as a highly complex error handling system).

1.4 The editions of Visual Basic

Visual Basic is offered in three different editions:

→ In the *Learning Edition* many additional controls and most of the designers are lacking. This version is not suitable for use by professional developers.

→ The *Professional Edition* has the full set of features apart from those specifically needed for developing client/server applications. With the aid of certain tricks and tools, however, it is possible to use the Professional Edition to create client/server applications as well. Incidentally, access to client/server database systems has nothing to do with this and presents no problem with the Professional Edition.

→ The *Enterprise Edition* has additional tools and libraries for developing client/server applications (distributed applications). This edition includes the RDO library for database access, a developer's version of the SQL server, a *Repository* for centralized administration of components, Visual Source Safe for developing in a team and for version control and other – in view of the Enterprise Edition's high price – rather less important tools. That you, as an independent developer, do not necessarily need the Enterprise Edition is made clear by the following comparison. You can generate client/server applications with the Professional Version by applying a little know-how; RDO has now been superseded by ADO, also supplied with the Professional Edition; and you can obtain a developer's version of the SQL server as the owner of a Visual Studio application on payment to Microsoft of the shipping costs.

1.5 Service Pack 4 and other updates

Just when I started putting the finishing touches to this book, Microsoft published Service Pack 4 for Visual Basic and for Visual Studio. Like every service pack, this one repairs a lot of bugs[2] in all the Visual Studio applications and/or in VB 6. Unfortunately, since I had no more time left to test the new service pack thoroughly, I can only recommend that you install Service Pack 3. And you should most definitely do this. Then perhaps you could try out the new version. The service packs from Microsoft are usually very stable. Aside from the service pack, on its website Microsoft also offers updates for a variety of tools and wizards.

---

2. The word "bug" used to denote a program error is said to have come about when programmers of one of the earliest computers were searching for the source of an error. They finally discovered that a bug had caused a short circuit between two of the machine's wires.

Introduction to VB

2.1 Object orientation in VB

In Section 2.1.1 below I explain what an object is.
Objects are extraordinarily important to programming in VB.

Now let us take a look at object-orientation. VB 6 is not *yet* a truly object-oriented programming language. For truly object-oriented programs, we will have to wait for VB.NET. The next version will fully support that which is missing in VB 6: true inheriting.

Even if true object-oriented programming with VB 6 is still difficult, you will continue working with ready-made objects (controls, forms, special objects for data processing, etc.). And if you use modern Microsoft features such as database access with ADO, or wish to exercise remote control over aspects of other applications like Word or Excel, you will not be able to avoid using objects.

2.1.1   What is an object?

The term "object" is not specific to OOP. Indeed, OOP has developed based on the actual properties of the real world. In the real world, we continually work and think with and in terms of objects. Therefore the examples in this section relate to the real world[1].

---

1. When talking about the real world, I mean the world we live in. I know the real world has a quite different meaning for some people.

An object is a self-contained, usually independently functioning unit. Of course, there are also objects that can only function in conjunction with other objects. Thus, for example, a printer is only functional together with another object, such as a computer. However, a person (an object belonging to the class `Human Beings`) functions on its own.

Seen from the logical viewpoint,[2] an object is defined by its *properties*, *methods* and *events*. The traditional definition of the term "object" makes do with just properties and methods. Modern objects also often possess events in addition.

Properties

Properties store the values of an object and thereby define its function and/or its appearance.

A particular car as an example of an object possesses (among other things) the properties `PaintColor`, `TireSize` and `EnginePower`. In a car, the properties `PaintColor` and `TireSize` partly determine its appearance. The property `EnginePower`, on the other hand, determines its behavior, specifically how fast the car can accelerate and what top speed it reaches. (The latter property can also influence the appearance if, for instance, the power is used too extensively on a very bendy road ;-). As a general rule, properties correspond to methods. The property `EnginePower` corresponds in our car example to the method `Accelerate`. If the car has a great deal of power, a call of the method `Accelerate` leads to a powerful acceleration. If the car has little power, the resulting acceleration will be weaker.

In each object, the values of the properties can be adjusted individually. In different car objects, for example, the manifestation of the property `PaintColor` is most probably set differently. Since the properties of objects in the computer – in contrast to the real world – can also be set from outside, we can also influence the behavior and appearance of objects in the computer.

For objects in the computer, properties are usually implemented by means of variables declared in the class of the object. However, certain environments, such as COM, always implement objects using two methods: one which reads the value of a property and one which sets the value of the property. This means that, for example, checking or calculation of set or read values can be carried out. The property `Age` for a person could, for instance, itself ensure at the time of setting that a negative value cannot be set.

---

2. There are a few other ways of looking at the term "object", such as the technical view, according to which properties usually do not exist at all but are implemented by using setting and reading methods, or else from an abstract standpoint.

Access to properties takes place in almost all programming languages via the reference operator (the dot). It is possible as a rule to set and read properties:

```
Variable = Object.Property ' Read property
Object.Property = Expression ' Write property
```

This is how my hair color can be set to red:

```
Jürgen.HairColor = Red
```

If my hair color is to be set to the `PaintColor` of my motorcycle, the following source code applies:

```
Jürgen.HairColor = JürgensBandit.PaintColor
```

However, many objects also possess properties that can only be read or only written. My property `Age`, for instance, can unfortunately not be written, only read:

```
MsgBox "Jürgen is " & Jürgen.Age & " years old"
```

Properties can themselves be objects. This can be neatly illustrated using our example of a person: the person possesses a property `LeftEye` and a property `RightEye`, both of which are also objects.

The setting and reading of properties that are themselves objects works, in principle, exactly as with simple properties, except that they have access to a further object. Thus the property `IrisColor` of my left eye could be set to red (I know, it could have been otherwise...):

```
Jürgen.Left_Eye.IrisColor = Red
```

Methods

With methods an object can be controlled externally. In order to work with an object, the programmer calls up methods for the object. For example, a car should at least have the methods `Start`, `Accelerate`, `Steer` and `Brake`, to make it at least half-way useful.

Some methods have arguments, by means of which you can control their execution. The method `Accelerate`, for example, has an argument that stands for the position of the gas pedal. Assuming the gas pedal can click into any of the positions 0 to 255, with `Call MyCar.Accelerate(30)`, you can accelerate normally (as we all want to, of course...), and with `Call MyCar.Accelerate(255)` you can burn rubber (but then you wouldn't want to do that).

You can either execute methods independently, or dependent upon the value of a property. The method `Start`, for example, is executed independently in conjunction with `Car`. On the other hand, the method `Accelerate` is carried out dependent upon the property `Power`.

Whether the method uses arguments or properties – or neither of these – to exercise control depends on how the object is programmed. We could conceive of a car object (in the computer) for which we have to convert the setting of the gas pedal before the "Accelerate" into a property:

```
MyCar.GasPedalSetting = 30
Call MyCar.Accelerate
```

For objects in the computer, methods are often very important, since it is only by calling up a method that you can work with the object. Methods are comparable to functions and procedures. Indeed, methods are programmed in the class of the object like normal functions or procedures. However, these functions and procedures are always executed in the context of the object.

There are also objects that possess no methods, or whose methods are pretty unimportant. These objects are often used for input and output. A text box control in which the user inputs text is an example of this. We can say that in principle for visible objects, methods are relatively unimportant, while for invisible objects they are relatively more important.

Events

Apart from properties and methods, many objects also possess events. By means of events, an object gives the programmer the possibility of reacting to particular occurrences with program code. This type of programming is known as *event-driven programming*.

In contrast to older, sequentially structured programs, modern Windows applications no longer run from a defined entry point to follow a strict order. Rather they tend to hang around stubbornly waiting for something to happen. If nothing happens, these programs wait eternally (or until the computer is switched off). If you write a Windows program using a modern programming environment, you create event procedures for all events that you want your program to evaluate. These procedures are executed when the event occurs in relation to the object concerned. Once the procedure has been completed, your application (or to be more precise, the active window) waits for further events. For this reason, all the controls and forms make several events available to you at once. Often, though, just a few will be sufficient for your programming task.

The majority of events affecting controls concern user inputs. In principle, it can be said that everything a user can do (with the application) can be evaluated in an event. For example, with a text box control you can react to the user's desire to leave a control by checking the input text for validity.

However, the most important things are often the OK and Close buttons, by means of which you can react, using the Click event, to the user pressing a button. But other events are also important for programming and when describing the various objects, I will also cover the most important events in each case.

Objects in the computer

Everything that forms a closed logical unit within the computer can be regarded as an object. Many objects, such as controls (text input fields, buttons, etc.) or a window, can be seen. Other objects are invisible, and these serve mainly in gaining simple access to the resources of the computer (e.g. the printer or the serial interface) or in making a program more transparent.

In modern operating systems, every application (e.g. Word, Excel, etc.) has now become an object. And each of these objects consists of many other objects (e.g. the individual workbooks in Excel) and, if necessary, can use other objects that are not stored in the application itself (e.g. the graphics object MSGRAPH in Word and Excel).

2.1.2 What is a class?

Every object belongs to a class. The class defines what properties, methods and events an object possesses. This is achieved in that these items are programmed within the class. Thus a class is the pattern used for creating objects. All instances of a class (an object is also designated as an instance of a class) therefore possess the same properties, methods and events. Properties can, however, be set individually for different instances.

On the one hand, classes can be defined as (or compiled into) class libraries, and on the other hand, they can be defined as class modules (in source code). You can very simply link both alternatives into your VB project or you can create them yourself. Some class libraries, such as the VBA and the VB library, are already linked into your project by way of prior settings, so that you can use these classes without further preparation.

2.2 Starting Visual Basic: the different project types

Once Visual Basic 6 starts, you will find yourself facing a range of options for the creation of a new project (see Fig. 2.1). Although in this book we are concerned purely with normal EXE files and the fundamentals of ActiveX components, I will briefly cover all the possibilities to give you a broader overview.

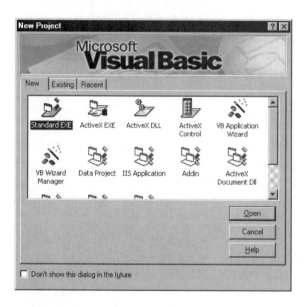

Figure 2.1 *The New Project dialog box*

Behind these options are templates for individual projects and, with some, assistants that will help you create the basic framework of an application. Table 2.1 lists the different project types. Explanations of the project types can be found in Section 1.3.

Symbol	Meaning
Standard EXE	Creates a project to develop a normal Windows application
ActiveX EXE ActiveX DLL	Creates a project to develop an ActiveX code component. A detailed description can be found in the article "OOP with Visual Basic" on the book website
ActiveX Control	A project to develop ActiveX controls
VB Application Wizard	This wizard creates the basic framework for an EXE application with start screen, toolbar, document window, integrated web browser, ODBC log-in window and/or database forms
VB Wizard Manager	Creates a project to program an addin structured as a wizard to extend the development environment
Data Project	Creates a Standard EXE project with previously integrated designers, which simplify work with a database
IIS Application	Creates the basis for an IIS application
Add-in	A project to develop a Visual Basic addin to extend the development environment

Symbol	Meaning
ActiveX Document DLL	A project to develop ActiveX documents
ActiveX Document EXE	
DHTML Application	Creates the basis for a DHTML application
VB Pro/Enterprise Edition Controls	Creates a project to develop a normal EXE file in which all the ActiveX controls supplied as standard are already linked in

Table 2.1   *The project options in Visual Basic*

This book is concerned exclusively with the creation of a Standard EXE and the fundamentals of creating and using ActiveX components.

Note also the tabs existing and recent, with which you can open saved projects.

Ready-made projects

Stored in the folder \Template\Projects within the VB folder are all the ready-made projects that appear in the New Project box as selection options. You can adapt these projects as required. You can also design your own ready-made projects and copy them into this folder. They will then appear in the dialogue box as additional options for creating a new project.

2.3 The development environment

2.3.1   Overview of the windows

The development environment is divided into several separate windows that are dockable – i.e. when they 'dock' onto other windows on contact. Figure 2.2 shows the windows you will see on starting Visual Basic. These are also the most important windows in the program.

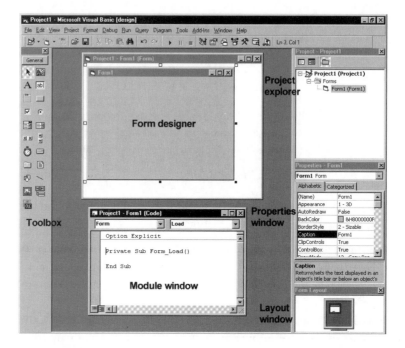

Figure 2.2 *The development environment*

The toolbox

The toolbox contains control objects that you can place on a designer. Depending on the project type (EXE, DHTML application, data project, etc.), the toolbox contains several registers – one with the general controls and others for application-specific controls (e.g. HTML controls for a DHTML application). To place a control on a designer (e.g. the form designer), click on it, release the mouse button and then pull a frame open on the designer.

The form designer

The form designer shows one project form at a time for processing. On the form you can place controls whose properties you can determine in the properties window. From the form designer you can also reach the module for the form. (Double-click on an object or on the form.)

The module window

The module window is where the VBA program code for a module is created. The module shown in Fig. 2.2 is a form module, though the module window can also display other modules. Forms and other objects, such as user-defined controls, each possess their own module for program code which relates exclusively to the object (form, etc.) in question. By using additional independent modules (standard modules) that can be integrated into the project, you can include procedures, functions, variables and other declarations that apply globally for the entire project.

The project explorer

The project explorer is an administration system for your projects. In this window, you can access all the components of a project. It also allows you to administer several projects of different types (Standard - EXE, ActiveX control, etc.) at the same time. The ability to open several projects at once is particularly important when developing COM components, in order to debug them. However, at the start and for simple Windows applications, one project in the project explorer is sufficient.

With a double-click on an object in project explorer or a click on the second button in the symbol bar, you can open the designer window (if a designer is involved) or the module window (if a standard module or a class module is involved). Should you explicitly wish to open the module window of an object, click on the left button in the symbol bar of project explorer. If you mark an object in the explorer window then, as a rule, VB shows the properties of this object in the properties window. But where the designer for the object is open (provided it has a designer) this does not apply if a control is marked on the designer. In such a case, you will need to click on a free space in the designer to see the object's properties.

The properties window

In the properties window you can set the properties of controls, forms and other objects. In order to set the properties of an object, mark the control or form (by clicking on a free area of the form) and either press **F4** or (↑) **Ctrl** + *letter*. **F4** takes you to the properties window, (↑) **Ctrl** + *letter* calls up the properties window and places the cursor on the first property that starts with that letter. The same key combination (usually) also functions within the properties window.

Certain properties are marked on the right in the properties window with an arrow. With these properties, you will only be able to set particular values that are specified in collections. These collections can be opened by clicking on the arrow. By double-clicking on the value of the property, you can step through the collection sequentially, though this only makes sense with short collections, such as Boolean properties (True, False).

With other properties, a switch with three points on it is displayed on the right side. These are object properties, i.e. properties that are themselves also objects. The property Font is an example of this. For properties of this kind, you must click on the button to set the sub-properties (for Font, e.g. Name, Size, Bold) in a dialogue box.

Tip Some of the properties that you can set during the development stage cannot be edited directly using the properties window. You can reach these properties by entering user defined in the properties window. You will, however, only find this entry for ActiveX controls. Further information about this can be found in Chapter 5.

The layout window

In the layout window, you can determine the position of a form on the screen and the size of the form in relation to smaller screen resolutions. (Tip: click with right mouse button on the layout window and select the command Resolution Guides).

Other windows

Aside from the windows mentioned above, the development environment also possesses some others that are used for debugging or for other types of project. Some of them can only be used in these special projects. For example, you would develop an ActiveX control in a *User Control designer*, or a DHTML page in a *DHTML designer*. For space reasons, I cannot give details of all the windows here. Some will be dealt with in later chapters and others concern topics that are not covered at all in this book (e.g. Internet programming).

2.3.2   Fundamentals of writing program code

Events and event procedures

As I said earlier, almost all controls possess events of which you will probably only have to evaluate a few to fill your program with life. Now, in order to react to an event, you will need to write an event procedure in the module for the object that contains the control (this is usually a form, although it could be an ActiveX document). It is normally sufficient if you write a procedure that complies with the convention for the naming of event procedures. Visual Basic then always automatically links procedures with an event if the name of the procedure obeys the following syntax:

```
Private Sub Control name_Event name()
```

However, since many event procedures possess arguments, it makes more sense to leave completion of the procedure to the development environment itself. To do so, double-click on the control or form and then select the event you wish to program from the (right-hand) procedure list in the form module. Figure 2.3 shows an example for a command button.

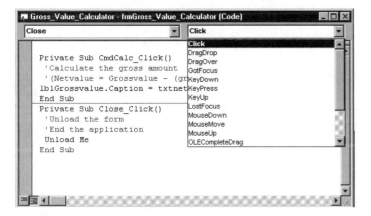

Figure 2.3 *Module of a form with procedure list for a command button opened out*

If you double-click on the form or an element, Visual Basic takes you straight to the Standard Events procedure for this control or form. However, if at least one event procedure for the object has already been provided with code, it takes you to the first defined event procedure in alphabetical order. Now simply select the relevant event from the (right-hand) procedure list. This process is often simpler than selecting objects from the (left-hand) object list if you want to program a particular event. Incidentally, you can simply leave empty event procedures created in this way inside the module. The compiler will then remove them automatically when you compile or test the project.

Alternatively, you can select the object in the module from within the (left-hand) object list of the module window instead of double-clicking on the form.

The syntax helper (IntelliSense)

The development environment offers a very good aid to syntax when writing code (Microsoft *IntelliSense*). For instance, if you write the name of an object and put in a dot, the environment shows you a list containing all the properties and methods (available at run-time) belonging to this object.

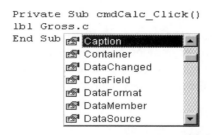

```
Private Sub cmdCalc_Click()
lbl Gross.c
End Sub
```

Figure 2.4 *IntelliSense when writing an object name*

Properties are identified in the list with a hand symbol and methods with a "flying box". You can select an item from the list by simply carrying on writing or using the cursor buttons. You can adopt the currently marked entry by simply writing the text that follows the property or method. This might be a space, for example, if no text follows.

Tip Normally all the properties and methods of the object used are given in the list, but IntelliSense has problems with graphics methods. The method Print is (as far as I know) the only one that does not appear on the list, although it is available for forms, the PictureBox control and the Printer object.

Another feature of IntelliSense is that, when you are writing procedures, functions or methods, their syntax is shown to you.

```
Private Sub asd_123_click()
If IsNumeric(txtNetValue.Text) And IsNumeric(txtVAT.Text) Then
  lblGrossValue.Caption = txtNetValue.Text * (1 + (txtVAT.Text / 100))
Else
    msgbox |
End MsgBox(Prompt, [Buttons As VbMsgBoxStyle = vbOKOnly], [Title], [HelpFile], [Context]) As VbMsgBoxResult
```

Figure 2.5 *IntelliSense when a procedure is called*

The current argument (that you are currently on in the code) is highlighted. An enormous advantage of this tool type is that you no longer have to concentrate on the syntax of functions, procedures and methods.

Tip As with the object element list, IntelliSense also has problems handling the syntax of graphics methods. The syntax of the methods Print, Circle, Line and PSet are not shown.

Tips and tricks

Selecting and positioning controls

You can select several controls simultaneously by pulling out a rectangle with the mouse. All controls that are touched by the rectangle will be selected.

By simultaneously pressing the buttons (↑) or **Ctrl**, you can select or deselect individual controls with a simple mouse click.

It is often necessary to place controls in a line or to adjust their size to each other. To do this, in the `Format` menu, use the commands `Align`, `Make same size`, `Horizontal spacing` and `Vertical spacing`. When aligning, you need to take account of a peculiarity of the VB development environment. It aligns the marked controls to the control that was marked last and not the leftmost, uppermost, lowest or rightmost (as is the case with other development environments). Therefore mark last the control to which you wish the alignment to take place.

Another useful trick is the moving and sizing of controls using the keyboard. Activate a control, press the **Ctrl** button and simultaneously the cursor buttons, and you will be able to move the control. Pressing the (↑) and cursor buttons at the same time changes the size of a control.

Alignment and resizing operations are based on a grid that you can set under Options (`Tools | Options | General`). The preset value of this grid is somewhat coarse. You may find it better to change the value to 40 (instead of 120).

IntelliSense with key combinations

You can use key combinations to get automatic completion of the current term. Press **Ctrl Spacebar**, and the development environment displays a list of the available elements. This does not only work if, when writing an object name, the list has disappeared, but also for normal instructions. If you use a naming convention for identifiers, then you will have no difficulty finding those identifiers again. If, for example, you want in the source code to read or write a text box (whose name always begins with "txt" according to the Reddik convention described on p.78), simply write "txt" and then press **Ctrl Spacebar**. In the list, you can now select the text box with the cursor and then write the program code, *which follows the identifier* (e.g. with the dot).

2.4 The Visual Basic project

An application written in Visual Basic is administered in a project file. The project file contains information about the components and various settings of the application. A project contains at least one form or one module. As a rule, however, several forms and modules are grouped together in a project.

A project can consist of the following components (files):

→ **forms** (.FRM)
Windows equipped with various controls that aid interaction between the user and the system.

→ **standard modules** (.BAS)
Standard modules contain global declarations (variables, constants, types, functions and procedures) that apply throughout the project.

→ **class modules** (.CLS)
Class modules define a class used in the program for creating objects.

→ **user-defined controls** (User controls) (.CTL)
User-defined controls store the definition of a control written by the user. They can be used in normal projects, although they also form the basis for creating ActiveX controls.

→ **user document files** (.DOB)
User document files store the definition of an ActiveX document created using VB.

→ **resource files** (.RES)
Resource files store pictures, text and any data in the Windows resource format[3]. You can read and use these resources in the program using special functions.

→ **WebClasses** (.DSR)
A WebClass defines an ActiveX object which is specifically intended for execution in the Internet information server and which, linked in via ASP documents, generates pure HTML code in the result.

→ **DataReports** (.DSR)
A DataReport enables the design of simple reports based on databases and other data sources.

---

3. Windows resources can be created using a resource compiler (in VB, supplied in the shape of the "Resources Editor" as an add-in). A resource of this type, when linked into a project, is attached to the EXE file. The data for a resource must be read out at run-time using special functions (e.g. LoadResString). The advantage of using resources is that they can be created to be multilingual (with automatic switching over of language) and a resource compiler can also subsequently amend the resource in the EXE file. It is therefore possible, for instance, to alter program text in the EXE file later on.

→ **DHTML designers** (.DSR)

DHTML designers store the definition of a VB-generated DHTML page.

→ **DataEnvironment** (.DSR)

A DataEnvironment is an object that can administer several ADO[4] data sources and simplifies access to the data with visual handling in the design.

Note: The frequently occurring ending .DSR stands for "Designer".

Forms

A form is a window. Contained within the form file is the program code necessary for the running of the program (in the *form module*). A form file has another file assigned to it having the same name, but with the ending .FRX. In this file are stored all the pictures and icons allocated to the form (in binary form).

> **Warning** The FRX file (and with other designers such as User Controls, a corresponding CTX, DOX, etc. file) must always be present if you want to use a form that possesses pictures or icons. If this file is not found on linking a form into the project, all the form's pictures and icons will be deleted.

Standard modules

Standard modules are used for global declarations that can be used by all parts of a program. Modules are comparable with the units of a Pascal program or the libraries of a C program. The difference, though, is that they do not have to be precompiled, nor do they have to be anchored explicitly. On anchoring of a module into the project, all common functions, procedures and global variables of the module immediately become accessible to all the other modules (including form modules).

The project file and the project group file

Visual Basic administers all the components of an application using a project file with the ending VBP. In this file, among other things, all the files assigned to the project are described. When a project is opened, Visual Basic loads all the associated files into the development environment.

---

4. ActiveX data objects allow work with databases and other data sources. ADO is covered in Chapter 10.

In addition, several projects are grouped together in a project group file with the ending VBG. You can do this within the development environment by putting together individual projects using Add file | Project. The grouping together of several projects is actually only usable when developing ActiveX components, in order that you can test these with a normal EXE project. At the beginning, it will probably often occur that you add in a project accidentally. If this happens, simply remove the project using Remove file | project. You will have to accept that, when saving, Visual Basic will want to save the project group file as well (or simply do not save this file).

Starting and ending a VB application

In the development environment, to start a Visual Basic program, simply use **F5** or the menu command Run | Start. Visual Basic needs to know with which form the program starts (alternatively, an application can start with a procedure Main in a standard module, although this is seldom used). You inform the development environment which form is the start form through the project properties (Project | Properties ...). The first of the created forms is entered here as standard. This setting will be stored in the project file.

Once the project has been compiled, you can start the EXE file as normal, of course.

When all the loaded forms have been unloaded again, a VB application is automatically ended. You can also explicitly end the program by putting the instruction End in the program code, although this is equivalent to a hard interrupt and should only be used in exceptional circumstances (sad to say, you can find End in all too many examples).

Warning When End is called, the Unload, QueryUnload and Terminate events (see "Shared events") of the loaded forms are not necessarily called. Possible "tidying-up" work that you perform with these events is then not carried out. Thus the instruction End used in many source codes to end the application is entirely out of place. Even if no tidying up work is done, it might be that in later versions your application will carry out some concluding actions in the Unload or QueryUnload event in one of the many forms of the project. If you think it right in principle that applications such as Word or Excel, etc. should ask you before closing down whether you want changes saved and not just thrown out, then use End only in very exceptional cases.

Using `Create file` | XYZ.EXE, you can create an EXE file out of an error-free VB project. The EXE file can then be executed without VB. You cannot assume, however, that your EXE file will also run on other computers. Visual Basic EXE files always need a few run-time libraries that must be present in their current version or a relatively new version on your computer. Since these are almost always ActiveX components, which must not only be copied but also registered, you can do nothing other than take the trouble to use the "Package and Deployment Wizard", as I describe in Chapter 11.

2.5 Important options

2.5.1   Options of the development environment

Before you really get started, you ought to "correct" a few options of the development environment. The pre-set values of the important options are, as so often with Microsoft, not particularly useful.

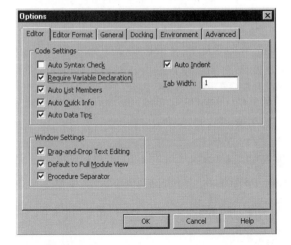

Figure 2.6 *The options of the development environment – the Editor tab with the corrected settings*

→ Under the `Editor` tab, you can specify under the option `Auto Syntax Check` whether syntax errors should be drawn to your attention immediately when writing code. With this option switched on, when you leave a faulty line, VB displays a message with the error description. This message can, after a time, become irritating, since you may well deliberately leave a line incomplete from time to time, with the intention of finishing it later. Switch off this option and use the following trick to recognize syntax errors. VB automatically reformats a correct line on leaving it, therefore always start the VB keywords with lower case letters. Now if no reformatting takes place, the line is faulty.

➔ Under the same tab is the option `Require Variable Declaration`, used for switching off the highly fault-laden implicit variable declaration. This is something that Visual Basic inherited from the first version of Basic for DOS. As explained in greater detail in Chapter 3, implicit variable declaration often leads to logical errors which are difficult to locate. Therefore, switch on this option.

➔ Under the tab `General` you can specify whether VB should compile your program code on starting the program in the development environment *on demand*. If this option is switched on, program code will only be compiled when the function or procedure containing this code is called. In this way, an extensive program can be opened quicker when testing than would be the case with complete compilation. In order to avoid problems, you should switch off this option. With compilation on demand, errors that occur at compilation time (e.g. syntax errors) will only be notified when the code containing the error is compiled. If the option is switched off, "Errors at Compilation Time" will be notified to you right at the start. If you had left a project containing a faulty procedure written with "Compile On Demand" switched on for, say, six months before compiling it into an EXE file, you would probably then no longer know why a particular error message cropped up there.

➔ Also under the `General` tab, you can set the grid spacing to which the development environment "attaches" the controls. I have found a value of 40 Twips (1440 Twips = 1 inch) to be useful.

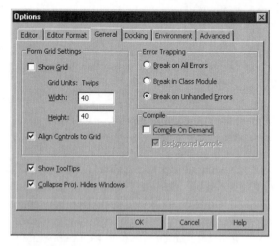

Figure 2.7 *The* `General` *tab under Options with the corrected settings*

➜ Another very important option can be found under the `Environment` tab. Using the setting `When a program starts| Save Changes`, you can make Visual Basic save your entire project when you test the program using **F5** in the development environment. At the beginning, this setting may not appear very important to you. However, when with larger projects VB crashes for the nth time due to an access error and all your most recent changes are lost, you will soon decide in favor of using this option.

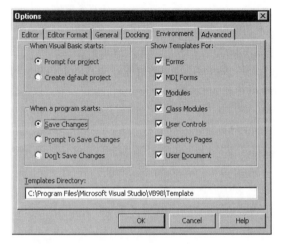

Figure 2.8 *The corrected options under the* `Environment` *tab*

2.5.2 Compiling options

In the Compile options (that you can find under Project Properties), you can firstly determine whether your EXE file is compiled with native code or P-code (packed code). With P-code, your programs are not compiled into machine code, but into a space-saving intermediate code. An "engine" simultaneously compiled into the application interprets this P-code at run-time and converts it to machine code. The advantage of P-code is the compact size of the executable file (about 40 percent smaller than native code). This may also be of interest for executable files that are to be transmitted over the Internet to a client. The disadvantage of it is a significantly lower execution speed (ca. 20 times slower), although this only applies to the execution of your own programs, and not to execution of the code in VBA functions and external objects.

You can optimize native code (the pre-set for new projects) with the aid of various options, even in certain cases for the (old-fashioned) Pentium Pro processor. Pentium Pro programs do also run on other processors, but more slowly. In the other optimizations, you can switch off various run-time checking functions, such as testing for integer overflow. These other optimizations accelerate your program running speed, but will have the result, in the event of a fault, that no run-time errors are generated. This in turn can lead to serious logical errors or even a program crash. You should therefore only switch on this optimization if you are absolutely sure that the relevant error cannot occur (and who is ever that certain? Not me, for sure!).

2.6 A first Visual Basic application

If you start Visual Basic and select the option "Standard EXE" from the project dialogue, Visual Basic creates a new EXE project with a form. In order to demonstrate the fundamentals of using the Visual Basic development environment, in this section I shall explain how you can create an executable program based on this new project. The example application shown here is a simple program that converts an input net monetary value into a gross value (Fig. 2.9).

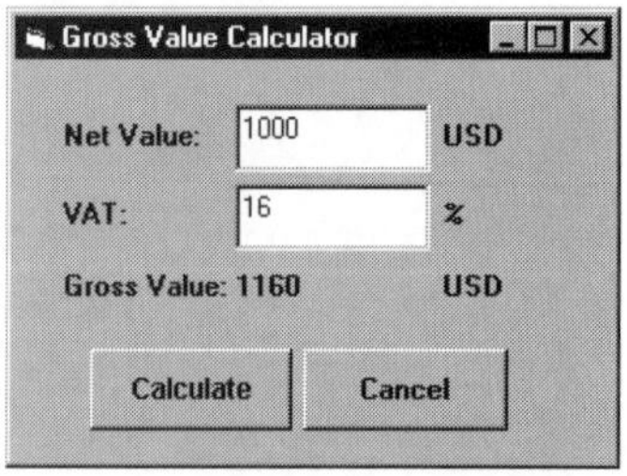

Figure 2.9 *A simple gross value calculator*

Firstly, create a new EXE project and place a text box (which is used as standard for the entry of input) on the form. To do so, click the text box symbol in the toolbox, release the mouse button and pull out a frame on the form (Fig. 2.10).

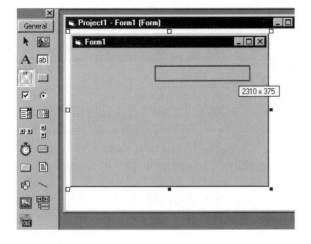

Figure 2.10 *Toolbox with text box activated and form designer with frame for the text box pulled out*

Apart from another text box, place *labels* (you can find the label to the left of the text box in the toolbox) and *Command buttons* (under the text box in the toolbox) on the form until it has the required number of controls (Fig. 2.11).

At this point, I would like to offer you some advice. If, as an experienced Windows user, you select previously positioned controls and copy and insert them via the Clipboard, a dialogue appears and asks whether you want to create a control field. Since you do not yet want to create a control, press the no button. But because, in 90 % of cases, no control is to be created, Microsoft has (as so often) used the yes button as the pre-set, so be careful. If the unfortunate event should occur, then name the controls individually and delete the value from the property Index.

Figure 2.11 *Form designer with the controls required for the example*

Now the labels and the buttons still need to be labeled. To provide text for a label, you will need to set its property `Caption`. To do this, mark the first label and then press **F4**. Alternatively, after selecting the label, you can click directly on the Property window. In the now activated property window, seek out the property `Caption` in the left column. Click in the right-hand column and overwrite the text there with "Gross:". Repeat this procedure for the other labels with the corresponding text. In order to give the button a label, switch its property `Caption` on as well. The text boxes should not otherwise contain any text. To make sure this is the case, in the property `Text`, of each text box, you should delete all text. To avoid a run-time error in the calculation (which occurs if no number is entered in one of the text boxes used for the calculation), enter a numerical value there. Later you will learn how to trap these run-time errors in the program. Then set the labeling of the form by clicking on a free space in the form and then again overwriting its property `Caption`.

Another important step before programming is the giving of suitable names to the controls, which you will later access in the program code. If you have not changed the name (by way of the property `Name`), then you will use the standard name used by VB (Text1, Text2, etc.). A line such as

```
Label1.Caption = Text1.Text * _
   (1 + (Text2.Text / 100))
```

does not, however, tell us much about the identifiers used. Questions such as "what kind of object is this?", "is this a variable perhaps?" or "what is the purpose of this object?" are not in any way clarified by this name. On the other hand, a line such as

```
lblGross.Caption = txtNet.Text * _
   (1 + (txtVAT.Text / 100))
```

is much more informative. The identifiers used simplify your – and other programmers' – access to the program (just try leaving a program for half a year and then attempt to follow your own logic). The prefix *txt* here, for example, indicates that what we are looking at is a text box. In Chapter 3, I explain the *Reddik naming convention* used here.

You should also give the form and the project itself helpful names. For example, call the form *frmGrossValueCalculator*, and the project itself simply *GrossCalculator*. To set the name of the project, you must click the project in the Project Explorer. Then you can set the name as usual in the properties window.

You could now start your program using the F5 button, although since you have not programmed anything yet, not much will happen ☺.

To program a calculation program, double-click on the button. This simplest of routes to the event procedures opens the module window of the form with an empty procedure. This procedure is the event procedure, which is called up when the event Click of the button takes place. Click is always called when a user operates the button in some way. Write the following source text:

```
Private Sub cmdCalc_Click ()
 lblGross.Caption = txtNet.Text * _
    (1 + (txtVAT.Text / 100))
End Sub
```

In this calculation, you will refer at run-time[5] to the property Text of the text boxes, in contrast to the setting of the values in the development environment. You address every text field with its *Name*. The text box to the right of "Net" is used as an output field and you will assign the results of the calculation to it.

Now you need only provide the End button with program code. In the click event procedure for this button, write the following source code:

```
Private Sub cmdClose_Click()
 Unload Me
End Sub
```

With the Unload procedure, you unload, with the aid of the Me operator, the form in which this instruction is written. With that the application is ended.

Before testing, you should save the project. To do so, select the command File| Save project. With this command, Visual Basic saves all open projects, i.e. the forms, modules and project data assigned to the project. If you have set all the options of the development environment as I suggest above, Visual Basic does also save your project automatically when you start the project with **F5**. For files that have not previously been saved, you must input the file name and path, so as to make things clearer for yourself later.

If you now start the program using **F5**, the calculation will be carried out as soon as you click the button. Make sure that the text field contains only numbers and is not empty, otherwise the program will be interrupted by a run-time error.

---

5. Run-time is the time when the program is executed, in contrast to the development phase.

In order to make the program at least partly reliable, add some code to check, before calculating, whether the input is numeric:

```
Private Sub cmdCalc_Click()
 ' Calculation of gross value
 ' (Net = Gross - (Gross* Tax/ 100)
 If IsNumeric(txtNet.Text) And _
    IsNumeric(txtVAT.Text) Then
    lblGross.Caption = txtNet.Text * _
                     (1 + (txtVAT.Text / 100))
 Else
    ' Empty output
    lblGross.Caption = ""
    ' Output message
    MsgBox "Your input is not purely numeric"
 End If
End Sub
```

When you have tested your program and found that it works, produce an EXE file by calling the command `Create gross value calculator.exe` in the `file` menu. This EXE file can now run without Visual Basic, but note that an EXE file of this type is usually not able to run on another computer. VB EXE files always use several different ActiveX components, which must be present in the version used on the development computer. In order to install applications created with VB on another computer, you must previously create an installation packet using the Package and Deployment Wizard. See Chapter 11 for coverage of this topic.

The use of other events taking the example of a USD-Euro converter

The gross value calculator used only the `Click` event of the button. In order to show that other events could also be used for calculations of this type, I will briefly show you the code for a USD-Euro converter. Whenever the user presses (ø) in the USD input, the program must always calculate the Euro value and, conversely, when he or she presses (ø) in the Euro input, it must calculate the USD equivalent.

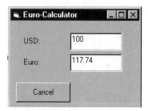

Figure 2.12 *The USD-Euro converter*

To program this behavior, use the `KeyPress` event of the text boxes. This event is always called up when a key is pressed in the text box. By means of an argument, you always receive information about the key code of the button pressed. The source code looks like this:

```
Private Sub txtUSDAmount_KeyPress(KeyAscii As Integer)
 ' When the RETURN button is pressed in
 ' the USD field, the Euro amount is calculated
 If KeyAscii = 13 Then
  If IsNumeric(txtUSDAmount.Text) Then
     txtEuroAmount.Text = txtUSDAmount.Text / 1.95583
  Else
     txtEuroAmount.Text = "Invalid Input"
  End If
  KeyAscii = 0 ' Trick, to suppress the beep
 End If
End Sub


Private Sub txtEuroAmount_KeyPress(KeyAscii As Integer)
 ' When the RETURN button is pressed in
 ' the Euro field, the USD amount is calculated
 If KeyAscii = 13 Then
  If IsNumeric(txtEuroAmount.Text) Then
     txtUSDAmount.Text = txtEuroAmount.Text * 0.85474[6]
  Else
     txtUSDAmount.Text = "Invalid Input"
  End If
  KeyAscii = 0 ' Trick, to suppress the beep
 End If
End Sub


Private Sub cmdClose_Click()
 Unload Me
End Sub
```

Incidentally, I achieved the output rounded to two decimal places as shown in Fig. 2.12 using the `Format` function:

```
txtEuroAmount.Text = Format(txtUSDAmount.Text / _
  1.95583, "0.00")
```

---

6. This factor should be changed to the factor that is valid at the date this program is used. The best way is, to store the factor in an ini file and read it when the program starts.

Part I

Take that!

Fundamentals of the VBA language

In this chapter, I shall describe the fundamentals of the VBA language and how VBA is used within Visual Basic, as well as certain features associated with VBA. You can also use this chapter as the basis for programming in Office applications or with VBScript. However, if you do so, you should note that VBScript does not recognize certain features of VBA. The VBA in Office 2000[1] is identical to the version that Visual Basic uses (because it is actually the same thing).

3.1 Modules

Because your programs will be written in modules, you ought to know what a module is. Visual Basic distinguishes fundamentally between *form modules*, *standard modules* and *class modules*:

→ **Form modules** each belong inseparably to a form and contain exclusively declarations, procedures and functions assigned to the form. The most important procedures in a form module are the event procedures for the form and the controls they contain. You can, however, include other declarations, procedures and functions in the form. Remember that a form is an object and the program code in the form module should therefore only relate to this form. The form module is stored within the form file beneath the form definition. I recommend that you take a look at a form file in a text editor.

→ **Standard modules** contain global declarations, procedures and functions that are not linked into any form but can be used throughout the entire project. A function written in a standard module can, for instance, be called within the project at any point simply by using its name. Standard modules are comparable with the Units in Delphi programs (without class declarations) or the C files in C programs. Standard modules are stored in files with the ending .BAS.

---

1. Office 97 uses VBA 5.0, which is also what Visual Basic 5.0 uses.

→ **Class modules** are special modules for declaration of a class. In VBA, you always declare a class in a separate class module. Later in the program code (e.g. in a form module) you can generate instances of this class.

There are also further module types for special objects, such as user-defined controls. These modules are very similar to form or class modules. Form and class modules do not differ very greatly when you consider that a form is also just an object.

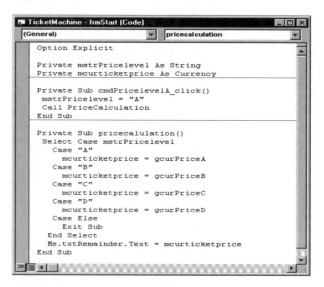

```
TicketMachine - frmStart (Code)
(General)                        pricecalculation

    Option Explicit

    Private mstrPricelevel As String
    Private mcurticketprice As Currency

    Private Sub cmdPricelevelA_click()
     mstrPricelevel = "A"
     Call PriceCalculation
    End Sub

    Private Sub pricecalulation()
     Select Case mstrPricelevel
       Case "A"
         mcurticketprice = gcurPriceA
       Case "B"
         mcurticketprice = gcurPriceB
       Case "C"
         mcurticketprice = gcurPriceC
       Case "D"
         mcurticketprice = gcurPriceD
       Case Else
         Exit Sub
     End Select
     Me.txtRemainder.Text = mcurticketprice
    End Sub
```

Figure 3.1 *A form module with variable declarations in the declaration area and event procedures in the procedure area*

The declaration area

Every module has a declaration area and a procedure area. The declaration area begins at the top and ends where the procedure area begins. The declaration area can be reached via the setting (General) in the object list and (Declarations) in the procedure list, or with the key combination **Ctrl Pos1**. In the declaration area, you can set up all the global and module-global declarations (variables, constants, types) and the module options (Option Explicit in the module in Fig. 3.1, for example, is a module option).

The procedure area

In the procedure area, situated directly beneath the declaration area, all the procedures and functions assigned to this module are implemented. You can create new procedures or functions anywhere in the procedure area by inputting Function *Name* or Sub *Name*.

3.2 Statements, expressions and operators

Statements

In VBA, statements are not delimited as in other languages. The end of a statement is indicated by the end of the written line. From this follows that an instruction cannot simply be broken up, and that several statements cannot be written on one line without further ado. In order to break up statements on multiple lines, you must add an underline character at the end of the line. The statement

```
txtEuroAmount.Text = txtUSDAmount.Text / 0.85474
```

can, for example, be broken up as:

```
txtEuroAmount.Text = _
    txtUSDAmount.Text / 0.85474
```

If, however, you wish to break up a line in the middle of a text constant, you cannot simply use the underline:

```
MsgBox "This is an unsuccessful attempt_
        to break up a text constant"
```

This example does not work, which you can recognize if you try it yourself from the fact that the source text appears in red. In the case of text constants, you must inform the compiler where the text constant ends and begins again. Add individual text constants using the text addition operator (&):

```
MsgBox "This is a functioning attempt at" & _
        "breaking up a text constant"
```

Should you wish to include several statements in one line, simply place a colon at the end:

```
lblGross.Caption = "": txtNet.SetFocus
```

Multiple statements on a single line make the source code difficult to read, so always write only one statement per line (with a few exceptions).

Otherwise, statements are constructed in principle just as they are in other programming languages. Assignments use the assignment operator = (which in VBA is identical to the comparison operator).

Comments

In VBA comments are introduced with a simple apostrophe:

```
MsgBox "Hello World" ' This is a comment
```

Everything that follows the comment symbol is not interpreted as program code. Multiple line comments are only possible in VBA if the comment symbol is inserted before each line:

```
' This is a
' multiple-line
' comment
```

In theory, instead of the apostrophe you can also use the keyword Rem, but hardly anyone uses it and I prefer to avoid it.

Calling-up functions and procedures

When procedures are called or if you wish to call functions so that the return value is not used, you are with two syntax possibilities in VBA. You can use the keyword Call:

```
Call MsgBox("Hello World", vbInformation)
```

Otherwise, you can leave out Call, although then you must not use the brackets:

```
MsgBox "Hello World", vbInformation
```

VBA beginners often make the mistake of leaving out Call and using brackets:

```
MsgBox ("Hello World")
```

Warning If only one argument is present, this version works in principle, but with multiple arguments, the attempt to bracket the arguments results in a syntax error. However, this version has a significant drawback. Arguments that are passed on using "Call by Reference" (which may only become clear to you after you read Section 3.6.2) are thereby explicitly passed on using "Call by Value" if they are bracketed. This can lead to logical errors in the program which are hard to trace. You should therefore note the following:

Tip If the arguments of a function or procedure are bracketed, there must be something to the left of the name of the function or procedure (apart from a colon, naturally). If the statement is not an assignment statement, the keyword Call can be used.

As a lazy person, I prefer to leave out `Call`, because I can then also do without the brackets.

Functions are called in the same way as in other languages if you wish to use the return value. For example, you call the `Format` function which formats numbers, among other things (in this case with two decimal places) like this:

```
txtEuroAmount.Text = Format(txtUSDAmount.Text / _
    0.85474, "0.00")
```

Many procedures and functions possess optional arguments that are signified in the syntax description by square brackets. The syntax of `MsgBox` is a good example of this:

```
MsgBox(prompt[, buttons] [, title] [, helpfile, context])
```

You can simply leave out the optional arguments if you wish. In the simplest case, you put in the comma if another argument follows:

```
MsgBox "Hello World", , "Message"
MsgBox "Hello World", vbInformation
```

You can also alter the sequence of the parameters passed on by using explicit naming. What is more important is the explicit naming of optional arguments, and here you can leave out the following commas. For every argument, write the name of the argument followed by a colon, an equals sign and the value:

```
Name:=Value
```

The MsgBox can, for instance, also be called up in this way:

```
MsgBox Prompt:="Hello world", _
       Title:="Example of explicit naming"
```

> **Tip** Explicit naming has not become established at all in the VB programming community. This is probably due to the fact that you just have to write more. Nevertheless, you ought to know about this option. Word and Excel use explicit naming very intensively when macros are recorded.

Arithmetic expressions and the VBA-specific problem

Arithmetic expressions produce a value (a number, a date, a text) that can be used in further expressions or assignments. In the case of arithmetic expressions, however, you should be aware of a VBA-specific problem. This is that the result of an arithmetic expression possesses a data type (in the memory a particular number of bytes is temporarily set aside for the result). The data type for the temporary intermediate result of an expression in VBA is always the same as the "largest" of the data types used in the expression. Constant numerical values in expressions are interpreted according to their value (in terms of data type). The number 10, for example, is an Integer constant; the number 10.1 is a Single, while 32768 is a Long constant. The problem arises when the individual data types in an expression are smaller than the final data type of the result. An expression like (32767+1) produces an overflow. The compiler reserves an Integer array in memory, although the result is of the type Long. The expression (32768+1) does not lead to an overflow because the compiler reserves a Long array for the result.

In order to avoid this problem, either use sufficiently large data types for the individual operands, convert the individual operands with the conversion function described on page 141 (such as CLng, CDbl, etc.), or attach type identifiers (& for Long, # for Double) to operands. In this way, you will force VBA to reserve a sufficiently large data type for the intermediate result:

```
Dim intNum1 As Integer
Dim intNum2 As Integer
Dim lngResult As Long
intNum1 = 32767
intNum2 = 1
' Use conversion
lngResult = CLng(intNum1) + intNum1
' Convert with type identifier
lngResult = 32767 + 1&
```

Comparison expressions

Comparison expressions produce a result just as arithmetic expressions do, but in their case these are restricted to the constants (defined in VBA) True (-1) and False (0). The result of a comparison expression can (as with every other expression) be used in other expressions or assigned to a variable. Thus, for example, you can assign the result of a comparison expression to a Boolean variable:

```
Dim blnEmptyInput As Boolean
blnEmptyInput = (txtInput.Text = "")
```

Arithmetic operators

VBA uses the arithmetic operators given in Table 3.1.

Operator	Operation
()	Brackets; shift the calculation priority
^	Exponentiation
*, /	Multiplication, division
\	Integer (whole number) division
Mod	Modulus (remainder) division
+, -	Addition, subtraction, negative and positive sign
&	String linkage operator

Table 3.1 *The arithmetic operators of VBA*

I do not intend to describe these well-known operators here. Operators such as \ and Mod might require some further explanation, however.

The \ operator leads to a whole-number division being carried out between two numbers. The result is always a whole number in which any figures after the decimal point are cut off. For instance, the operation 5 \ 2 gives a result of 2. If the operands are decimal numbers, these are rounded beforehand. The whole-number division 5.7 \ 2 therefore produces the result 3 (6 \ 2).

The Mod operator, on the other hand, produces the remainder of the left operator that is no longer divisible by the right operator. The result of 5 Mod 2 is therefore 1. Decimal numbers are rounded exactly as with \: 5.7 Mod 2 gives a result of 0.

For the linking of strings, you can use both the + and & operators. The & operator has one distinct advantage. When linking normal strings with Variant variables, the outcome is a Null value if at least one of the Variants contains the value Null. This usually leads to the run-time error "Invalid use of Null" if the resulting string is to be further utilized. For example, the linking of a text constant with the input in text boxes (whose data type is Variant) leads to this run-time error:

```
Dim varFirstname As Variant
Dim varSurname As Variant
varFirstname = "Zaphod"
varSurname = Null
MsgBox "Your name is: " + varFirstname + " " + _
    varSurname ' generates a run-time error
```

However, if linking is carried out with &, `Null` is automatically converted into an empty string:

```
Dim varFirstname As Variant
Dim varSurname As Variant
varFirstname = "Zaphod"
varSurname = Null
MsgBox "Your name is: " & varFirstname & " " & varSurname
```

Therefore, when linking strings, only use & (unless a `Null` result is explicitly allowed for, but that is seldom the case).

Comparison operations

To perform comparisons, VBA uses the operators given in Table 3.2. Most of these should already be familiar to you. If you compare strings with each other, they are checked character by character using their ANSI codes, whereby the first character is given the highest priority. The string "100" is therefore *smaller* than the string "20", because the ANSI code of the character "1" is smaller than that of the character "2". When comparing strings, it is standard procedure for VBA to distinguish between upper and lower case letters. The expression `"a"` > `"A"` is therefore initially true. However if, in the declaration area of a module, you specify the option `Option Compare Text`, for this module, VBA no longer distinguishes upper and lower case letters. For the comparison of strings the `Like` operator is also of great interest because it allows you to utilize the usual wildcards in the strings. The following comparison operations produce the value `True`:

```
"Meier" Like "M??er"
"Meier" Like "M[a,e][i,y]er"
"Mayer" Like "M[a,e][i,y]er"
"Mayer" Like "Ma*"
```

The `Is` operator is mainly used when you wish to find out whether an object belongs to a particular class or whether the object variable even points to a valid object:

```
' Check whether an object belongs to the class Collection
If objTest Is Collection Then
    ...
' Test whether an object is valid
If Not (objTest Is Nothing) Then
    ...
```

In addition, using Is, you can check whether two object variables point to the same object, although you will probably seldom need to do this.

Operator	Operation
=, <, <=, > , >=, <>	Arithmetic comparison. Strings are compared from left to right on the basis of their ANSI code.
Like	Compares two string expressions. Wildcards (*, ?, #, [charlist]) can be used for the comparison.
Is	Determines whether an object belongs to a particular class or points to Nothing, or whether two object variables point to the same object.

Table 3.2 *The comparison operators in VBA*

Logical and bit-by-bit operations

The operators for logical and bit-by-bit operations are identical in VBA. VBA recognizes – mostly from the context – whether a logical or a bit-by-bit operation is to be performed. But when this automatic recognition fails, you will need to help by using brackets.

Operator	Significance for expressions	Significance for numerical values
Not	Negates an expression.	Flips all bits over (e.g. 00001111 becomes 11110000).
And	*Expression1* And *Expression2* gives True if both expressions give True. If one of the expressions gives Null, then And also gives Null.	*Num1* And *Num2*: In the result, bit *n* is set if bit *n* in both numerical values is also 1 (e.g. 0101 And 0100 gives 0100).
Or	*Expression1* Or *Expression2* gives True if either of the two expressions gives True. If an expression is Null and the other is False, then the result is Null. In all other cases, it is False.	*Num1* Or *Num2*: In the result, bit *n* is set if bit *n* is 1 in either of the two numerical values (0101 Or 1001 therefore gives a result of 1101).

Operator	Significance for expressions	Significance for numerical values
Xor (Exclusive Or)	*Expression1* Xor *Expression2* gives True if one of the two expressions is True and the other is False. If an expression is Null, the result is Null. Otherwise, it is False.	*Num1* Xor *Num2*: In the result, bit *n* is set if bit *n* is 1 in one and 0 in the other (e.g. 0101 Xor 1001 produces a result of 1100).
Eqv (logical comparison)	*Expression1* Eqv *Expression2* results in True if both expressions are True or False. If one expression is Null, the result will be Null. In all other cases, it will be False.	*Num1* Eqv *Num2*: In the result, bit *n* is set if bit *n* in both values is 0 or 1 (e.g. 0101 Eqv 1001 produces 0011).
Imp (logical implication)	*Expression1* Imp *Expression2* gives True if *Expression2 is* True or *Expression1 is* False. Imp produces a logical Or, whereby however *Expression1* is logically negated beforehand.	*Num1* Imp *Num2*: In the result, bit *n* is set if *n* is either 0 in *Num1* or 1 in *Num2* (e.g. 0101 Imp 1001 gives 1011).

Table 3.3 *The logical and bit-by-bit operators of VBA*

The most important operators here are Not, And and Or. When you use the logical meaning of these operands, note the priority of the operators if using several operators in one expression: Not is evaluated before And, while And is carried out before Or. For the sake of certainty, always use brackets when combining logical operations. An expression like

```
datInceptiondate< "01.01.90" And _
 intOrderphase = 100 OR intOrderphase = 200
```

does not produce the expected result, as you can see if you bracket the operations according to their priority:

```
(datInceptiondate < "01.01.90" And _
 intOrderphase = 100) OR intOrderphase = 200
```

Therefore, always include suitable brackets:

```
(datInceptiondate < "01.01.90") And _
  ((intOrderphase = 100) OR (intOrderphase = 200))
```

This applies in particular if you use `Not`. You must also beware in cases where the compiler is additionally able to evaluate an operator as a bit-by-bit operator. As a general rule, brackets help with this.

3.3 Declaring variables

As with all other programming languages, VBA supports variables for storing intermediate results, for holding set data and for other programming techniques. Unfortunately, VBA still allows implicit declaration whereby you do not have to declare variables yourself (i.e. explicitly). Luckily, however, you can switch off the implicit declaration function by means of a module option.

3.3.1 Implicit declaration

If you have not switched on compulsory explicit declaration, variables that are not explicitly declared are declared implicitly by Visual Basic on their first use in the source text as local variables with the Standard data type (default setting: `Variant`). See also page 72.

> **Tip** You should always avoid implicit declarations. Using them, you are certain to create errors that are difficult to locate. If, for example, you accidentally spell a variable name wrongly, VBA simply declares a new, empty variable and your statement does not use the correct value.

3.3.2 Explicit declaration

Using the module option `Option Explicit` in the declaration area of a module, you can set up VBA so that no implicit declarations are permitted in this module. The result, if non-explicitly declared variables are used, will then be that an error occurs on compilation. The instruction `Option Explicit` ought really to be burned into every module, so that it could never be removed again. Other programming languages do not entertain such a nonsense[2] as implicit variable declaration. You should in any event switch on the setting `Require Variable Declaration` in the Options, so that `Option Explicit` will be automatically added to every mo-

---

2. Please do not misunderstand me. I consider VBA to be a very good programming language, but Microsoft has carried huge quantities of padding over from the first version of Basic for DOS. It is about time that this purposeless baggage was finally jettisoned.

dule. You should definitely check existing modules and, if necessary, set `Option Explicit` for them by hand.

With explicit declaration, variables are declared as follows:

```
{Dim | Static | Private | Public} Name1 [As Data type] _
             [, Name2 [As Data type]] [...]
```

The various declaration variants differ with respect to area of validity and life-span. Table 3.4 describes the different types of declaration.

Declaration	Where ?	Validity	Life-span
Dim	In a procedure or function	Automatically local	Only for as long as the procedure or function "lives"
Static	In a procedure or function	Static local	For as long as the program runs
Private	In the declaration area of a module	Module global	For as long as the program runs
Public	In the declaration area of a module	Program global	For as long as the program runs

Table 3.4 *The areas of validity and life-spans of variables*

```
' Program global integer variables
Public gintLeft As Integer
' Module global string variable
Private mstrFirstname As String

PrivateSub Test()
 ' Automatic local integer variable
 Dim intIndex As Integer
 ' Static local long variable
 Static slngPosition As Long
End Sub
```

A common error on declaration

If several variables are declared in a line, programmers often make the mistake of not quoting the data type for all the variables. If, for instance, you wish to declare three long variables on one line, you must declare them as in the following example:

```
Dim lngZ1 As Long, lngZ2 As Long, lngZ3 As Long
```

The usual mistake would look like this:

```
' if you are used to working with Delphi
Dim lngZ1, lngZ2, lngZ3 As Long
' if you usually work with C
Dim lngZ1 As Long, lngZ2, lngZ3
```

In the first faulty declaration, only the third variable is of the Long type, while in the second declaration only the first one is. All the other variables are of the default data type Variant. Therefore, take care that you always specify the data type.

Automatic local variables

Automatic local variables only apply within the procedure or function in which they are declared. With every call of the procedure/function, a variable of this type is created afresh and initialized with a null value. For numerical values, this is the figure 0, while for strings it is an empty string ("").

You should choose local variables if you only need the variable within the procedure or function. Many programmers make the mistake (usually out of laziness) of always declaring variables in the declaration area of the module. You may also make the mistake yourself if you want to reduce the legibility of your program (which can, after all, be intentional). If so, then a few long nights of searching for the cause of errors resulting from logical inconsistencies built in like this are sure to convince you that variables should be declared as locally as possible. If a module global variable is described in a procedure and then read in another procedure, really unpleasant logical errors can be the result. A simple example involving two procedures, each of which executes a loop, should illustrate the problem clearly:

```
Private i As Integer

Private Sub cmdLoop1_Click()
  While i < 3
    MsgBox i
    i = i + 1
  Wend
End Sub

Private Sub cmdLoop2_Click()
  While i < 3
    MsgBox i
    i = i + 1
  Wend
End Sub
```

If one of the buttons is pressed first, for every further press, no further loop is executed. This example is very simple, but it demonstrates the problem. Of course, you could solve the problem with a simple initialization of the variables, but believe me, in bigger projects, this problem will occur in a similar form. Therefore, use local variables wherever possible.

Static local variables

Static local variables are, just like automatic local variables, valid only within the procedure or function, although they are not removed from memory as long as the program is running. Therefore, these variables possess the same value on the next call of the procedure or function as when the procedure or function was last exited. You can therefore lastingly note values in a procedure or function without having to declare the variables module globally.

A simple program is designed to increment a variable on clicking a button and output the result in each case:

```
Private Sub cmdCount_Click()
 Static slngCount As Long
 slngCount = slngCount + 1
 MsgBox slngCount
End Sub
```

By setting Static before the procedure header, you can declare all the variables of a procedure to be static. You should not do this, though, unless you want specifically to worsen the legibility of your source text.

Module global variables

Module global variables (declared with Private) apply within the module in that they are declared in all procedures and functions and keep their value for as long as the program is running. You should always use module global variables when you have to exchange data between several procedures and functions within the module and the exchange cannot be done using arguments. This is particularly the case with event procedures in which you cannot extend the argument list. The counter in the last example should count via one switch and output the counter value through another switch:

```
Private mlngCount As Long

Private Sub cmdCount_Click()
 ' Increment the counter
 mlngCount = mlngCount + 1
End Sub


Private Sub cmdOutput_Click()
 ' Output the number
 MsgBox mlngCount
End Sub
```

Program global variables

Module global variables apply only within the module in which they are declared. If you need to exchange the value of a variable between several modules, you should use program global variables. These can be declared in a standard module using `Public` declarations. Program global variables apply throughout the program. A good example of a program global variable is the name of a database that you need to open in your project within several forms. On starting the application, you write this file name in a program global variable (e.g. by letting the user find the name in a dialogue box). You will then always use this when you have to open the database. The counter example could be extended so that outputting takes place in a separate form, and you will then need a program global variable there.

Declarations in forms

Within a form module, the same goes for `Private` declarations as for these declarations in standard modules. `Public` declarations of variables, however, automatically become new properties of the form (and not program global variables). You can access these properties from outside via the object syntax. New properties of this type should always be used if a form is to pass back some value or other to the caller after closing. An example to illustrate this is given in Chapter 5.

Priority of declarations

When a variable is declared whose identifier has already been used for a variable from a higher area of validity, the new declaration is always used in the current block, without overwriting the higher declaration going outwards.

In the case of variables having the same name and different areas of validity, access takes place in order of the priorities: *local*, *module global*, *program global*.

```
' Declaration in the declaration area
Private x As integer

Sub Test ()
  ' Declaration in the procedure. Since the variable x
  ' is declared locally, at this point the local
  ' and not the module global variable is used
  Dim x As integer
  x = 10
  ...
End Sub
```

> **Tip** If you use the Reddik naming convention for identifiers, this type of thing cannot happen to you, because module global and global variables have different prefixes ("m" and "g"). The Reddik naming convention is explained from page 78 on.

3.4 The data types

The standard data type

If, when declaring variables, you give no data type or permit implicit declaration to take place, the variable will be assigned the standard data type. If a default data type is not set using Def *data type*, then VBA uses the data type Variant. In the declaration area of a module, the standard data type can also be set, using the Def *data type* statement for variables beginning with a particular character, to other data types. (This is something that no one does any longer, because other people tell them they must never do it.)

Tips and tricks

Always make declarations with the data type

Declare all variables with the data type, even when the data type is Variant. Your source text will then become more transparent and less prone to errors.

3.4.1　The VBA data types

If you declare variables explicitly and would like to do without the slow and un-
certain data type `Variant`, then use the data types described in Table 3.5 when
declaring variables, arguments, properties and function return values.

Data type	Value	Value range
Byte	1 Byte whole number	0 to 255
Integer	2 Byte whole number	−32,768 to +32,767. Warning: In most other programming languages, an integer is 32 Bits long, whereas in VBA it is only 16 Bits.
Long	4 Byte whole number	−2,147,483,648 to +2,147,483,647
Single	4 Byte floating point number	$-3.4 * 10^{38}$ to $-1.4 * 10^{-45}$ for negative numbers $+1.4 * 10^{-45}$ to $+3.4 * 10^{38}$ for positive numbers
Double	8 Byte floating point number	$-1.8 * 10^{308}$ to $-4.9 \ 10^{-324}$ for negative numbers, $4.9 * 10^{-324}$ to $1.8 * 10^{308}$ for positive numbers
Currency	8 Byte fixed point number for financial calculations	−922,337,203,685,477.5808 to 922,337,203,685,477.5807
Date	8 Byte floating point number	1.1.100 to 31.12.9999 A `Date` variable can have, on the one hand, a double value and, on the other hand, a string value assigned to it. The string must only contain a valid date.
Boolean	2 Byte Truth value	True, False
String * n (fixed string)	Character sequence of fixed length (Dim s As String * n)	1 to 65,535 characters long
String (dynamic)	Character sequence of dynamic length	0 to 2,147,483,648 (2^{31}) characters long
Variant	Variable data type: Date/time, numerical value, character sequence, Null, array or objects	Date: 1.1.100 to 31.12.9999 Numerical value: as Double Character sequence: as string

Data type	Value	Value range
Decimal (sub-group of Variant)	Highly precise 12 Byte floating point data type with up to 28 decimal places. A maximum of 29 digits can be used	Largest value: $+/- 7.9228162514 * 10^{28}$. Smallest value: $1 * 10^{-28}$

Table 3.5 *The VBA data types*

As a relic from the prehistory of Basic, for certain data types, in the declaration instead of "As *data type*", you can also input a type label. Thus it is also possible to declare an integer variable with

```
Dim i%
```

Do not, however, do this. First of all, your source text will become untransparent and, second, relevant type labels do not exist for all the data types. For the identification of the data type of a variable, you would do better to use the Reddik naming convention (see page 78).

Floating point data types

Floating point data types always store a specified maximum number of digits. The possible number of decimal places depends on how many digits are stored before the decimal point. For example, Single can only store two decimal places if five digits are stored before the decimal point. Single is therefore normally not very suitable. You should preferably use Double, since with five figures before the point this data type can store nine decimal places. With one digit before the point Double can store about 15 decimal places, while Single can only manage about seven. Incidentally, the data type Decimal, if correctly used, can store up to 28 decimal places.

If you would like to try it out for yourself, test the following source code in the direct window:

```
? CSng(1 / CDec(3)) ' Decimal points using Single
? CDbl(1 / CDec(3)) ' Decimal points using Double
? CDec(1 / CDec(3)) ' Decimal points using Decimal
```

Numerical constants

If you use numerical constants in the source code, very large or very small numbers can also be written using scientific notation. For example, 1E3 corresponds to $1 * 10^3$ (1000), and 1E-3 represents $1 * 10^{-3}$ (0.001). Hexadecimal notation is also possible, of course, and in that case the numbers need to be preceded by &H e.g. &HFF represents 255. According to the VB documentation this is adequate, but in practice you should add another "&" onto the number: &HFFFF gives the value (goodness only knows why) –1, whereas &HFFFF& correctly gives the value 65535. If, in this notation, you swap the "H" for an "O", you will then be using the octal notation (the need for which I have never understood).

Decimal

The data type Decimal is a sub-group of Variant and cannot be declared separately. You can generate a Variant of this type by using the CDec function:

```
Dim varDecimal As Variant
varDecimal = CDec(0)
```

Decimal is a special data type with a fixed number of digits (29). You can rapidly calculate how many decimal places this data type can store if a particular number of digits before the decimal point is supported. You can use Decimal if you want to perform highly precise calculations. You need only to take care that at least one Decimal data type occurs in the calculation, so that the compiler will reserve a sufficiently large storage area. If you do not use any such variable in the calculation or you work with constants, you can also simply convert the operands using the CDec function. The following calculation, for example, does not produce a Decimal value but rather a Double value:

```
Dim varResult As Variant
varResult = 1 / 3
```

With a conversion, a Decimal value results, as required:

```
Dim varResult As Variant
varResult = 1 / CDec(3)
```

Decimal is also required for access to fields of this data type in SQL server and Oracle databases.

Date values

For the storage of date values, VBA uses a Double value, in which the portion before the decimal point represents the days elapsed since 30.12.1899 (thus 1.1.1900 has the value 2) and the portion after the decimal point gives the number of seconds elapsed since 00:00:00. Thus a day has a value of 1 and a second a value of $1.1574074 * 10^{-5}$ (corresponds to 1 / (24*60*60)). Since a date value can also be negative, VBA supports date and time values between 1.1.100 and 31.12.9999.

Warning If you wish to exchange date values between VBA and external systems, in rare cases problems can arise with the database. Excel, for example, calculates dates from a starting point of 31.12.1899. The number 2, therefore, which in VBA represents 1.1.1900, stands in Excel for 2.1.1900! As a result, if you communicate with such systems, you may have to convert dates.

Strings

Strings are automatically administered dynamically within VBA if when declaring you do not force a fixed string to be defined:

```
Dim strDynamic As String   ' dynamic string
Dim stfFix As String * 80 ' fixed string
```

A fixed string is always automatically filled with spaces if fewer than the maximum number of characters are stored in the string. Fixed strings are actually only needed when you wish to write to and read your own files using VBA functions. In other cases, you should not use fixed strings, since they are awkward to use due to the automatic filling with spaces.

Dynamic strings are much more flexible. If necessary, when a dynamic string is written to, VBA sets up a new memory area corresponding to the length of the string and copies the string into it. What is more, dynamic strings are not filled with spaces and are able to store more characters. I therefore recommend that you use only these strings. If you have doubts about the performance of dynamic strings, the fact is that they are often processed even quicker than static strings.

An important function in connection with strings is the comparison of two strings. In VBA, string comparisons are case-sensitive, so if you do not wish letter case to be taken into account in comparisons, you should include the option `Option Compare Text` in the module. Quite apart from this, you can also determine the comparison type individually by using functions like `StrComp`:

```
StrComp(string1, string2[, compare])
```

Like many other string functions, `StrComp` has a setting in the third argument that determines which comparison type will be used. `vbBinaryCompare` signifies a comparison taking account of the difference between upper and lower case, while `vbTextCompare` is not case-sensitive.

Variant

The `Variant` data type can store numerical, date/time and string data, the value `Null` (which other data types cannot store) and arrays, and it can also refer to objects (i.e. it can do everything). If you use Variants in expressions, VBA automatically converts the data in the Variant into a data type that is usually appropriate and corresponds to the expression. Automatic conversion does have its advantages. For instance, it is only in this way that you can be sure of the `Text` property of a text box, as was the case at the start in the gross value calculator. The disadvantages, however, are not insignificant either. For example, the compiler decides which data type will be used for the operation. In certain cases, unfortunately, this decision is the wrong one. An example would be a situation where you create a form with two text boxes and one button with the following source code:

```
Dim dblResult As Double
If IsNumeric(txtNum1.Text) And _
    IsNumeric(txtNum2.Text) Then
    dblResult = txtNum1.Text + txtNum2.Text
    MsgBox dblResult
End If
```

If, say, in the one text box, the number 100 is input and, in the other one, the number 200, the result is not, as expected, 300, but 100200! The compiler evaluates the data type as String and then joins the two strings together.

> **Tip** When performing calculations with Variants, you should therefore always explicitly convert them. To this end, a variety of *Cxyz* functions is provided (such as `CLng` and `CDbl`).

```
Dim dblResult As Double
If IsNumeric(txtNum1.Text) And IsNumeric(txtNum2.Text) Then
    dblResult = CDbl(txtNum1.Text) + CDbl(txtNum2.Text)
    MsgBox dblResult
End If
```

Naturally enough, you must take care that the data in the Variant corresponds to the basic data type for the operation concerned. An arithmetic operation using Variants will generate a "Type Mismatch" run-time error if one of the Variants has a non-numerical value (e.g. a string not consisting of digits). If you wish to ascertain the basic data type before calculations or assignments, you can use the functions `IsNumeric`, `IsDate`, `IsEmpty` and `IsNull`. The function `VarType` gives you more precise information about the data type received, but you do not actually need this information (personally, I have never yet used the `VarType` function). The functions for ascertaining data type are described in Chapter 4.

> **Tip** Whenever you can avoid them, you should preferably not use Variants. The ability to store any data type does not exactly make working with Variants simple. In addition, they always require more space than other VBA data types and operations involving them are very slow. Since, however, the properties of all controls and particularly the property Value of the field objects with which you read and write to the fields of database tables are of the `Variant` data type, you will need a basic knowledge of this type.

Variant is the only data type that can store the value `Null`. Under normal circumstances, you cannot do anything with this value which represents "nothing". Nevertheless, the `Null` value appears very frequently in database fields. In this case, you will need to determine, usually with the aid of the `IsNull` function, whether a Variant has normal data in it or if it contains `Null` before you can carry out any operations with the content of the database field.

3.4.2   The Reddik naming convention

The Reddik naming convention, which is now used by a great number of VBA programmers, was originally developed by Greg Reddik, President of Gregory Reddik & Associates, which specializes in development work using Access, Visual Basic and C++. He worked in the Access development team for four years and his "Reddik VBA Name Conventions" are derived from the Hungarian notation and adapted to VBA. To lend your programs an extra level of quality and to make them easier to read and edit, I urge you to use this convention – and use it consistently.

The fundamental form of the Reddik naming convention is:

```
[Prefix]Type abbreviation[basic name[Suffix]]
```

The *Type abbreviation* comprises a lower case character sequence – usually three characters long – that specifies the data type of the variable or object. The *Prefix*, also written in lower case, attaches additional information onto the abbreviation, such as the area of validity of a variable. The *basic name* is the actual name of the variable or object. In order to separate it from the type abbreviation, the first character is written in capitals. The *Suffix* attaches additional information to the basic name. To distinguish it, again the first character is put in capitals.

For reasons of space, I have not set out the complete convention here, only the most important part.

Prefixes for area of validity and life-span

In order to identify the area of validity and the life-span of a variable, use the prefixes shown in Table 3.6.

Prefix	Area of validity and life-span	Example
(none)	Local automatic	intIndex
s	Local static	sdblSum
m	Private (module global)	mintPosition
g	Public (global)	gstrName

Table 3.6 *Prefixes for area of validity and life-span in the Reddik naming convention*

Prefixes for arrays

For arrays use the prefix "a":

```
aintFontSizes ' local array of integer values
mastrNames   ' module global array of strings
```

Type abbreviations for variables

The type abbreviations shown in Table 3.7 are taken from the Visual Studio documentation (look in the index under "Programming conventions"). For some of the type abbreviations, I have used a different one than that given by MSDN, in which case the original is also shown in brackets.

Data type	Type abbreviation	Example
User-defined type (with `Type` **declared)**	udt (User-defined type)	udtAddress
`Boolean`	bln	blnOK
`Byte`	byt	bytAge
`Currency`	cur	curFee
`Date`	dtm (**D**ate**T**ime)	dtmBirthday
`Double`	dbl	dblDiscount
`Integer`	int	intYear
`Long`	lng	lngIndex
`Object`	obj	objWord
`Object`	obj	objAddress
`Single`	sng	sngPrice
`String`	str	strFilename
String of fixed length	stf	stfPath
`Variant`	var	varTemp

Table 3.7 *The type identifiers for variables*

Type abbreviations for forms and menus

Control	Type abbreviation
Form	frm
MDI form	mdi
Menu	mnu

Table 3.8 *The type identifiers for forms and menus*

Type abbreviations for standard controls

Control	Type abbreviation
CheckBox	chk
ComboBox	cbo
CommandButton	cmd
Control, general	ctl
Data	dat

Control	Type abbreviation
DirListBox	dir
DriveListBox	drv
FileListBox	fil
Frame	fra
HScrollBar	hsb
Image	img
Label	lbl
Line	lin
Listbox	lst
OLE	ole
OptionButton	opt
PictureBox	pic
Shape	shp
Textbox	txt
Timer	tmr
VScrollBar	vsb

Table 3.9   *The Reddik type abbreviations for standard controls*

Type abbreviations for ADO objects

Control	Type abbreviation
Command	cmd
Connection	con
DataEnvironment	env
Field	fld
Recordset	rst
Report	rpt

Table 3.10   *The Reddik type abbreviations for ADO objects*

Constants

Constants can be given the type abbreviation con. Usually, however, programmers write constants with capital letters without a type identifier:

```
Private Const VAT = 15
```

User-defined types and classes

For user-defined types and classes, you should use an abbreviated form of the type or class name. If, for instance, you have a class XPrint, use the type abbreviation *xpn* or similar. If you cannot find a suitable type identifier, you could simply use *udt* (user-defined type).

Procedures / functions

When declaring procedures, you should always specify the applicable area of validity (`Private` or `Public`). For all arguments, you should use the supplement `ByRef` or `ByVal`. Arguments are named like variables of the same type, with the difference that arguments which are passed on *by Reference* (see from page 102) have an "r" in front of them.

```
Private Sub TestValue(ByVal intInput As Integer, _
    ByRef rlngOutput As Long)
Public Function GetValue(ByVal strKey As String, _
    ByRef rgph As Glyph) As Boolean
```

Tip Since procedures and functions will often also be used by other programmers, the naming conventions for the arguments of procedures and functions are frequently not used. The reason for this is that you should not force other programmers to use your convention.

Suffixes

Suffixes are used to provide extra information with a variable. As well as the standard suffixes given in Table 3.11, you can use your own.

Suffix	Meaning
Min	The very first element of a field or a list.
First	The first element used in a field or a list during the current operation.
Last	Like First for the last element.
Lim	The upper limit of elements used in a field or list. Comparable with the UBound function.
Max	The very last element of a field or list.
Cnt	Used in database applications to identify a data field of the type Counter (Counter, Auto Value).

Table 3.11 *The suffixes of the Reddik naming convention*

3.4.3   Static arrays

The term *Array* as used in Visual Basic signifies a field of several variables. In C, such a field would be called a vector. Arrays permit the coherent saving of several pieces of information of the same type, so that the individual information items can be accessed via an index. VBA differentiates between static and dynamic arrays.

> **Tip** Before you concern yourself too intensively with arrays, you should look at the `Dictionary` class from page 114 on. This is significantly more flexible and even faster for searching than a static or dynamic array.

Static arrays are declared as follows:

```
{Dim | Static | Private | Public} Name ( _
       Number Dimension1 [, Number Dimension2] [...] ) _
       [As Data type]
```

The area of validity (`Dim` and `Static` in procedures, `Private` and `Public` in the declaration area of modules) corresponds to that of variable declarations. You must, however, take care that in a form module, no `Public` arrays can be declared. Arrays can have the same data types as variables. In principle, therefore, you can save anything in an array.

Number gives the number of data fields for each dimension. In VBA, a maximum of 60-dimensional arrays are possible. Multi-dimensional arrays are hardly ever needed nowadays and in place of these, many programmers prefer to use `Collection` objects or `Dictionary` objects.

If you declare an array without using the `To` convention, the array normally begins with 0 (as so often, you can again set the start index in VBA with an option `Option Base`...) and ends with the number given. An array that is declared as follows:

```
Dim aintTest(3) As Integer
```

therefore has four elements (with index 0 to 3). In order to avoid such confusion, you should always use the `To` convention:

```
Dim aintTest(1 To 4) As Integer
```

Now the index goes from 1 to 4.

Access to an array then takes place via the index:

Arrayname(Index Dimension 1 [, Index Dimension 2] [...])

```
' One-dimensional array
Dim aintTest1(1 To 4) As Integer
' Two-dimensional array
Dim aintTest1(1 To 2, 1 To 4) As Integer
Dim intNum As integer
' Write 2nd element into a one-dimensional array
aintTest1(2) = 11
' Read 2nd element in a one-dimensional array
intNum = aintTest(2)
' Write 3rd element of the 2nd level in a two-dimensional array
aintTest1(2, 3) = 11
' Read 3rd element of the 2nd level in a two-dimensional array
intNum = aintTest(2, 3)
```

Using the functions `LBound` and `UBound`, you can determine the limit indices of the array. Both functions are important for the passing of arrays to procedures and the evaluation of dynamically created arrays.

In the examples in the book you will find the program *Lotto*, in which a simple array is used.

3.4.4   Dynamic arrays

In contrast to static arrays, you can redimension dynamic arrays during run-time, and even keep the old contents in the process. But before you read on, I should point out that even dynamic arrays are being replaced to an ever greater extent by `Collection` and `Dictionary` objects. These are filled more slowly, but they have certain advantages, such as significantly faster searching.

If, nevertheless, you still wish to use dynamic arrays, declare this in principle just like a static array, only without any dimension details:

{Dim | Private | Public} *Name* () [As *Data type*]

The area of validity (`Dim` in procedures, `Private` and `Public` in the declaration area of modules) corresponds, as with static arrays, to that of variable declarations.

With the `Redim` statement, you can adjust the array to the required size at run-time:

```
ReDim[Preserve] Arrayname(Number Dimension1_
 [, Number Dimension2] [...] ) [As Data type]
```

> **Warning** Every `ReDim` statement results in all array contents being lost if you do not also include the statement `Preserve`. For redimensioning, always use the `To` convention with a starting value of 1 if you wish to avoid problems.

Read the names of all the files stored on drive `C:\` into a dynamic array:

```
Dim astrFilenames() As String
Dim strFilename As String, lngCounter As Long
lngCounter = 1
' Read first file name from C:\
strFilename = Dir("c:\*.*")
Do While strFilename > ""
    ' for as long as files are found:
    ' Redimension array
    ReDim Preserve astrFilenames(1 To lngCounter)
    ' Store file name
    astrFilenames(lngCounter) = strFilename
    ' Increment counter
    lngCounter = lngCounter + 1
    ' Find next file name
    strFilename = Dir()
Loop
```

Deleting a dynamic array

Using `Erase Array`, you can remove all the elements of a dynamic array from memory. Do not use the statement `Redim Array(0)`. This redimensions the array to 0 elements, after which the array can no longer be redimensioned.

How many elements can a dynamic array store?

The number of possible elements is limited only by the available memory space. If, on redimensioning, too little memory is available, this results in run-time error 7 "Out of memory". In this case, the last condition of the array remains preserved. You can trap this run-time error and still make use of the array.

3.4.5 Initializing arrays

Unfortunately, so far it is not possible to initialize static arrays (although in VBA 7, it probably will be). You must therefore set the predetermined value of a static array in the program code. Alternatively, instead of a static array, you can simply create a dynamic array with the aid of the `Array` function. Since this returns a `Variant` data type, you must use a suitably declared variable:

```
Dim avarColors As Variant
avarColors = Array("Blue", "Red", "Green")
```

Unfortunately, the index of an array created in this way begins at 0.

3.4.6 Allocation of arrays

From VBA 6, you can allocate another array to a dynamic array:

```
Array1 = Array2
```

The effect of this is that all the elements of the right-hand array are copied into the left-hand array, and any elements and dimensions previously present in the left-hand array are thereby deleted.

```
Dim aint1(1 To 2) As Integer, aint2() As Integer
aint1(1) = 111
aint1(2) = 222
aint2 = aint1
MsgBox aint1(2) & ", " & aint2(2)
```

The array to which the allocation is done must be a dynamic array, otherwise VBA generates a run-time error "Can't assign to array".

This technique simplifies and optimizes the copying of one array to another, where otherwise each item would have to be copied individually using a loop. Since the assignment probably takes place internally by straightforward copying of the memory that defines the array, direct assignment is significantly faster than sequential copying. In a test, I found that sequential copying of 1,000,000 elements took 1.1 seconds, while direct allocation needed only 0.05 seconds.

3.4.7 Structures

Structures are assemblies of data types that are very similar to objects. In contrast to objects, though, structures only possess "properties" and do not have to be generated dynamically (as is the case for objects in VBA). Structures are identical to the Records in Delphi and the Typedefs in C and are also designated as *User-defined data types*. You declare a structure with the keyword `Type`:

```
[{Private | Public }] Type Structurename
    Element1 As Data type
     [Element2 As Data type]
     [Element3 As Data type]
     [...]
End Type
```

You can then simply use the structure as a data type for variables and arrays:

```
Dim Variable As Structure type
Dim Array(1 To n) As Structure type
```

The declaration must take place in the declaration area of a module. `Type` cannot be used in procedures or functions. In class modules (to which form modules also belong) only `Private` declarations are possible. Private structures, like variables, apply only in the module in which they were declared. If you need the structure in several modules of your project, you must declare this in a standard module using `Public`.

Access to the individual fields takes place as with objects via the reference operator (.). The following example uses a structure for the storage of address data:

```
' Declaration of the Structure TAddress
Public Type TAddress
 Name As String
 City As String
 Zip As Long
End Type

Private Sub Test ()
 Dim udtAddress As TAddress
 udtAddress.Name = "Jürgen Bayer"
 udtAddress.City = "Kamp-Lintfort"
 udtAddress.Zip = 47475
End Sub
```

3.4.8   Symbolic constants

Symbolic constants stand for a constant value. In the program source text, the use of symbolic constants in place of text or numeric constants has its advantages:

→ The source text is more legible.
→ If the underlying value is used more than once in the program, when changing this value you must only change the declaration of the symbolic constants.

You declare symbolic constants with the keyword `Const`:

```
[Public | Private] Const _
    Name1 [As Data type] = Expression _
    [, Name2 [As Data type] = Expression]
```

The area of validity of a symbolic constant corresponds to that of a variable. Within functions or procedures, you declare the constant quite simply by using `Const`. If you declare a constant at the module level, by default its area of validity is `Private`. In a form or class module, you cannot declare `Public` constants. If you do not specify the data type, VBA assigns to the constant a data type that matches the value. However, using `As Type`, you can set a data type explicitly.

```
' The private constant PI is of the Single type
Private Const PI = 3.14159


Sub Test()
 ' the local constant LEFT_MARGIN
 ' is of the data type Long
 Const LEFT_MARGIN As Long = 100
End Sub
```

Tip Always (and consistently) use symbolic constants if you have the least suspicion that a set value could change at some time. If you declare these constants in a separate module, then any change of value required later can be carried out very easily by changing the symbolic constants. In addition, you can later convert the symbolic constants into variables without great difficulty if, for instance, you want to make the stored values editable by a user, in a dialogue box.

3.4.9   Enumerations (Enums)

Enumerations are in principle also symbolic constants. They exclusively possess the data type `Long` and are grouped together into an enumeration type. If you declare a variable with this enumeration type, then Visual Basic will help you with assignments and similar actions by using IntelliSense and a list of the possible constants. The declaration conforms to the following pattern:

```
Public Enum EnumName
 Constant1 [= Long value]
 [Constant2 [= Long value]]
 [...]
End Enum
```

If you specify no value for the individual constants, VBA automatically assigns them an incrementing value starting at 0.

Enumeration of possible traffic light colors:

```
Private Enum TrafficLightColors
  tlcRed
  tlcAmber
  tlcGreen
End Enum

Private Sub cmdLights_Click()
 Dim udtLightColor As TrafficLightColor
 udtTrafficLightColors = Red
 ...
End Sub
```

You can now assign to a variable that you declare with this data type all the constants contained within the type, though unfortunately all the other Long values are also included. The enumeration has the sole purpose of making the writing of program code easier by using a constant list. But it works so well that I no longer want to do without enumeration. I must say, though, that I use it less for variables than for the arguments of procedures and functions.

Tips and tricks

Enumeration for arguments and properties

You should preferably use enumeration for the arguments of functions, procedures and for properties and methods so that the programmer using it will be provided with the available constants via IntelliSense. Figure 3.2 shows an example of this.

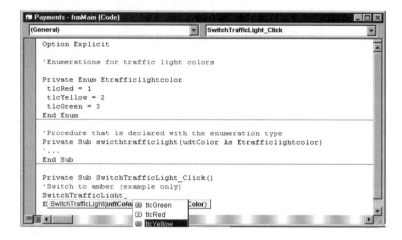

Figure 3.2
Example of the use of enumerations as the argument of a procedure

3.5 Loops and branches

3.5.1 Conditional branches

Like every other programming language, VBA uses the most common types of conditional branches.

If Then

Compared with other languages, the If Then branch in VBA is enhanced with optional ElseIf blocks:

```
If Condition1 Then
    [Statement block 1]]
[ElseIf Condition2 Then
    [Statement block 2]]
[...]
[Else
    [Statement block n]]
End If
```

The optional ElseIf block can be inserted as often as required into the If-Then branch. The condition of an ElseIf block is only tested if none of the conditions of previous blocks was fulfilled. The same applies for the Else block, except that here no further condition is tested. A simple If Then branch that tests whether today is a weekend or a working day looks like this:

```vba
Dim intWeekday As Integer
intWeekday = Weekday(Now)
If (intWeekday = 7) Or (intWeekday = 1) Then
   ' Saturday or Sunday
   MsgBox "It's a weekend, " & _
         "only authors have to work"
Else
   MsgBox "It's not a weekend - everyone has to work"
End If
```

Using `ElseIf` blocks, you can test several different conditions in a branch. The possibility of testing *different* conditions also distinguishes the `If Then` branch from the `Select Case` branch (with which you can test only one condition). The following example tests whether it is possible to go shopping right now:

```vba
Dim intWeekday As Integer
intWeekday = Weekday(Now)
If (intWeekday = 7) And _
   (Time > "10:00") And (Time < "16:00") Then
   ' Saturday between 10:00 and 16:00
   MsgBox "You can go shopping, but only until 16:00"
ElseIf (intWeekday > 1) And (intWeekday < 7) And _
      (Time > "09:00") And (Time < "20:30") Then
   ' Normal weekday between 9:00 and 20:30
   MsgBox "You can go shopping"
ElseIf intWeekday = 1 Then
   ' Sunday
   MsgBox "Today you can only do your" & _
         "shopping at gas stations"
Else
   MsgBox "It is either too early or too late" & _
         "for shopping. " & _
         "Go shopping at the gas station"
End If
```

Short form of the If - Then branch on one line

It is possible to write the `If Then` branch on just one line, but only if there are no `ElseIf` blocks:

```vba
If Condition Then Statement [Else Statement]
```

By using a trick, you can use several statements in a block for this branch: simply separate the individual statements with a colon.

Select Case

The `Select Case` branch tests an expression for several possible outcomes:

```
Select Case Test expression
   [Case Expressionlist 1
      [Expressionblock 1]]
   [Case Expressionlist 2
      [Expressionblock 2]]
   [...]
   [Case Else
      [Expressionlist n]]
End Select
```

The `Select Case` statement has also been extensively expanded compared with other languages. For the test expression, for example, you can specify any arithmetic or logical expression. (Other programming languages only allow whole-number data types.)

The individual `Case` blocks test whether the result value of the test expression agrees with one of the values in the expression list. The expression list can contain, separated by commas, individual values and ranges (*Value1* To *Value2*). In contrast to some other programming languages, with VBA you can also include complex expressions and strings in the expression list. Usually in practice, however, only simple values and lists of values are utilized.

If one of the values in the expression list is identical to the test expression, the relevant statement block is then executed. Following this, unlike the process in C, the `Select Case` branch is ended. The optional `Case Else` block is executed if none of the previous blocks has been executed.

When closing the form, ask whether it should be saved:

```
Private Sub Form_Unload(Cancel As Integer)
 Select Case MsgBox("Save?", vbYesNoCancel)
   Case vbYes
      ' Save
      Save
   Case vbNo
      ' Do nothing
   Case Else
      ' Cancel close
      Cancel = True
 End Select
End Sub
```

What is special about this example is that the `MsgBox` is simply used here as a test expression. `Select Case` evaluates the test expression once only and temporarily stores the result in order to make the comparisons. Therefore the `MsgBox` is only called once.

Tips and tricks

Select Case in place of If Then

Wherever possible, use `Select Case` if you want to test several cases. `Select Case` is executed significantly faster than an equivalent `If Then` enquiry with several `ElseIf` blocks. With `Select Case`, the test expression is evaluated just once, whereas `ElseIf` conditions are evaluated sequentially and individually.

Optimizing If Then branch statements

Should you require an `If Then` enquiry with several `ElseIf` blocks because the conditions differ, then save the result of function calls in variables if this result is to be tested using several conditions. The examples of the `If Then` enquiries use this technique.

3.5.2 "Branch" functions

VBA has some functions that are similar to branches and will therefore be described here.

IIf

The IIf function (Inline If) evaluates a logical expression and, depending on the result, returns one of two possible `Variant` values:

```
IIf(Expression, TruePart, FalsePart)
```

`IIf` is comparable with the `If` function in Excel and Access. This function is very useful if, depending on the outcome of a condition, the one or the other value should be used. The following example determines whether it is a weekend:

```
Dim intWeekday As Integer
intWeekday = Weekday(Now)
MsgBox Today is " & IIf((intWeekday = 1) Or _
      (intWeekday = 7), "a weekend day", "a working day")
```

Switch

The Switch function performs a similar test to `IIf` logical expressions, although in this case you have the possibility of using up to seven expressions:

```
Switch(Expression1, Value1 [, Expression2, Value2] [...])
```

If *Expression1* is `True`, then *Value1* will be returned; however, if *Expression2* is `True`, then *Value2* will be returned, etc. An `Else` value does not exist, but you can simulate this very easily by just putting `True` in the last expression. The following example determines whether today is a Saturday, a Sunday or a working day:

```
Dim intWeekday As Integer
intWeekday = Weekday(Now)
' Evaluation of the day of the week using the
' Switch function
' Note: an Else value is simulated with the True
' in the last expression
MsgBox "Today is " & _
    Switch(intWeekday = 1, "Sunday", _
           intWeekday = 7, "Saturday", _
           True, "a weekday")
```

Choose

The Choose function is given a numerical value as an index, followed by as many variant arguments as required:

```
Choose(Index, Expression1 [,Expression2] [...])
```

`Choose` returns the expression found at the position given by the index value in the parameter list:

```
MsgBox Choose(1, "a", "b", "c") ' returns "a"
MsgBox Choose(3, "a", "b", "c") ' returns "c"
```

3.5.3   Unconditional branches

VBA also has a number of unconditional branch statements, which you should preferably not make use of. `Goto` and `Gosub` are a relict of the prehistory of Basic, when there were no such things as procedures and functions. For that reason, I will not consider these here. Unfortunately, you still need `Goto` for error handling, but that will finally change with the arrival of VB.NET.

3.5.4   Loops

VBA has a number of loop statements for repeated execution of program blocks. Some of these loops are redundant with a syntactically similar form.

Do While loops

The Do While loop runs for as long as a condition is fulfilled:

```
Do While Condition
  Statements
Loop
```

Since the condition is given in the loop head, the loop is carried out only if the condition is true at the time of first entry into the loop.

Loop for as long as a variable is smaller than 4:

```
Dim intCount As Integer
intCount = 1
Do While intCount < 4
  MsgBox intCount
 intCount = intCount + 1
Loop
```

The Do While loop is functionally identical to the While Wend loop:

```
While Condition
  Statements
Wend
```

The Do While loop, in contrast to the While Wend loop, can be explicitly exited using Exit Do.

Do Until loops

The Do Until loop is not very different from the Do While loop. The only difference is that the Do Until loop runs *until* the condition is fulfilled:

```
Do Until Condition
  Statements
Loop
```

Should you wish to convert a Do Until loop into a Do While loop, you need only to reformulate the condition. The example loop above could, for instance, also be formulated as follows:

```
Dim intCount As Integer
intCount = 1
Do Until intCount > 3
   MsgBox intCount
   intCount = intCount + 1
Loop
```

Do loops with condition testing at the foot of the loop

The Do loops also exist in a version that tests the condition at the loop foot:

```
Do
    Statements
Loop While Condition
```

```
Do
    Statements
Loop Until Condition
```

Condition testing at the loop foot has the effect that the loop must run through at least once. If you want the program code in the loop to be executed at least once in any event, then use a loop of this type.

Do loop without conditions

The Do loop also exists in a version without condition testing:

```
Do
    Statements
Loop
```

You can use this "endless" loop if the condition is too complex to be tested at either the head or the foot of the loop, or if on occurrence of the condition, additional statements must be carried out. Simply test the condition within the loop and then leave the loop with Exit Do.

Loop that draws circles on the form for three seconds, then outputs a message and ends the loop:

```
Dim datStart As Date, lngRadius As Long
datStart = Now
lngRadius = 0
Do
    lngRadius = lngRadius + 1
    ' Draw circle
    Me.Circle (ScaleWidth / 2, ScaleHeight / 2), lngRadius
    If Now - datStart > CDate("00:00:03") Then
        ' end after 3 seconds
        MsgBox "Finished"
        Me.Cls ' delete drawing
        Exit Do ' and exit the loop
    End If
Loop
```

For Next loop

The For Next loop is a simple counting loop which automatically increments a numerical variable until it has a value that is larger than the end value given in the loop:

```
For Counter = Start value To End value [Step Step size]
    Statements
Next [Counter]
```

The standard value for the step size is 1. Using the optional Step, however, you can also use larger or negative values, or decimal values. You could, for example, count from 3 to 1 backwards:

```
Dim lngCounter As Long
For lngCounter = 3 To 1 Step -1
    MsgBox lngCounter
Next
```

You can explicitly exit a For Next loop using Exit For.

The For Each loop

With the For Each loop, you can go through all the elements of an array (including control arrays) or a listing (say a collection or a dictionary) without knowing the number of stored elements.

```
For Each Element In {Array | Collection}
    [Statements]
Next [Element]
```

When used with an array, *Element* is a variable of the Variant type. In the case of listings, variables of the types Variant or Object or belonging to the class of the stored objects are permissible. Information on using the For Each loop in listings can be found in Section 3.8.2.

Go through an array with For Each:

```
Dim i As Integer, varTemp As Variant
Dim aintTestArray(1 To 10) As Integer
' Fill array
For i = 1 To 10
    aintTestArray(i) = i
Next
' Go through the array using For Each
For Each varTemp In aintTestArray
    MsgBox varTemp
Next
```

Just as with the `For Next` loop, you can explicitly end a `For Each` loop with `Exit For` before its implicit ending.

`For Each` has an advantage over iteration with an integer index. This is that if during the iteration the number of elements changes, perhaps because you delete elements, `For Each` *does not* produce an error. If, for instance, you iterate through a listing with

```
For intIndex = 1 To colTest.Count
```

and delete elements in the loop, a run-time error will be generated at the end of the list, since the number of elements is evaluated only on entering the loop.

3.5.5 Exiting a program block

You can exit a program block explicitly with the statements shown in Table 3.12.

Event	Description
Exit For	exits a For loop
Exit Do	exits a Do loop
Exit Sub	exits a procedure
Exit Function	exits a function

Table 3.12 *Statements for exiting a program block*

`Exit For` and `Exit Do` are often needed to exit from loops when the condition within the loop is tested. `Exit Sub` and `Exit Function` are frequently used to avoid the need for several layered tests in a procedure being programmed with complicated interlinked `If` enquiries:

```
Private Sub cmdOK_Click()
 If txtFirstname.Text = "" Then
    MsgBox "You have not entered a first name"
    Exit Sub
 End If
 If txtSurname.Text = "" Then
    MsgBox "You have not entered a surname"
    Exit Sub
 End If
 If txtPlace.Text = "" Then
    MsgBox "You have not entered a place name"
    Exit Sub
 End If
 ' Do something with the input
 ' ...
 ' Close form
 Unload Me
End Sub
```

3.5.6 The With statement

Using the `With` statement, you can call the elements of an object or of a structure using statements, without having to specify the object anew each time.

```
With {Object | Structure variable }
    [Statements]
End With
```

You can input methods and properties for the object within the `With` block with just a dot as prefix. This lessens the amount of writing to be done and relieves the compiler of some programming work. You can also nest `With` statements:

```
With frmMain
  .Height = 1000
  .Caption = "Hello world!"
  With .Font
    .Size = 12    ' represents frmMain.Font.Size = 12
    .Bold = True ' represents frmMain.Font.Bold = True
  End With
End With
```

Tips and tricks

Using With to access objects

Use With wherever you can. Access to objects is accelerated by using With if you address several elements. This is particularly true if you address nested objects, since VBA does not then always have to search its way through the higher-order objects all over again.

3.6 Procedures and functions

You will always need procedures when almost identical source code is required over and over again at several places in the program. Simply make a procedure out of this source code and call it using its name. If the source code also needs to be controlled, declare the procedure with arguments to which you can pass the appropriate values when you call it. Functions are needed if a value needs to be returned. Simple functions calculate a value and pass it back. But functions can also, like procedures, contain complex program segments and, together with the return value, report back with a message about its success or failure.

Another reason for writing procedures and functions is to divide up other procedures or functions. Normally, procedures should contain only 50 or at most 100 lines of source code (not including comments and blank lines). If procedures exceed 100 lines of source code, they rapidly become difficult to follow. Therefore, divide these up into several smaller procedures.

This brief explanation will have to suffice at this point, as space simply does not allow more.

3.6.1   Declaring procedures and functions

Functions are declared with the keyword Function, and procedures using the keyword Sub. The declaring of procedures follows the syntax below:

```
[{Private | Public}] [Static] Sub Name_([Argument list])
 ' Definition of the code
 ' ...
End Sub
```

Functions are declared in the following way:

```
[{Private | Public}] [Static] Function Name ([Argument
list]) [As Data type]
 ' Definition of the code
 ' ...
 ' Return of the function value
 [Function name = Expression]
End Function
```

The optional argument list is a comma-delimited list with individual arguments. Declare the individual arguments according to the following syntax:

```
[[{ByVal | ByRef}] Argument [As Data type]
```

As data type, you can use all the data types that are possible for variables. For example, a procedure that receives a date and outputs the day of the week in a MsgBox is declared as follows:

```
Private Sub MsgWeekdayName(ByVal datDate As Date)
 Dim intWeekday As Integer, strWeekdayName As String
 intWeekday = Weekday(datDate, vbUseSystemDayOfWeek)
 strWeekdayName = WeekdayName(intWeekday, , _
                   vbUseSystemDayOfWeek)
 MsgBox "Today is " & strWeekdayName
End Sub
```

When calling it, you must supply it with a suitable data type:

```
MsgWeekdayName Now
```

If you do not declare a data type for individual arguments, VBA uses the standard data type (`Variant`). Functions can also return all data types (including arrays, structures and objects).

Through the optional prior specification of `Static` before the name of the procedure or function, you turn all the variables declared in the procedure or function into `Static` variables. This procedure is not recommended, however, since this makes the source code very untransparent. If you do need `Static` variables though, you would do better to declare them with `Static` rather than `Dim`.

The return value of functions

In a function, you pass back the return value by writing it in the function name. Within the function, the function name represents a local variable. The value of this variable is then passed back by the compiler to the caller at the end of the function.

Function to determine the day of the week:

```
Private Function GetWeekdayName(ByVal datDate As Date) _
                As String
 Dim intWeekday As Integer, strWeekdayName As String
 intWeekday = Weekday(datDate, vbUseSystemDayOfWeek)
 strWeekdayName = WeekdayName(intWeekday, , _
                vbUseSystemDayOfWeek)
 ' Return the day name as determined
 GetWeekdayName = strWeekdayName
End Function
```

Note that inside the function you can use the function name like a normal local variable.

Calling of this function takes place just as with every other function:

```
Dim strWeekdayName As String
strWeekdayName = GetWeekdayName(Now)
MsgBox "Today is " & GetWeekdayName
```

Private procedures / functions

Using the keyword `Private`, you can declare a private procedure or function. Like a private variable, this function or procedure applies only within its own module and cannot be called from other modules. Private procedures can have the same name as other procedures in other modules. VBA allows the use of a previously declared procedure name, provided the new procedure is privately declared.

Public procedures / functions

Using the keyword `Public`, you can declare a public procedure or function. Public procedures or functions can also be called from outside. A `Public` function or procedure in a form module or class module, however, becomes a new method of the form or class. `Public` procedures are still frequently used in VBA 6 to initialize forms and other objects after their creation (unfortunately, VBA 6 still does not offer constructors, whereas VB.NET will do so).

3.6.2   Call by Value and Call by Reference

The standard method for passing arguments is "by reference" for parameters that are variables, while value parameters or properties are always passed "by value". You can explicitly set the passing type with the keywords `ByVal` and `ByRef`. On passing "by value", the compiler always generates program code which has the effect that the value of that which is passed from this argument to the procedure or function is copied into a local variable. Of course, the compiler generates this local variable in the background. Using the name of the argument, you can access this variable in the procedure or function. If you change the value of the argument in the procedure, this causes no change in the value of a variable passed during the call.

With the "by reference" passing type, the compiler generates no local variable if a variable is passed at the call itself. Instead, the compiler simply passes the address of the passed variable. If the argument is changed in the procedure, this always also brings about a change in the passed variables. You will always need Call by Reference:

→ if a function is to return more than one value;
→ if you want to pass an object, a structure or an array to a function (objects, structures and arrays can only be passed by reference).

Example of Call By Reference: procedure that increments a variable:

```
Private Sub Inc(ByRef lngNumber As Long, _
                ByVal lngAddition As Long)
 lngNumber = lngNumber + lngAddition
End Sub
```

When making the call, you must pass a variable of the correct type in order to receive the value returned:

```
Dim lngCount As Long
lngCount = 1
Inc lngCount, 2
```

> **Warning** Since passing "by reference" can lead to logical errors which are difficult to locate if you modify an argument within a procedure or function and thereby alter a variable passed outwards at this point, you should always pass "by value", making it necessary to specify `ByVal` before every parameter. However, if you need explicit reference arguments, then pass by reference. In this case, for better transparency, you should use the keyword `ByRef`.

In some cases, passing by reference can bring performance advantages. The reason is that on calling a function or procedure, Visual Basic need only place the address of the passed variables on the stack and not the potentially larger value in memory. This advantage would only be felt on frequent calling of a procedure or function. You could test whether passing by reference brings speed advantages. The drawback remains, however, that you risk generating errors that are difficult to locate.

3.6.3   Functions that return objects

Apart from the standard data types, functions can also return objects. Declare the return type of the function with the appropriate class. In the function, you should ideally use the function name, so as to generate an object of this class and then return it automatically.

Generating a collection from several country designations:

```
Private Function CreateCountryCollection() As Collection
 Set CreateCountryCollection = New Collection
 CreateCountryCollection.Add "England"
 CreateCountryCollection.Add "Germany"
 CreateCountryCollection.Add "USA"
End Function
```

Call:

```
Private Sub GetCountryCollection
 Dim col As Collection
 ' Call of the function and assignment of the return object
 Set col = CreateCountryCollection
End Sub
```

3.6.4   Functions that return arrays

From VBA 6 on, functions can also return arrays. Declare the return type with empty brackets. In the function you create a local array which you fill and then finally assign it to the function. The idea which could arise, of generating a dynamic array instead of the local array with the function name, cannot be realized (for reasons unknown to me).

Function that returns an array made up of country designations:

```
Private Function CreateCountryArray() As String()
 Dim astrCountries(1 To 3) As String
 astrCountries(1) = "England"
 astrCountries(2) = "Germany"
 astrCountries(3) = "USA"
' Assignment of the array to the function
 CreateCountryArray = astrCountries
End Function
```

Call:

```
Private Sub GetCountryArray
 astrCountries() As String
 ' Call of the function and assignment of the return array
 astrCountries = CreateCountryArray
End Sub
```

3.6.5   The passing of arrays

If you wish to pass an array to a procedure or function, declare it as an argument with brackets, but without specifying the elements and dimensions. For analyzing the passed arrays in the function, use the functions LBound and UBound. LBound gives the lower array index, and UBound the upper one. Note that for an empty array (0 elements), both functions will generate error 9, "Subscript out of range".

Function to add all the values in an array and return the result:

```
Public Function ArrayTest(aintArr() As Integer) As Long
 Dim i As Integer
 ArrayTest = 0
 For i = LBound(aintArr) To UBound(aintArr)
    ArrayTest = ArrayTest + aintArr(i)
 Next
End Function
```

When the procedure is called, the array is also passed with empty brackets:

```
Dim lngResult As Long
ReDim aintArr(1 To 2) As Integer
aintArr(1) = 10
aintArr(2) = 11
lngResult = ArrayTest(aintArr())
MsgBox lngResult
```

3.6.6   Parameter arrays

Parameter arrays are useful if you want to pass an unknown number of arguments on declaration of a function or procedure. In the place of a declared parameter array, you can pass any number of separate values, separated by commas, to a procedure or function. The declaration is similar to that of a normal array:

```
{Sub | Function} Name(ParamArray Identifier () _
        As Variant) [As Data type]
```

The data type of the parameter array must be Variant. You can only declare one parameter array. Furthermore, this must be the last of the arguments passed. During the evaluation, you can determine the upper and lower bounds of the parameter array, as with a normal array, by using LBound and UBound. Since the data type of the parameter array is Variant, for evaluation of the individual elements, you should use the functions for determining the data types of Variants.

Function to determine the total of any number of passed values:

```
Function Sum(ParamArray avarNumbers() As Variant) As Long
 Dim i As Long
 For i = LBound(avarNumbers) To UBound(avarNumbers)
   If IsNumeric(avarNumbers(i)) Then
      Sum = Sum + avarNumbers(i)
   End If
 Next
End Function
```

Call:

```
Dim lngResult As Long
lngResult = Sum(1, 2, 3, 4, 5, 6, 7, 8, 9, 10, 11)
MsgBox lngResult
```

3.6.7 Optional arguments

You have most probably already met some VBA functions that possess optional arguments. The MsgBox, for example, has only one compulsory argument. All other arguments are optional. Naturally enough, you can write functions of this type. Optional arguments are signified with the keyword Optional:

```
{Sub | Function} Name([...] Optional Identifier_
As Data type [...]) [As Data type]
```

Within the procedure or function, the presence of the parameter is determined with the functionIsMissing if the argument possesses the data type Variant. Using this Variant is usually long-winded, however:

```
Public Sub Inc(ByRef lngNumber As Long, _
      Optional ByVal varAddition As Variant)
 Dim lngAddition As Variant
 ' Evaluation of the optional passing
 If IsMissing(varAddition) Then
    lngAddition = 1
 ElseIf IsNumeric(varAddition) Then
    lngAddition = varAddition
 Else
    lngAddition = 1
 End If
 lngNumber = lngNumber + lngAddition
End Sub
```

It is usually better to make the declaration with a normal data type. In this case, you can even specify a default value as well:

```
Public Sub Inc(ByRef lngNumber As Long, _
      Optional ByVal lngAddition As Long = 1)
 lngNumber = lngNumber + lngAddition
End Sub
```

Only if you have to detect in the procedure whether perhaps no value has been passed do you have to use the declaration with `Variant`. An optional argument with another data type is always initialized with a default value if no value has been passed at this point.

The call takes place as I have already described in the first part of this book:

```
Dim lngCount As Long
lngCount = 1
Inc lngCount ' Call without the optional argument
MsgBox lngCount
Inc lngCount, 10 ' Call with the optional argument
MsgBox lngCount
```

3.6.8   Recursion

VBA permits the recursive call of a procedure or function. In the process of recursion, the procedure or function calls itself again and again until an End condition is reached. Recursions are always needed if a procedure has to work its way through a hierarchy that is not clearly defined (e.g. if all the sub-folders of a particular folder, including its sub-folders, need to be searched for a particular file).

Tip Recursive calls are slow and use up a great deal of stack space. If you can do without a recursive process, you should try to avoid it.

You must program the End condition yourself. For example, a simple function for recursive calculation of the factorial of a number first tests the number passed to ensure it is > 1:

```
Public Function Faculty(ByVal lngNumber As Long) As Long
  If lngNumber > 1 Then
     ' Recursive call
     Faculty = lngNumber * Factorial(lngNumber - 1)
  Else
     Faculty = 1
  End If
End Function
```

A complex example that finds all the files in a folder and all the sub-folders is included in the examples in this book.

Tip The return values and argument values of functions are always stored in the stack. Regrettably, VBA only supports a stack size of 64KB, with the result that incursions often come up against the limits of available memory space.

3.7 Conditional compilation

You can cause compilation of program code to be carried out conditionally upon fulfillment of particular criteria using a branch structure similar to the If branch:

```
#If Condition1 Then
    Statements
[#ElseIf Condition2 Then
    [Statements]]
[#Else
    [Statements]]
#End If
```

The method corresponds to that of the If Then branch, but with the difference that code in blocks whose conditions are not met will not be taken into account by the compiler. This code may also contain statements not usable in the current environment.

The condition expression must only include literals, operators and constants for conditional compilation. You can set up these special constants in the module using #Const Name = Value or define them via the Project Properties under the Make tab. You cannot use any symbolic constants here, such as True or False. In place of these, you must use their numerical values (–1 for True, 0 for False).

Conditional compilation was important in the days of Visual Basic 4.0, when 16-bit programs were still being developed. With the constants Win16 and Win32 defined in VB from VB 4.0 on, it has been possible to use the same project for 16-bit and 32-bit Windows. Until the change-over to 64-bit or 128-bit Windows, conditional compiling is of less importance. It could conceivably be used, though, for compiling a restricted Shareware or test version of an application:

```
#Const SHAREWARE = True

Public Sub Save()
 #If SHAREWARE Then
    MsgBox "Sorry, but saving is not" & _
           "implemented in the Shareware version"
 #Else
    ' Program code for saving
    ' ...
 #End If
#End If
```

3.8 Working with objects

If you intend (or have) to undertake programming with objects, you will need to take a few points into account. Firstly, naturally enough, you need the class from which you will create the object. This class may exist in the source code, in a class module, or be contained in a class library. The classes contained within VB or VBA are, without exception, stored in class libraries. In the VB library, for instance, you can find the classes of the standard controls, and in the VBA library the important class Collection.

The peculiarity of object variables lies in the fact that, after its declaration, such a variable receives assigned to it either a reference to a newly *created* or an *existing* object:

```
' Declare object variable
{Dim | Private | Public} Object variable As Object type

' Create new object and assign reference to it
Set Object variable = New Object
```

```
' Assign reference to an already existing object
Set Object variable = Object
```

However, you cannot create objects from all classes in the source code. The control classes, for instance, are not allowed to be instantiated. You will need variables of the control class types only in special situations, such as when you wish to pass to a function a reference to a control. Far more frequently, you will probably create normal invisible objects such as objects of the class `Collection`:

```
Dim colTest As Collection
Set colTest = New Collection
```

In place of this long version, a short form is also possible:

```
Dim colTest As New Collection
```

Doing this, you save precisely one line, but your program is sure to run more slowly. For object variables declared in this way, the compiler generates program code every time the object is accessed, to test whether an instance already exists. If no instance already exists, a new one is quite simply created. The additional checking on every access to an object declared in this way costs time, of course. Do not, therefore, declare your object variables with `As New`.

Tip Should you forget, with the long form of declaration and creation of the assignment using `Set`, VBA returns a run-time error 91 on accessing an object variable, "Object variable or With Block variable not set".

In many cases, for assigning an object to an object variable, you will use the return of a suitable function or method. The method `Execute` of a `Connection` object from the ADO library, for example, always returns a `Recordset` object if you pass to the method an SQL selection query:

```
Dim rst As ADODB.Recordset
Set rst = conn.Execute("SELECT * FROM Addresses")
```

Generic object data types

Most object data types are type-secure. With these objects, you can only use the properties, methods and events that have been defined in the class. An attempt to use a non-existent property or method in the source code causes the compiler to return an error.

VBA also recognizes some generic data types that can reference objects of various classes. The data type `Object`, for example, can reference all types of object, while the data type `Form` can reference all objects that are "derived" from a form. The data type `Control` can reference all controls. But since the compiler can no longer tell with these objects which properties, methods and events are actually present with a referenced object, you can also use objects in the source code that are not present at all. When compiling, no error messages will be output, and the error "Object does not support this property or method" will only be generated at run-time. If, for example, you generate a form dynamically and declare the form variable with the generic data type Form, you can also use methods in the source code that may not exist at all:

```
Dim frm As Form
Set frm = New frmDemo
frm.Init ' This method doesn't exist at all,
         ' but the compiler doesn't recognize that fact
```

It is always better to use a non-generic data type. In the example above, for instance, it would be better to use the form name as the data type:

```
Dim frm As frmDemo
Set frm = New frmDemo
frm.Init ' The compiler can now check
         ' whether this method exists
```

Sometimes you do not know to which type of object you want to refer, in which case you can use a generic data type. With the aid of the function `TypeOf`, you can determine the type of an object. If, for instance, you want to search through all the controls of a form to change the font of all the labels, then test each control to see whether it is a label:

```
Dim ctl As Control
For Each ctl In Me.Controls
   If TypeOf ctl Is Label Then
      ctl.Font.Name = "Times New Roman"
      ctl.Font.Size = 12
      ctl.Font.Bold = True
   End If
Next
```

The `For Each` loop used in this example has already been described on page 97. Collections, such as the `Controls` collection used here, are covered from page 113.

3.8.1 Class libraries

Class libraries are compiled COM components installed and registered on your system, which in principle contain nothing other than classes. You can use the classes of a class library to generate objects of those classes. Since the class library is not directly available in Visual Basic, however, you must make it known with a reference before using it. Select the `Menu project | References` to open the dialogue box where references to the class libraries installed on your system can be created.

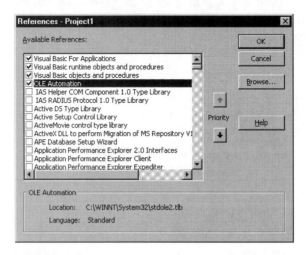

Figure 3.3 *The dialogue box for adding references to class libraries*

Do not be alarmed at the large number of class libraries. Every modern application installs the odd class library or two, and these are often used only for applications from the same manufacturer. Since you probably do not have the right documentation for this and you are unlikely to have a development license for these libraries, you often cannot even begin to use them. The class libraries of importance to Visual Basic are restricted to just a few. The most important of these – apart, that is, from the VB, VBA and other VB standard libraries – are those you will use for data access with ADO ("Microsoft ActiveX Data Objects 2.x Library") and when working with the filing system via FileSystemObjects, or with the Dictionary Class ("Microsoft Scripting Runtime").

You can instantiate the classes of a class library in the same way as for a normal class. When doing so, however, you should enter not only the class name but also the abbreviation for the class library. If, for example, you create an object of the dictionary class, cite the Scripting Library:

```
Dim dic As Scripting.Dictionary
Set dic = New Scripting.Dictionary
```

If you do not give the abbreviated name, but refer instead to several class libraries, it can happen that the same class name occurs in different class libraries. The result, if you do not also cite the component, is that the compiler will not necessarily use the class you require. You can find out the abbreviated names of the class libraries and the classes they contain from the object catalogue.

3.8.2   Collections

A collection is an object that stores a sequence of elements that can be referred to as a unit. Elements in a collection can be of any data type, and can also include objects. The individual elements in a collection may also store *different* data types, because they have the data type Variant. You can access the individual elements in the same way as for an array. Of assistance here is the property Count.

Read out the opened forms of the current application from the collection Forms:

```
Dim intIndex As Integer
For intIndex = 0 To Forms.Count - 1
 MsgBox Forms(intIndex).Name
Next
```

You can also use the For Each loop to address all the elements of a collection (further information on For Each can be found on page 97). To do this, declare a variable of the same type as the elements stored in the collection and use this in the For Each loop. The following example goes through all the currently loaded forms and shows the name of each in turn:

```
Dim frm As Form
For Each frm In Forms
 MsgBox frm.Name
Next
```

Many collections have additional key strings for the entries, so that you can reach each element via the key. For instance, in the Controls collection, which refers to all the controls in a form, it is the name of the control:

```
MsgBox frmMain.Controls("cmdOK").Caption
```

This admittedly useless example reads out the label of the button *cmdOK*.

> **Tip** The index in one of the older of VB's own collections (Forms, Controls, etc.) starts at 0. According to Microsoft, the index of newer collections starts at 1. Unfortunately, Microsoft does not always keep to this and some of the newest collections still begin at 0.

The data type of elements in a collection is `Variant`, so you can store in them all the data types that are possible with Variant. To ascertain the data types of individual elements stored in a collection, you can use the function for discovering the data type of a Variant (see page 143).

3.8.3 Your own collections using dictionary objects

VBA allows you to create your own collections with the classes `Collection` and `Dictionary`. `Dictionary` is the newer class and offers more possibilities. And since objects of this class are not only significantly more flexible but often faster than `Collection` objects, I will not go into details here about the `Collection` class. In any case, `Collection` is interesting for creating your own collection classes that can be equipped with special methods and properties.

As the name suggests, a `Dictionary` object is suitable not only for storing objects but also for storing string pairs (e.g. German/English texts for the translation of terms). However, in this section I am assuming that it is mostly objects that will be stored.

Creating Dictionary objects

Since the `Dictionary` class is a component of the "Microsoft Scripting Runtime" library, you will first of all need a reference to this (see page 112). Then you will be able to create a `Dictionary` object:

```
Dim dic As Scripting.Dictionary
Set dic = New Scripting.Dictionary
```

Adding elements

You can add values or objects to a collection with the `Add` method:

```
dic.Add Key, Item
```

Item is the value or object to be stored. If you insert an object, only one pointer to the object is stored. *Key* is an identifier with which you will be able to access the element later. The key can contain not only letters but also numbers (and probably other data types as well). The key must be unambiguous amongst the stored elements. The new element is added to the end of the list.

Adding of new person objects:

```
' Create some persons and
' add them to the dictionary
Dim objPerson As clsPerson

' Create and define new person
Set objPerson = New clsPerson
objPerson.FirstName = "Zaphod"
objPerson.LastName = "Beeblebrox"
objPerson.Hobby = "Travelling through the galaxy"
' and add it to the list;
' the name will be used as the key
mdicPersons.Add objPerson.FirstName & _
  " " & objPerson.LastName, objPerson

' Create and define another person
' Note: the creation of another person
' in objPerson removes the reference to
' the first person, but because it is
' referenced in the collection, the
' object is retained
Set objPerson = New clsPerson
objPerson.FirstName = "Ford"
objPerson.LastName = "Prefect"
objPerson.Hobby = "Travelling through the galaxy"
mdicPersons.Add objPerson.FirstName & _
  " " & objPerson.LastName, objPerson
```

Automatic addition

One feature of the `Dictionary` class is that it automatically creates a new element when an as yet non-existent key is passed to the `Item` property (which is used to access individual elements):

```
Dim dic As Scripting.Dictionary
Set dic = New Scripting.Dictionary
dic.Item("Car") = "Porshe 911"
dic.Item("House") = "One family house with 42 chambers"
dic.Item("Cat") = "Regular house cat"
MsgBox dic.Item("Dog")
```

Naturally, you must keep this feature in mind. If you wish to access existing elements and pass an as yet non-existent key, the `Dictionary` object possesses a new element with an empty Variant value (`Empty`). The last `MsgBox` call in the above example generates just such an element. But happily, a `Dictionary` object has available to it an `Exists` method with which the presence of an element having a particular key can be checked.

Deleting elements

For the deleting of elements, the `Dictionary` class makes use of the `Remove` method:

```
dic.Remove Key
```

`Remove` deletes the element which possesses the *Key*. Unfortunately, you can only quote the key, not the integer index of the element (which is possible, for instance, with `Collection`):

```
' delete the entry with the key "Dog"
dic.Remove "Dog"
```

Using `RemoveAll`, you can delete all the elements in the list (which is an advantage over `Collection`, which does not have any such method).

Accessing the elements

Access to the elements takes place via the `Item` property with inclusion of the key:

```
MsgBox dic.Item("Dog")
```

Since `Item` is the standard property, you can leave it out:

```
MsgBox dic("Dog")
```

Because `Item` is a property of the `Dictionary` object, you can also – in contrast to `Collection` – overwrite the element using a key.

```
dic.Item("Dog") = "Bobtail"
```

> **Tip** Unfortunately, you can pass only one key and no integer index to an `Item` property. If, for example, you wish to access the first element and you pass the number 1 as the key, the `Dictionary` object simply creates a new element with the key 1 if no element yet exists with this key.

Checking whether elements exist

Using the `Exists` method, you can discover whether an entry is stored with a particular key in the list:

```
dic.Exists(Key)
```

For example, you can enquire about Zaphod Beeblebrox's telephone number as follows:

```
If mdicPersons.Exists("Zaphod Beeblebrox") Then
  MsgBox mdicPersons.Item("Zaphod Beeblebrox").PhoneNumber
Else
    MsgBox "Zaphod Beeblebrox does not " & _
           "exist in the collection, but that" & _
           "can't actually be so."
End If
```

The `Exists` method is a significant advantage over the `Collection` class, which possesses no comparable method.

Sequential stepping

If you want to go through a `Dictionary` object sequentially, you cannot initially use an integer index, because with an `Item` property, a `Dictionary` object will interpret an integer value as a key and simply create a new element if the key is not found:

```
Dim dic As Scripting.Dictionary
Set dic = New Scripting.Dictionary
dic.Add "a", 1
dic.Add "b", 2
dic.Add "c", 3
Dim i As Integer
For i = 1 To dic.Count
    MsgBox dic.Item(i)
Next
```

This example does not output anything, since the existing elements are not addressed, but new ones are created.

You can go through a `Dictionary` object directly using `For Each`. But if you try to use a `Dictionary` object like a `Collection` object, you will end up with egg on your face:

```
Dim varElement As Variant
For Each varElement In dic
    MsgBox varElement
Next
```

This example outputs the keys and not the values themselves. The reason for this is simply that the `Keys` method is the standard method for the `Dictionary` class[3].

You should therefore use the `Items` method if you want to go through a `Dictionary` object sequentially with `For Each`:

```
Dim varElement As Variant
For Each varElement In dic.Items
    MsgBox varElement
Next
```

---

3. It seems that the Dictionary class has a standard property (Item) and a standard method (Keys), which are used depending on the context, if no property or method are cited. We cannot do something like this with our own classes. Only a standard property or a standard method is possible.

The Items method returns an array containing all the elements of the Dictionary object. The Keys method does a similar job for the keys. Since these arrays have the data type Variant, they can, unfortunately, use only one Variant variable for the For Each loops (with Collection, you can also use variables whose data type is the class of objects stored in the Collection).

If you do indeed now wish to go through a Dictionary object using an integer index, simply read the elements, using Items, into a Variant array:

```
Dim dic As Scripting.Dictionary, avarItems As Variant,
intIndex As Integer
Set dic = New Scripting.Dictionary
dic.Add "E1", 1
dic.Add "E2", 2
dic.Add "E3", 3
' Assignment of the item array to a Variant variable
avarItems = dic.Items
' Step through with an integer index
For intIndex = LBound(avarItems) To UBound(avarItems)
  MsgBox avarItems(intIndex)
Next
```

Specifying the comparison method

With the CompareMode property, you can specify whether the comparison of strings in a Dictionary object will be binary (vbBinaryCompare), according to text (vbTextCompare) or dependent on the Option Compare statement in the module (vbUseCompareOption). The constant vbDatabaseCompare, also permissible here, applies only if you use a Dictionary object in Access 2000 programs, and is therefore of no significance for VB programmers.

Time comparison between arrays, collections and dictionary objects

If time plays a role, you should consider carefully whether to use an array, a Collection or a Dictionary object for storing. However, you must decide whether what is required is to fill the list as quickly as possible or to search in the list as quickly as possible. Filling can be performed fastest with a static or dynamic array, while searching is most rapidly done with the key of a Collection object or of a Dictionary object.

Tips and tricks

For Each instead of For Next

In order to step sequentially through a `Collection`, always use `For Each` and not `For Next`. `For Each` is significantly faster. In a test with 10,000 stored objects, going through a `Collection` object sequentially with `For Each` took about 0.07 seconds, while doing the same thing using `For Next` took all of 7.9 seconds!

VBA functions and VB objects

This chapter is concerned with the functions and procedures integrated into VBA and with the pre-defined objects included within VB. To avoid duplication, I shall, where possible, only use the term *function*, even where what we are talking about is one of the few procedures.

VBA now contains a large number of functions, most of which are extremely usable. Particularly in the area of string functions, VBA 6 has gained much ground compared with VBA 5 and the date, formatting and conversion functions also leave little to be desired. Statisticians will probably miss some statistical functions; VBA does not have any at all. Financial mathematicians, on the other hand, will probably be more than satisfied with the financial functions (although these are not covered in this book). If you miss one or the other, remember that you can still buy these in other manufacturers' function libraries.

The pre-defined objects in VB (which do not belong to VBA but to the VB library) are somewhat more meagerly provided than the VBA functions. The important `Printer` object, for example, is often not easy to use in practice, because the preview option (which is probably very easy for Microsoft to program) is missing.

4.1 The object browser

The object browser will be of great help to you by giving you an overview of the content of any libraries you wish to see. You can even use it to give you an overview of the VBA functions. It also helps with searching through other libraries, such as the ADO library, for data access. You can open the object browser by pressing **F2**.

Figure 4.1 *The object browser with the VBA library*

At the top of the object browser window, you can input the library you wish to explore. Figure 4.1 shows the object browser with the VBA library selected.

The class list on the left-hand side shows some entries which catalogue the VBA functions (Table 4.1).

Class	Meaning
Conversion	Conversion functions
DateTime	Date/time functions
FileSystem	File and folder functions
Financial	Financial functions
Information	Functions that supply information
Interaction	Functions that are used for interactions with objects, applications and systems
Math	Mathematical functions
Strings	String functions

Table 4.1 *The function catalogue of the object browser*

Tips and tricks

Fast listing of all the available VBA functions

You can get a rapid listing of all the available VBA functions simply by including "VBA" in the program code. Since VBA is a library, you will receive a list of all the available functions, procedures, variables and constants.

4.2 File and folder functions

This section describes the most important file and folder functions in VBA. Some of them are not covered, as they are only needed for the writing and reading of files with VBA functions. The reading and writing of files in VBA is now very old-fashioned. You can read and write text files much more easily with FileSystemObjects and files for direct access are better replaced with databases. Some of the functions described here (such as MkDir) have now been replaced by corresponding methods of the FileSystemObjects class. Since this class can also do substantially more (such as checking whether a file exists), for file operations you would do better to use a FileSystemObjects object. I will explain how these objects should be handled in Chapter 9. Sometimes, however, the creation of a FileSystemObjects object can be simply too laborious. If, for example, you just want to delete a file quickly, you might do better to use the VBA functions described here.

Functions for reading, copying, deleting and renaming

Function	Purpose
Dir[$][(*Pathname* [, *Attributes*])]	Returns the first file or folder name matching the file pattern supplied in the *Pathname* and having the attribute supplied in *Attributes*. In *Pathname*, you can also use wildcards. The attributes should be supplied with constants such as vbArchive, and IntelliSense will help you here. Dir("C:*.txt", vbNormal), for example, seeks the first text file in C:\ that is normal, is not hidden or write-protected and is not a system file. vbNormal is the preset if you do not input anything in *Attributes*. If you input vbNormal, files will also be found for which the Archive Bit is set. You can combine individual attributes with each other by simple addition. You will find all other files after the first call by calling Dir without arguments.

Function	Purpose
FileCopy Source, Destination	Copies a file. Should the file or the target folder not be present, a run-time error is generated. You must input the complete name of the target file – that is, together with its folder.
Kill Pathname	Deletes a file irretrievably (i.e. not into the Recycle Bin). If the file does not exist, a run-time error will be generated.
MkDir(Path)	Creates the directory given in Path.
RmDir(Path)	Deletes the folder given in Path as a string. The folder must not contain any files.

Table 4.2 *Functions for reading, copying, deleting and renaming of files and folders*

Information functions

Function	Purpose
FileDateTime (Pathname)	Returns the date of the last amendment of a file as a Variant of the type Date.
FileLen(Pathname)	Determines the size of a file in bytes.
GetAttr(Pathname)	Determines the attributes of a file. What are returned are the attribute constants used in Dir (vbNormal, vbArchive, vbSystem, vbHidden, etc.). Note that a file can possess several attributes. Should you wish to test an attribute, you must use And for filtering.
SetAttr(Pathname, Attributes)	With SetAttr, you can set the attributes of a file.

Table 4.3 *File information functions*

Functions for the current drive or folder

Function	Purpose
ChDir(*Path*)	Changes the current directory. You do not actually need this function, since the current directory is not normally of any importance to the VB programmer.
ChDrive(*Drive*)	Changes the current drive to the one given. The same applies here as I have already said in connection with ChDir.
CurDir[**$**][(*Drive*)]	Determines the current directory on the current or the specified drive.

Table 4.4 *Functions for the current drive or the current directory*

4

TAKE THAT!

Examples

Determine all files (including hidden and system files, etc.) on C:\ and put them in a list box:

```
Dim strFilename As String
' Determine first name from the files on C:\
' with normal attributes
strFilename = Dir(txtPathName.Text, _
    vbNormal Or vbHidden Or vbSystem Or vbReadOnly)
Do While strFilename > ""
   ' for as long as files are found
   ' add them to the List Box
   lstFilenames.AddItem strFilename
   ' Determine name of the next
   ' appropriate file
   strFilename = Dir()
Loop
```

Copy the file C:\Boot.ini to C:\Temp:

```
FileCopy "C:\Boot.Ini", "C:\Temp\Boot.Ini"
```

Determine the attributes of the file C:\Boot.Ini:

```
Dim udtAttributes As VbFileAttribute ' Enum data type
        ' of VBA with the file attribute constants
Dim strAttributes As String
' Read the attributes
udtAttributes = GetAttr("C:\Boot.Ini")
' Evaluate the attributes
If (udtAttributes And vbArchive) = vbArchive Then
   strAttributes = strAttributes & "Archive" & vbCrLf
End If
If (udtAttributes And vbHidden) = vbHidden Then
   strAttributes = strAttributes & "Hidden" & vbCrLf
End If
If (udtAttributes And vbSystem) = vbSystem Then
   strAttributes = strAttributes & "System" & vbCrLf
End If
If (udtAttributes And vbReadOnly) = vbReadOnly Then
   strAttributes = strAttributes & "ReadOnly" & vbCrLf
End If
' Output
MsgBox "The file has the following attributes " & _
        vbCrLf & strAttributes
```

The VBA string functions are often implemented in two versions, of which one has a "$" attached to it. The function without "$" returns a character sequence of the data type `Variant`, while the version with the "$" returns a character sequence of the data type `String`. In pure string processing operations, the $ version probably works better than the Variant version, since the string does not have to be converted first from a `Variant` to a `String`.

4.3.1   Extracting partial strings and shortening strings

With the functions `LTrim`, `RTrim` and `Trim`, you can remove blank spaces from the left, the right, or both sides of a string.
For example, `LTrim(" abc ")` produces "abc", `RTrim(" abc ")` gives `"abc"` and `Trim(" abc ")` results in "abc".

With the `Left` and `Right` function, you can extract a left or right partial string. For example, `Left("abcdef", 3)` gives "def". You can use the `Mid` function if you want to read out a partial string from the middle of another string. `Mid("abcdef", 3, 2)` returns "cd".

Function	Purpose
LTrim[$](String), RTrim[$](String), Trim[$](String)	The Trim functions return the entered string without any left-hand blanks (LTrim), right-hand blanks (RTrim), or without either left or right-hand blanks (Trim).
Left[$](String, Length) Right[$](String, Length)	These functions find the left-hand or right-hand partial string with the length given by Length.
Mid[$](String, Start[, Length])	Mid returns the partial string that begins from the position given by Start and has the length given by Length. If Length is not given, the string is returned up to the end.

Table 4.5   *Functions for reading partial strings and for shortening strings*

4.3.2   Compare strings and search for partial strings

The functions which compare strings with each other often use an optional argument *Compare*. In this argument, you can specify how the comparison should be made. To do so, use the constants given in Table 4.6.

Constant	Purpose
vbBinaryCompare	When comparing, a distinction is made between lower and upper case letters ("a" is not equivalent to "A").
vbTextCompare	When comparing, a distinction is not made between lower and upper case letters ("a" is equivalent to "A").
vbDatabaseCompare	This constant can only be used in the VBA of Access from version 2000. In this case, the comparison option set in the database is used.

Table 4.6 *The constants of the Compare argument for string comparisons*

Tip If you input nothing for the *Compare* argument, then for comparison operations, the old string functions use the setting in the `Option Compare` option of the module. With this option, you can make a fundamental setting for string comparisons to say whether they distinguish between upper and lower case letters (`Option Compare Binary`) or not (`Option Compare Text`). Newer string functions (`Filter`, `Join`, `Split`), however, possess another preset according to IntelliSense (`vbBinaryCompare`). This implies that for these functions, the string comparison ought to be binary – that is, distinguishing between upper and lower case if you do not stipulate *Compare*. But that is not actually the case: these functions, too, use the setting in the `Option Compare` option. The constant `vbUseCompareOption` described in the Help text simply does not exist (at least not on my system). If I use the value of the constant (–1), I get a run-time error.

If, when making a pure comparison of strings, you wish to skip the `Option Compare` option of the module, in place of a normal comparison, you can use the `StrComp` function, as set out in Table 4.7. Since in practice it is often sufficient for you to discern whether the two strings are equivalent or not, the return by `StrComp` of 0 is actually sufficient. In the argument *Compare*, you stipulate whether you wish to distinguish between upper and lower case letters or not.

```
i = StrComp("abc", "ABC", vbTextCompare)
'returns 0 (both strings equivalent)
i = StrComp("abc", "ABC", vbBinaryCompare)
'returns 1 (String 1 is greater than String 2)
```

With the `Instr` and the `InstrRev` functions, you can search through a string for a partial string from left to right. Both functions reveal the position of the first character of the sought string within the string being searched. `InstrRev` is newer than `Instr`, so that the call syntax of the two functions is somewhat different. `Instr` uses an old-fashioned syntax with an optional first argument, and you must leave out the comma if you do not wish to use this argument.

```
' Search from the 1st character towards the right
i = InStr("1aa4aa7", "aa") 'gives 2
'Alternatively
i = InStr(1, "1aa4aa7", "aa") 'gives 2
'Search from the 3rd character towards the right
i = InStr(3, "1aa4aa7", "aa") 'gives 5
'Search from the last character towards the left
i = InStrRev("1aa4aa7", "aa") 'gives 5
'Search from the 5th character towards the left
i = InStrRev("1aa4aa7", "aa", 5) 'gives 2
```

> **Tip** Note that the strings can be split up very simply using the `Split` function and that, without much trouble, you can replace partial strings with the `Replace` function. Many search functions, which in VB 5 were still very complex, using `Instr` and `InstrRev` for the splitting or replacement of strings, are therefore no longer necessary from VBA 6 on.

With the `Filter` function which at first sight also appears somewhat complicated, you can search in a list of strings for those that contain a particular partial string. You should pass the strings in which the searching is to take place as an array in the argument *SourceArray*. In *Match*, you pass the partial string that is to be sought. With *Compare*, you define the comparison type. `Filter` returns a one-dimensional array made up of the strings that contain the partial string. I think an example will serve to explain this function better than a verbal description:

```
Dim astrSource(1 To 4) As String
Dim astrResult() As String, intIndex As Integer
astrSource(1) = "ABC"
astrSource(2) = "abd"
astrSource(3) = "123abc123"
astrSource(4) = "abc123"
astrResult = Filter(astrSource, "abc", _
            True, vbTextCompare)
For intIndex = LBound(astrResult) To UBound(astrResult)
   MsgBox astrResult(intIndex)
Next
```

The result of this example is a string array with the strings "**ABC**", "123**abc**123" and "**abc**123".

Function	Purpose
InStr([*Start,*] *String1,* *String2* [, *Compare*])	InStr returns the position of the first occurrence of *String2* in *String1*. If *Start* is not specified, searching starts from the first character, or otherwise from the position given by *Start*. *Compare* specifies the type of the comparison. Somewhat unique with this function is the fact that the first argument is optional although the two subsequent arguments are not. This frequently leads to misinterpretations if the last argument is used. For safety, therefore, always input 1 for *Start* if you wish to search from the first character.
InstrRev (*StringCheck,* *StringMatch* [, *Start*] [, *Compare*])	InstrRev searches through a string in a similar manner to Instr, but from right to left. *StringCheck* is the string to be searched. With the argument *Start*, you can specify from which position in the string the searching should take place. With this set to −1 (default), searching starts with the last character. Note that the argument order is different from that of Instr.
StrComp(*String1, String2* [, *Compare*])	StrComp compares two strings. If *String1* is smaller than *String2*, then StrComp returns a value of −1. If both are equal, the value returned is 0. If *String1* is larger than *String2*, 1 is returned. If you pass Variants and one of the Variants contains Null, then Null is returned. Using StrComp, you can make string comparisons independently of the Option Compare statement of the module.
Filter(*SourceArray, Match* [, *Include*] [, *Compare*])	Filter enables searching through a list of strings for those that contain a particular partial string. You pass the strings in which the searching is to take place as an array in the argument *SourceArray*. With *Match*, you pass the partial string that is to be searched for. In the case of *Compare*, you define the comparison type. Filter returns a one-dimensional array with the strings that contain the partial string.

Table 4.7 *The constants of the Compare argument for string comparisons*

4.3.3 Replacing strings

The most powerful function for replacing strings within strings is Replace. You pass at least one character sequence being the partial string that is to be replaced and the character sequence that is to replace the partial string. If you input nothing further, then Replace returns a string in which all the searched-for partial strings have been replaced by the substitute character sequence:

```
MsgBox Replace("1aa2aa3aa", "aa", "bb")
'produces "1bb2bb3bb"
```

Normally the replacing of all the sequences found is sufficient. But you can do more with the Replace function. In the fifth argument (*Count*) you can state how many replacements should be undertaken:

```
MsgBox Replace("1aa2aa3aa", "aa", "bb", , 1)
' results in "1bb2aa3aa" (1 replacement from the 1st charac-
ter)
```

In the fourth argument (*Start*), you can specify from where Replace should start acting:

```
MsgBox Replace("1aa2aa3aa", "aa", "bb", 5, 1)
' gives "bb3aa" (from the 5th character, 1 replacement)
```

> **Tip** What is baffling to me is the fact that Replace cuts off the left side of the string if you specify a *Start*, as the above example shows.

If you know exactly from where in a string you want to replace a partial string, you can also use the Mid statement (not to be confused with the Mid function), as described in Table 4.8. In principle, this is not very useful, because Mid always replaces a certain number of characters with a string of the same length.

Function	Purpose
Mid[$](*String1*, *Start* [, *Length*]) = *String2*	The Mid statement replaces a partial string in *String1* from the position given by *Start* with *String2*. If you specify a length with the argument *Length*, only the stipulated number of characters will be replaced. Otherwise, it will be as many characters as *String2* contains.
Replace(*Expression*, *Find*, *Replace* [, *Start*] [, *Count*] [, *Compare*])	Replace replaces all partial strings in the string contained in *Expression* that are identical to the string contained in *Find* with the string contained in *Replace*. The resulting string will then be returned. If you do not specify *Start* and *Count*, all the found sites will be replaced. Using *Start*, you can decide from which character searching should begin. *Count* defines how many replacements are to be made altogether. The preset value (−1) causes all partial strings found to be replaced. Note that the string is cut off at the left side if you do specify a *Start* value. *Compare* lays down the type of replacement.

Table 4.8 *Functions for replacing strings*

4.3.4   Conversion and creation of strings

VBA has several functions for converting strings (in numbers, capital letters, lower case letters, etc.), determining the ANSI value of a character, determining the character belonging to a particular ANSI value, and creating strings with a specified number of characters. Given the simplicity of these functions, I would simply draw your attention here to Table 4.9.

Function	Purpose
Asc(*String*)	Asc returns the ANSI code of a character. If you enter a relatively long string, the code of the first character is returned.
Chr[$](*CharCode*)	Chr returns the character corresponding to the ANSI code entered in *CharCode*.
LCase(*String*), UCase(*String*)	These functions return the string converted into lower case (LCase) or upper case (UCase).
Space[$](*Length*)	Space returns a string with the number of space characters specified in *Length*.
Str[$](*Number*) CStr(*Expression*)	These functions produce a string with the number supplied as its content. Warning: Str adds a space before the number. You would be better advised to use CStr.

Function	Purpose
String[$](*Number*, *Character*)	Returns a string with the number of characters given in *Number*. You specify the characters in the argument *Character* in ANSI code or as a string.
StrReverse(*Expression*)	StrReverse returns the string supplied in *Expression* reversed. Thus "abc" becomes "cba".

Table 4.9 *Functions for converting and creating strings*

4.3.5 Separating and joining strings

In practice, strings must often be disassembled into individual partial strings. If the partial strings are separated from each other by one or more separators, you can simply use the Split function. Split separates a string into several individual strings, which are then returned in an array. You input the string and the separator in the first two arguments. In the third argument (*Limit*), you can define how many partial strings are to be found, although in practice, this is seldom needed. The last argument (*Compare*) is more important, and if the separator(s) are simple letters, you can use it to specify whether upper and lower case are to be distinguished. However, since separators are often not letters (they may be semicolons, for instance), this argument is often not significant in practice. The following example demonstrates the functioning of Split:

```
Dim astrResult() As String, intIndex As Integer
astrResult = Split("123aa456aa789", "aa", , vbTextCompare)
For intIndex = LBound(astrResult) To UBound(astrResult)
   MsgBox astrResult(intIndex)
Next
```

The result of this example is a string array with the strings "123", "456" and "789".

Should you wish to reassemble a string disassembled with Split (e.g. after some processing), you can use the Join function. In order to demonstrate the functioning of Join, the following example uses a user-defined string array:

```
Dim astrResult(1 To 4) As String
astrResult(1) = "Trillian"
astrResult(2) = "Arthur"
astrResult(3) = "Ford"
astrResult(4) = "Zaphod"
MsgBox Join(astrResult, ";")
' gives "Trillian;Arthur;Ford;Zaphod"
```

TAKE THAT!

Function	Purpose
Join(*SourceArray* [, *Delimiter*])	Join reverses what Split takes apart. The strings stored in the array entered as the *SourceArray* are joined together using the separator specified in *Delimiter* and returned as a single string. The preset value of *Delimiter* is a space.
Split(*Expression* [, *Delimiter*] [, *Limit*] [, *Compare*])	Split separates an entered string into individual partial strings. These partial strings are recognized from the separators input in *Delimiter*. The default value of *Delimiter* is a space. The result of Split is a one-dimensional string array. In *Limit*, you can enter the maximum number of partial strings to be found. −1 (preset value) represents all partial strings found. *Compare* relates to the separator and defines the type of comparison made.

Table 4.10 *Functions for separating and assembling strings*

Tips and tricks

Processing text databases with Split and Join

With Join and Split, you can very simply process or create text databases with separators.

4.3.6   The left-over Len function

I have not been able to assign the Len function, which finds the length of a string, to either of the other tables. This important function is therefore all on its own here.

Function	Purpose
Len(*String*)	Len determines the length of a string.

Table 4.11 *The Len function*

4.4 Formatting functions

VBA now contains a few functions for the formatting of values. The most important of these is the `Format` function, with which you can actually format anything. Although you can use this function with any character sequences, the formatting of numbers having a fixed number of decimal points and the formatting of date values are probably its most important uses in practice. `Format` returns the value supplied in the first argument (string, numerical value or date) with the formatting stipulated in the second argument. You can specify the formatting as a string with formatting symbols or with a number of pre-defined formatting strings. Since there are very many of these symbols, I shall set out only the most important ones below in the examples. VB Help describes the available symbols and character sequences very well. Look in the Help text for the `Format` function and look at the associated topics via the link see also.

```
strDemo = Format(0.345, "0.00")
' returns "0.35"
strDemo = Format(12.345, "0.00")
' returns "12.35"
strDemo = Format(1234.567, "0.00")
' returns "1234.57"
strDemo = Format(1234.567, "#,#0.00")
' returns "1,234.57"
strDemo = Format(0.567, "#,#.00")
' returns ".57"

strDemo = Format(36525, "Short Date")
' returns "31/12/99"
strDemo = Format(36525, "Long Date")
' returns "Friday, 31 December 1999"
strDemo = Format(36525, "Medium Date")
' returns "31-Dec-99"
strDemo = Format(0.5, "Short Time")
' returns "12:00"

strDemo = Format(36525, "dd.mm.yy")
' returns "31/12/99"
strDemo = Format(36525, "dd.mm.yy hh:mm:ss")
' returns "31/12/99 00:00:00"
strDemo = Format(36525, "dddd, dd. mmmm yyyy")
' returns "Friday, 31 December, 1999"
```

```
strDemo = Format(36525, "yyyymmdd")
' returns "19991231"
strDemo = Format(36525, "yyyy-mm-dd")
' returns "1999-12-31"
```

The functions `FormatCurrency`, `FormatDateTime`, `FormatNumber` and `FormatPercent` are specialized for currency values, date values, numbers and percentage values and often simpler to use than the format function. Take the syntax from Table 4.12. Due to the simplicity of this function, I offer only a few examples:

```
strDemo = FormatCurrency(-0.235, 2, False, False)
' returns "-.24 USD"
strDemo = FormatCurrency(-0.235, 2, True, False)
' returns "-0.24 USD"
strDemo = FormatCurrency(-0.235, 2, True, True)
' returns "(0.24 USD)"
strDemo = FormatCurrency(1000.235, 2, True, True)
' returns "1,000.24 USD"
strDemo = FormatCurrency(1000.235, 2, True, False)
' returns "1000.24 USD"

strDemo = FormatDateTime(Now)
' returns "29/06/00 12:17:12 PM"
strDemo = FormatDateTime(Now, vbLongDate)
' returns "Thursday, June 29, 2000"
strDemo = FormatDateTime(Now, vbLongTime)
' returns "12:17:41 PM"
strDemo = FormatDateTime(Now, vbShortDate)
' returns "29/06/00"
strDemo = FormatDateTime(Now, vbShortTime)
' returns "12:18"
strDemo = FormatPercent(0.00123, 2, False, False)
' returns ".12%"
strDemo = FormatPercent(-0.00123, 2, True, False)
' returns "-0.12%"
strDemo = FormatPercent(-0.00123, 2, False, True)
' returns "(.12%)"
strDemo = FormatPercent(-0.00123, 2, True, True)
' returns "(0.12%)"
```

Function / Procedure	Purpose
Format[$](Expression [, Format] [, FirstDayOfWeek] [, FirstWeekOfYear])	Format returns a formatted number, date or string value. In the argument Format, you specify how the formatting will take place. For the formatting process, Format uses special formatting characters, separators and certain pre-determined character sequences for standard formatting. You can, in addition, insert your own character sequences in the format string. The formatting symbols are well explained in VB Help. You can find the most important of them in the examples in this section. If you simply enter the expression without any format information, then the transformation corresponds to that of CStr. The arguments FirstDayOfWeek and First-WeekOfYear concern date formatting. I describe these arguments in the date function section from page 138 on.
FormatCurrency (Expression [, NumDigitsAfterDecimal] [, IncludeLeadingDigit] [, UseParensForNegativeNumbers] [, GroupDigits])	Formats the currency value given in Expression. In NumDigitsAfterDecimal, you can specify how many places should be output after the decimal point. Rounding works reliably here, in contrast to the Round function. If you do not specify anything, two decimal places are output. IncludeLeadingDigit defines whether a leading 0 should be output. Apart from True and False, you can also specify vbUseDefault, which is also the pre-set value. With this setting, FormatCurrency takes the value set in the system's country setting. UseParensForNegativeNumbers defines whether negative numbers should be output in brackets. Again, the setting here is True, False or vbUseDefault. GroupDigits defines with the same constants whether the thousands separator is used or not.
FormatDate- Time(Expression [NamedFormat])	Formats the data value given in Expression. In NamedFormat, you can specify a named format: vbGeneralDate (Default), vbLongDate, vbLongTime, vbShortDate or vbShortTime.
FormatNumber (Expression [, NumDigitsAfterDecimal] [, IncludeLeadingDigit] [,UseParensForNegativeNumbers] [, GroupDigits])	FormatNumber works exactly like FormatCurrency, with the difference that the currency sign is not added.

4

TAKE THAT!

Function / Procedure	Purpose
FormatPercent (*Expression* [, *NumDigitsAfterDecimal*] [, *IncludeLeadingDigit*] [,*UseParensForNegativeNumbers*] [, *GroupDigits*])	FormatPercent works like FormatNumber and FormatCurrency. The value given in *Expression* is divided by 100 and output followed by a % symbol.

Table 4.12 *The formatting functions*

4.5 Date functions

The extensive but mostly user-friendly date functions are briefly described in Table 4.15. When using these functions, however, you must often take account of two arguments: the *FirstDayOfWeek* argument is important when you perform calculations with the time intervals "w" (day) and "ww" (week). In the absence of any input, VBA usually (though not always) uses the American format, where the first day of the week is Sunday. In other countries where Monday is regarded as the first day of the week, this setting leads to miscalculations. Therefore, you should ideally input the constant vbUseSystem, so that your application always uses the system setting. If, however, you want to specify the weekday, you can use the constants given in Table 4.13.

Constant	Description
vbUseSystem	VBA uses the system setting
vbSunday	Sunday
vbMonday	Monday
vbTuesday	Tuesday
vbWednesday	Wednesday
vbThursday	Thursday
vbFriday	Friday
vbSaturday	Saturday

Table 4.13 *The constants for the argument FirstDayOfWeek*

The argument *FirstWeekOfYear* defines which week is the first week of the year. Depending on the country concerned, a different first week of the year is used (e.g. the week including 1st January or the first week that includes at least four days of the new year). You can use the constants set out in Table 4.14. However, the ideal is that you simply use vbUseSystem, so that your application uses the Windows system setting.

Constant	Description
vbUseSystem	VB uses the system setting
vbFirstJan1	Start in the week including 1st January (preset)
vbFirstFourDays	Start in the first week that includes at least 4 days in the new year
vbFirstFullWeek	Beginning in the first complete week of the year

Table 4.14 *The constants of the FirstWeekOfYear argument*

If you do not specify *FirstWeekOfYear*, the week that includes 1st January will be taken as the first week.

Function	Purpose
Date**$** = *"Specified date"*	Date sets the system date.
Date[$], Time[$]	This function supplies the system date and time. If you use the $-variant, the date is returned in the English format, or otherwise as a Variant of the type Date (which is automatically converted to the system format for outputting).
DateAdd(*Interval, Number, Date*)	Returns a value of the Variant type, containing a date to which a specific time interval has been added. *Date* is the date to which the adding should take place, *Interval* defines the interval to be added (day = "d", month = "m", year = "yyyy" etc.); *Number* is the number of intervals to be added. Note that the interval symbols partly differ from those of the Format function. The interval symbols are very well described in the Help text on DateAdd and DateDiff, so I have not included a list of them here.
DateDiff(*Interval, Date1, Date2* [, *FirstDayOfWeek* [, *FirstWeekOfYear*]])	Specifies the number of time intervals between two particular events. The symbols used for *Interval* are the same as those used in the DateAdd function. Note that DateDiff unfortunately always rounds up. For instance, if you wish to calculate a person's age in years, the result is not always correct. DateDiff("yyyy", "30.6.70", "1.1.00"), for example, wrongly returns a result of 30.
Format[$]	With Format date values, among other things, can be converted into a string. Format is described in the section on formatting functions.

TAKE THAT!

VBA FUNCTIONS AND VB OBJECTS **139**

Function	Purpose
Hour, Minute, Month, Second, Weekday, Year	Supplies an integer value representing the hours, minutes, etc. of the input data value.
MonthName(*Month* [, *Abbreviate*])	Returns the full month name, or if *Abbreviate* is True, the abbreviated month name, that the number supplied in *Month* represents.
Now	Supplies the system date including the time as a Variant of the type Date. Now is actually not a function, but a variable.
Timer	Finds the number of milliseconds that have elapsed since midnight and can therefore be used for time measurement. Timer returns a value of the type Single. Note that Timer is reset again at 24:00 if you intend to make time measurements with it.
TimeValue, DateValue	These functions transform date and time details from strings into numerical values.
WeekdayName (*Weekday* [, *Abbreviate*] [, *FirstDayOfWeek*])	Returns the full weekday name, or if *Abbreviate* is True, the abbreviated weekday name, that the number supplied in *Weekday* represents. With *FirstDayOfWeek*, you can specify which day is taken to be the first day of the week. The preset (vbUseSystemDayOfWeek) reads this setting from the system.

Table 4.15 *The date functions*

4.6 Arithmetic functions

Naturally enough, VBA has a few arithmetic functions that I shall now list briefly, but without giving examples.

Function	Purpose
Abs(*Number*)	Returns the absolute value of the *number* given in *Number* (i.e. without a sign).
Atn, Cos, Sin, Tan	Calculate arc tan, cosine, sine and tan. Supply: angle in radian measure, (radians = degrees * PI / 180).
Exp(*Number*)	Returns the exponent from e and the *number* given in *Number* (inverse function to Log).
Hex[$](*Number*)	Outputs a string with the hexadecimal value of the *number* given in *Number*.
Log(*Number*).	Returns the natural logarithm of the *number* given in *Number*.
Oct[$](*Number*)	Returns a string corresponding to the octal value of the *number* given in *Number*.
Round(*Number, NumDigitsAfterDecimal*)	Round rounds a number to a specified number of decimal places, although unhappily not the way we are used to. In *Number*, you supply the number to be rounded. *NumDigitsAfterDecimal* stipulates to how many decimal places the rounding should be performed. Unfortunately, Round rounds mathematically (and not according to commercial practice). With mathematical rounding, if the figure to which rounding takes place is followed by a 5, then the figure is rounded up if it is odd, and rounded down if it is even. Therefore, Round(1.35, 1) rounds to 1.4 and Round(1.45, 1) also rounds to 1.4. Round(1.45001, 1), however, rounds to 1.5. This ensures that when rounding, no imbalance arises in the rounded numbers (as it does with the commercial rounding method).

Table 4.16 *The arithmetic functions*

4.7 Conversion functions

Although VBA usually converts automatically and correctly for operations, explicit conversion is still sometimes necessary. In Chapter 6, I will describe how calculations and comparisons with numerical inputs in text boxes are not carried out correctly if the text is not explicitly converted.

Floating point in Long

Function	Purpose
Int(*Number*)	For positive numbers, this supplies the whole number, while for negative numbers, it returns the rounded-up whole number.
Fix(*Number*)	For positive numbers, this supplies the whole number, while for negative numbers it returns the rounded-down whole number.

Table 4.17 *Functions for converting floating-point values into Long values*

Examples:

```
Int(-1.4) ⇒  -2
Fix(-1.6) ⇒  -1
Int(1.6)  ⇒   1
Fix(1.6)  ⇒   1
```

Strings to numbers and vice versa

Function	Purpose
Format$ (*Number*)	Converts the supplied number into a string.
Val(*String*)	Converts a string into a numerical value. Val uses the American number format. Example: 123.456,789. Val also converts strings that do not represent a numerical value, and in this case the left-most valid numbers are returned. Example: Val("abc") ' gives 0 Val("123abc") ' gives 123

Table 4.18 *Functions for converting strings into numerical values and vice versa*

General conversion

VBA has a few functions for general conversion, the names of which always begin with "C". The functions CCur, CDbl, CInt, CLng, CSng, CStr, CVar and CBool convert any expression into the relevant data type. If the expression cannot be converted, a run-time error results.

In contrast to `Val`, `CDbl` uses the numerical format pre-set in Windows. Using `CDbl`, you can also convert a user's input. `CDbl` generates a run-time error, however, if the value cannot be converted. Therefore check using `IsNumeric`, before conversion, whether the value to be converted is numeric.

`CInt` and `CLng` round decimal numbers mathematically correctly, as does the `Round` function. This rounding system which seems unusual to us has the effect, for instance, that 0.5 is rounded to 0 and 1.5 to 2. As we would expect, though, 0.51 is rounded to 1.

4.8 Information functions

Information functions supply information about input values or variables. The Is functions (`IsNumeric`, `IsDate`, etc.) check, for example, whether an entered variable possesses a basic data type. But the functions `RGB` and `QBColor`, which calculate a color value, are also included among the information functions.

Function	Purpose
`IsArray(`*VarName*`)`	Tests whether an input Variant variable contains an array.
`IsDate(`*Expression*`)`	Checks an expression or a variable for a valid date. Warning: if the date cannot be recognized as being in system format, `IsDate` also tries the English format. Thus `IsDate("12.31.00")` returns `True`.
`IsEmpty(`*Expression*`)`	Checks whether an entered `Variant` variable or `Variant` property is `Empty`, i.e. has never been initialized.
`IsError(`*Expression*`)`	Checks whether an expression is an error value. An error value can only be stored in a `Variant` variable. One could therefore write functions that either return a valid value or, with the aid of the `CVErr` function, return an error value and then evaluate this error after the function call with `IsError`. (One could, although this is not usually done.)
`IsMissing(`*ArgName*`)`	Checks in functions and procedures whether the caller has input a value in place of an optional variant argument (see under Functions and Procedures).
`IsNull(`*Expression*`)`	Checks whether an expression returns `Null`. `Null` can only be stored by Variant data types and stands for "empty".
`IsNumeric(`*Expression*`)`	Checks whether an expression is numeric. `IsNumeric` uses the decimal separator symbol as set in the system.

4

TAKE THAT!

Function	Purpose
IsObject(*Expression*)	Checks whether an input variable points to an object. The only variables coming into consideration are Variant and object variables.
QBColor(*Color*)	Returns the RGB color value for the 16 standard colors. You input the number as a value between 0 and 15. This is well explained in Help.
RGB(*Red*, *Green*, *Blue*)	With the RGB function, you can determine a color value given values for its red, green and blue components. The individual components are represented by values between 0 and 255.
TypeName(*VarName*)	TypeName returns the data type of a variable input as a string. Particularly for object variables, TypeName is very helpful if you need to find out to which class an object belongs.
VarType(*VarName*)	VarType determines the data type of an input variable as a number. The number 2, for example, stands for integer. For the comparison, it is better to use symbolic constants such as vbInteger or vbDouble. VarType is helpful if you wish to find out the exact data type of a Variant variable.

Table 4.19 *The information functions*

4.9 Interaction functions

At this point, I will only briefly describe the VBA functions for interaction with the user and the system, since some of these are covered in greater detail in other chapters and others are very simple to use.

Function	Purpose
AppActivate(*Title*, [*Wait*])	Activates an application window.
Beep	Creates a beep tone.
CallByName(*Object*, *ProcName*, *CallType*, *Args()*)	This function gives you the possibility of calling a method or property of an object, whereby you can input the name of the same as a string. This Variant, which is of little importance in practice, allows you to leave specifying the method or property until run-time (for instance, by letting the user input the name in a dialog box).

Function	Purpose
Choose(*Index, Choice()*)	Choose returns the expression found at the nth position in the parameter list (where n is the Index value) that you enter in the argument *Choice* as individual values. Choose is described in more detail in Chapter 3.
Command[**$**]	Command supplies the string that was input on calling your EXE file as the command line argument string. Using this function, you can evaluate command line arguments.
CreateObject(*Class* [, *ServerName*])	CreateObject is the alternative to creating objects with the New operator. You would do better not to use this function, which returns the created object, because its execution is slower than the execution of New.
DeleteSetting(...), GetSetting(...), GetAllSettings(...), SaveSetting(...)	These functions are used for the administration of data in the registry. I shall describe SaveSetting and GetSetting in greater detail in Chapter 6.
DoEvents	This function leads to the processing of all events and is used in processor-critical loops in order to give Windows time to work through the events. More information about DoEvents can be found in Chapter 6.
Environ[**$**](*Expression*)	Returns the value of an environment variable, whose name you specify in the argument *Expression*.
GetObject ([*PathName*], [*Class*])	With this function you can either fetch an already existing instance of a COM-capable application (e.g. Word) in that you specify the class (e.g. "Word.Application"), or you open a file in an instance of a COM-capable application by giving the file name. You will need this function if you wish to control other COM-capable applications remotely. That, however, is beyond the scope of this book.
IIf(*Expression, TruePart, FalsePart*)	IIf returns the value entered in the argument *TruePart* if the condition given in *Expression* is true, and otherwise the value entered in the argument *FalsePart*.
SendKeys(*String* [,*Wait*])	With SendKeys, you can simulate the pressing of buttons. Further information about this can be found in Chapter 6.

Function	Purpose
Shell(*PathName* [, *WindowStyle*])	Shell executes an EXE file given in *PathName*. In the argument *WindowStyle*, you can specify whether the application appears minimized or maximized, etc. The constant vbNormalFocus (application opened at normal size with focus) probably has the greatest significance here.
Switch(*Expression1*, *Value1* [, *Expression2*, *Value2*] [...])	Switch works with expression-value combinations input in pairs. If *Expression1* is True, then *Value1* is returned; if *Expression2* is True, then *Value2* is returned, etc. An Else value does not exist, but you can simulate it simply by putting True in the last expression. An example of this function can be found in Chapter 3.

Table 4.20 *The VBA interactive functions*

4.10 Functions for output and input

4.10.1   The MsgBox function

With the MsgBox function, you can output messages and force the user to make decisions. The user has to operate one of the buttons offered in order to close the dialog box.

MsgBox(*Prompt*[, *Buttons*][, *Title*][, *Helpfile*, *Context*])

In the argument *Prompt*, you input the actual message. *Buttons* defines the button surfaces, the icon style and the standard button for the dialog box. *Buttons* is a summand from the constants given in Table 4.21. *Title* defines the text in the title line of the message box. If you leave out this argument, the message box uses the title of the application (which you can set in the project properties). If *Helpfile* has been specified with a file name and *Context* with a help context number, when the F1 button is pressed, the message box calls this help text. The MsgBox function returns the button operated by the user as an integer value.

Constants for the buttons

Symbolic constant	Button
vbOKOnly	OK
vbOKCancel	OK & Cancel
vbAbortRetryIgnore	Abort, Retry and Ignore
vbYesNoCancel	Yes, No and Cancel
vbYesNo	Yes and No
vbRetryCancel	Retry and Cancel

Table 4.21 *The constants for the buttons in the MsgBox*

Constants for the icon

Symbolic constant	Icon	Meaning
vbCritical	Stop sign	Critical error
vbExclamation	Exclamation mark	Warning
vbInformation	Information sign	Information
vbQuestion	Question mark	Question

Table 4.22 *The constants for the icon in the MsgBox*

Constants for the default button

If you do not input a constant for the default button, the first button is the default button. This button will automatically be actuated if the user presses (ø). You can, however, redefine the default button if you wish (Table 4.23).

Symbolic constant	Meaning
vbDefaultButton1	The first button is the default
vbDefaultButton2	The second button is the default
vbDefaultButton3	The third button is the default

Table 4.23 *The constants for the default buttons in the MsgBox*

The return value

The return value of the MsgBox function stands for the button pressed by the user (Table 4.24).

Symbolic constant	Button pressed
vbOK	OK
vbCancel	Cancel
vbAbort	Abort
vbRetry	Retry
vbIgnore	Ignore
vbYes	Yes
vbNo	No

Table 4.24 *The constants for the return value of the MsgBox*

Example

Or how can I annoy the user when he attempts to close the program?:

```
If MsgBox("Close?", vbQuestion Or vbYesNo _
      Or vbDefaultButton2, "Quit") = vbYes Then
  If MsgBox("You are about to " & _
          "close the program. Proceed?", _
          vbOKCancel + vbExclamation, _
          "Finish") = vbOK Then
      Unload Me
  End If
End If
```

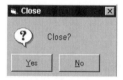

Figure 4.2 *MsgBox with vbQuestion Or vbYesNo Or vbDefaultButton2*

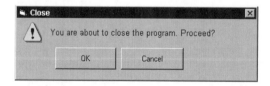

Figure 4.3 *MsgBox with vbOKCancel Or vbExclamation*

4.10.2   The InputBox function

You can use the `InputBox` function to input a single value:

```
InputBox(Prompt[, Title][, Default][, XPos][, YPos] _
        [, Helpfile, Context])
```

Prompt defines the message text. *Title* is optional and defines the title. If *Default* is entered, this value is pre-set in the input field. With *XPos* and *YPos*, the position of the box can be determined. *Helpfile* and *Context* function as with `MsgBox`.

```
strTemp = InputBox("Enter zip code:", "Zip code", "47475")
```

If the user presses the Cancel button, an empty string is returned, otherwise input takes place in the form of a string.

> **Tip** Evaluation of the Cancel button is almost impossible with the `InputBox` function, since the function returns an empty string when, on the one hand, the Cancel button is pressed or, on the other hand, the OK button is actuated with simultaneous null input. Therefore for simple input, it is better to use a separate form.

4.11 The VB objects

In Visual Basic certain objects are pre-defined and already created. You can use these objects very simply in any VB application.

The screen object

The `Screen` object provides information about the screen. The most important properties are `Height` and `Width`, giving these dimensions of the screen in twips[1], and `MousePointer`, with which it is possible to set the mouse pointer[2] for the whole screen. A frequent application is setting the mouser pointer to an "hour-glass":

```
Screen.Mousepointer = vbHourglass
```

Of course, you can change the mouse pointer back again:

```
Screen.Mousepointer = vbNormal
```

---

1. 1 cm = 567 twips.
2. See "Changing the mouse pointer" on page 221.

The App object

Using the App object, you can access your application. The most important properties are described in Table 4.25.

Command	Description
Path	The complete path of the directory in which the EXE file is stored. Warning: if the EXE file has been saved in a master directory, then Path is completed with a backslash, though not in all other cases.
ExeName	The name of the EXE file without file ending; in the development environment, this is the project name.
Helpfile	The name of the help file for your application, should you want to use Help. This can also be set in Options.

Table 4.25 *The most important properties of the App object*

If you include a Help file with your application, the complete name of the Help file must be written in the property Helpfile. To do this, you will use all the properties described in Table 4.25:

```
If Right$(App.Path, 1) = "\" Then
  App.HelpFile = App.Path & App.EXEName & ".hlp"
Else
  App.HelpFile = App.Path & "\" & App.EXEName & ".hlp"
End If
```

Using the properties Comments, CompanyName, FileDescription, Legal-Copyright, LegalTrademarks, ProductName and Revision, you can write Windows version information in the EXE file. This information can then be read in Windows Explorer in the file properties and provides information about the file's use and its creator.

Warning In certain situations (though I don't know why), `Path` does not return the long path, but only the short (DOS 8.3) path. This probably has to do with the storage of the folder in Windows and is not a fault of the `App` object. In certain applications, short path details suddenly appear on opening files. Unfortunately, under Windows 95 / NT 4, there is no API function for conversion of short file names into long file names. You should therefore use the function *GetLongFilename* described in the Knowledgebase article Q154822 or Q163227, which you can also find (in an improved form) in the module Fileprocs. Bas in the example files with this book. From Windows 98 / 2000 on, you can also use the API function `GetLongPathName`.

The Clipboard object

Using the `Clipboard` object, you can gain access to the clipboard. You can find more information on this in Chapter 6.

The Printer object

Using the `Printer` object, you can print text and graphics. You can find more information on this from page 278 on.

Controls and forms

5

This chapter describes how to handle standard controls, the most important ActiveX controls and forms. As you probably only experiment with simple applications at first using one form, I will initially describe the most important controls. The conclusion of the chapter is a description of how you program applications using several forms.

5.1 Standard controls, ActiveX and windowless controls

In the meantime Visual Basic comes supplied with very many controls. Some of them belong to *standard controls*, which are always available in the tool set. The others, the *ActiveX controls*, have to be integrated into the current project as needed using the `Project | Components` menu. Almost all the important standard controls are also available again in *Microsoft Windowless Controls*, though rather limited without Windows Handler, but consequently not so demanding on resources.

The multitude of controls supplied is perhaps somewhat confusing, but no need to worry. You should perhaps know the basic function of individual controls, but you only need to master this when you really need one of the controls. This is particularly true for the ActiveX controls. Just think, you can often buy or download controls free of charge which offer considerably more functions and are often easier to program than the controls supplied with VB. Important addresses here are www.activex.com and www.zoschke.com.

Also, due to the multitude of controls, I cannot describe all of them in this book. I do of course describe all standard controls, but when it comes to ActiveX controls I have to cut back. For this reason only the most important ActiveX controls from my point of view appear in this book.

Control elements are important just for the fact alone that they solve complex problems. For example, if you need a complex part program to show a table calculation, check first to see whether possibly an ActiveX control or an ActiveX object library solves the problem. Difficult problems are usually solved like this with a little download time from the Internet and some money, but without the stress. Consider how much time problem solving yourself (programming) can cost you (more than you think). Also it makes little sense to solve a problem again which has been solved already.

Standard controls

All standard controls are available in Windows, and for this reason these all look the same in all applications. As creating and calling a standard control is achieved in Visual Basic internally using the API functions, standard controls unlike ActiveX controls do not require any special files. Direct production of controls using Windows API functions is very complicated which is why Visual Basic reduces this work for you and encloses the controls so that they are visible already in the design process. Unfortunately in so doing, some functions of the basic controls are often lost. So the text box for example in Windows recognizes an Undo function, which Visual Basic unfortunately cannot claim as a method. This lack of available functions is however no problem for you as a true Visual Basic programmer. In spite of this, you can call these special functions usually by sending a relatively simple Windows message to the control. I explain how to do this in the "Tips and tricks" section for the individual controls.

ActiveX controls

ActiveX controls are stored in OCX files, which as a rule are filed in the Windows system directory and itemized as ActiveX components in the registry. Manufacturers other than Microsoft (e.g. Apex) have developed some of the ActiveX controls. You can frequently obtain the professional variant of these controls with considerably upgraded features from the manufacturer. An example is the DBGrid developed by Apex, which you can buy in the upgraded version *True DBGrid Pro*. However, that ActiveX controls supplied with VB often have limited functionality only because you are meant to buy the professional variant is only a rumor.

Using ActiveX controls you can easily solve almost any problem. You only have to obtain the suitable control and install it. So before you spend days programming a solution to a problem, which then has to be intensively tested and supported, consider whether a purchased control or object library already solves the problem and would save you a lot of time and effort. I myself have had lamentable experiences programming intrinsic ActiveX components[1]. It often takes too long before they function reliably under any circumstances.

---

1. Problems are often solved today with objects compiled in a COM component or as a control, and can be reused as you like.

Windowless controls

Windowless controls unlike "normal" controls do not possess a window handle and therefore use considerably fewer resources. If you have placed 50 normal controls on a form and wonder at how slowly the form loads and is displayed, you will understand why there are windowless controls. They do have one disadvantage however: as they do not possess a handle you cannot call any of the Windows API[2] functions for these controls and therefore cannot use any of the upgrades which the API offers.

Extend functionality with SendMessage

In the "Tips and tricks" section I frequently refer back to the Windows API function SendMessage, with which you can send a message to a control. In order to be able to use this function, you must firstly declare it, which occurs in the declaration area of the module.

```
Private Declare Function SendMessage Lib "user32" _
   Alias "SendMessageA" (ByVal hwnd As Long, _
   ByVal wMsg As Long, ByVal wParam As Long, _
   lParam As Any) As Long
```

You can take the declaration from the API Viewer, which can be found in the StartMenu in the VB folder. SendMessage works with constants, e.g. LB_FINDSTRING. Its declaration likewise can be found in the API viewer. You can find more information on working with API functions in Chapter 6.

5.2 Common elements of all controls

5.2.1   The most important common properties

Many controls have properties which most other controls also have. So these do not have to be listed over and over again. In Table 5.1 I describe common properties and only special properties in the control information.

Property	Meaning
Appearance	Determines whether the control appears flat (0) or in 3D-Look (1; presetting).
AutoSize	Using True determines whether a control automatically adapts itself in size to the internal area of the text or graphics content.

---

2. Application interface: Windows offers the programmer and sometimes also VB programmers about 1,000 important API functions in different DLL files, which combined represent the Windows API.

Property	Meaning
BackColor; ForeColor	Defines the fore and background color of the element as an RGB value.
BorderStyle	Sets the type of border. For controls you can only choose between no border or a simple border. Forms allow other settings. These are described in Chapter 5.
Caption	Defines the title and caption. An "&" defines a hotkey for switches, labels and menus (which can then be used with **Alt** + letter).
CausesValida- tion	Defines whether the Validate event of the control which the user has left before entering this control is called. With CausesValidation and Validate you can very easily enable input validation. You will find more information in "Checking inputs".
DataField; DataSource; DataMember; DataFormat	These properties are used when linking controls with ADO data sources in order, for example, to enable the user to edit the contents of a database table. Fundamental information on this can be found in Chapter 10.
DragMode	Defines whether a Drag&Drop operation is implemented automatically (1) or manually (0).
Enabled	Defines whether the control is activated or deactivated. A deactivated control is shown in paler colors and cannot receive focus.
Font; FontColor	Defines for controls which have a text property (Caption, Text) or can output text (e.g. picture field) which type of font is to be used.
HelpContextID	Defines the ID number for context-sensitive Help. The ID number must be present in the Help file allocated to the program (in the Options or in the App object). If the user presses **F1**, when the control has the focus, the relevant Help topic is displayed in Windows Help.
HideSelection	Defines with True, that marked text is then highlighted, when the control no longer has the focus.
Index	Defines a control's index using a control array.
KeyPreview	Defines whether keystrokes firstly go to the form (True) or to the object which currently has the focus (False). Using this property you can make a form react to a keystroke before the active control receives it. With KeyPreview = True for example you can program a cancellation of any action you like using the **Esc** key, independent of which control currently has the focus.

Property	Meaning
Left; Top	Defines the position of the object.
MousePointer	Determines the type of MousePointer for an object (vbNormal = normal, vbHourglass = hourglass). Screen.Mousepointer defines the mouse pointer, for example, for the screen.
Name	The program name of the object.
Parent	Identifies the form where a control is located.
ScaleHeight; ScaleLeft; ScaleTop; ScaleWidth	These properties define the dimensions for the internal coordinate system of a form, a Picture or a Printer object and are used whenever a user-defined coordinate system is set. Important for graphics output.
TabIndex	Defines the index for focusing with (⬅). The element with 0 in TabIndex automatically has the focus at the start of the form.
TabStop	True defines that this element can be reached with (⬅).
Tag	An additional variant data field that you can use for your own purposes. As the property Name cannot be queried at run-time, Tag for example can be used to identify an object.
Text	Contains the input text of a Text box, List box or Combo box.
ToolTipText	The ToolTip is displayed when the user holds the mouse for a while on an object.
Value	Sets or ascertains the current status of a scrollbar, pushbutton, an OptionButton or a CheckBox.
Visible	Determines whether the element is visible.
WhatsThisHelp	Defines whether the pop-up direct Help is being used (True) or not (False).
WhatsThis-HelpId	Defines the ID number for a pop-up direct Help facility.

Table 5.1 *The common properties of controls*

The default property

Every control has a default property, which as a rule is the property that is most used (*text box*.Text, *HScrollBar*.Value, *Label*.Caption). If you use only the name of a control in the source text, the compiler (usually) automatically uses the default property, if this matches the context of current programming.

```
txtFirstName = "Donald"
' is identical to
txtFirstName.Text = "Donald"
```

Tips and tricks

Do not rely on the default property

For clean programming and in order to guarantee compatibility with other languages which are not familiar with default properties, you should always specify the properties you are addressing. In some cases omitting the default property also leads to problems. In addition it may be that you will have to compile your source code again in the year 2199 with "Galaxy Basic 42"[3]. What do you do then if "Cosmosoft" has simply changed the default property? When changing from ADO 1.0 to 1.5 Microsoft did precisely that for the Field objects important for data access (out of Value became Properties), which caused a great deal of problems for some programming (after ADO 2.0 however Value is once again the default property).

5.2.2 Common events

Just like properties, most controls have certain events. The most important are listed in Table 5.2.

Event	Meaning
Change	Called whenever the content of a control is changed.
Click	Called when you click with the mouse, with the CommandButton, or when you activate the switch using the keyboard, you use List and Combo boxes and also when you select a new item.
DblClick	Called by double-clicking with the mouse.
DragDrop; DragOver	Called through a normal Drag&Drop operation ("normal" means *no OLE Drag&Drop*). You can find more on this in Chapter 6.

---

3. Name changes here are pure speculation ...

Event	Meaning
GotFocus; LostFocus	Called whenever the object receives or loses the focus.
KeyDown	Called when you press a key on an object (that has the focus). In this event you can evaluate all keys, even the special keys.
KeyPress	Called when activating an ASCII key on an object. KeyPress is only called using keys which have an ASCII Code. Non-ASCII keys are the function keys, the cursor keys and the keys **Pos1**, **RollUp**, **RollDown**, **Delete**, **Insert**.
KeyUp	Called when releasing a key on an object. As with Key-Down you can evaluate all keys in this event.
MouseDown	Called when operating a mouse button on an object.
MouseMove	Called when moving the mouse on an object.
MouseUp	Called when releasing a mouse button on an object.
OLEStartDrag; OLECompleteDrag; OLEDragDrop; OLEDrag-Over; OLEGiveFeedback; OLESetData	Called with an OLE Drag&Drop operation.

Table 5.2 *The common events of controls*

5.2.3 Common methods

The most important common methods for controls are listed in Table 5.3.

Method	Meaning
Drag	Starts, ends or cancels a normal Drag&Drop operation.
Hide	Hides the object (makes it invisible). Identical to setting the property Visible to False.
Move	Shifts an object on the screen, which can be important for example when finishing a Drag&Drop operation. Instead of using Move, you can set the Left, Top, Width and Height properties.
OLEDrag	Starts an OLE Drag&Drop operation.
Refresh	Updates the contents of an object. This usually happens automatically it is true, but in some situations an explicit Refresh is necessary (it is usually clear when).
SetFocus	Sets the focus on an object.

Method	Meaning
Show	Displays the object, provided that it is invisible. Is identical to setting the property Visible to True.
ZOrder	Using ZOrder you can place a control right at the front within its level (ZOrder 0) or place it at the back (ZOrder 1). ZOrder is important for overlapping controls, if you want to place one of them at the front.

Table 5.3 *The most important common methods for controls*

5.3 Standard controls

5.3.1   The label

A label is a pure text output field, which is used as a description or output field. Besides this you can transfer text using Drag&Drop to a label, but this is probably not done very often.

The most important property is certainly Caption, which is where you put the text of the label. Depending on the preferences in the AutoSize and WordWrap properties the size of the label is automatically adapted in height and width, which in practice is not all that important. As the label is not too concerned about space, it can happen that the label extends beyond the form and the text then becomes unreadable. Unfortunately you cannot respond to a change in size, as the label is missing an appropriate event. If you have to reserve the maximum space necessary in any case, you can also define a static size and leave AutoSize alone. WordWrap is interesting when it comes to labels which are going to have several lines. If you do not want to define the lines yourself by linking the individual strings using vbCRLF, set WordWrap to True, so that the label automatically wraps the text.

If the label serves as a caption for another control that can receive the focus you can create a shortcut by simply putting an "&" in front of the character. However UseMnemonic needs to be True and the label to be exactly one position in front of the other control in the TAB order.

One more tip: the type of label background is non-transparent by presetting. If you change the color of the form, the label stands out because of its ugly gray color. The label takes its color exactly like the form from the same setting in the system control. Changing the system setting therefore will not cause any problem. If, however, you want to change the background color of the form itself, change the type of label background to transparent.

The most important properties

Property	Meaning
AutoSize	With `Autosize = True` the size of the label is automatically adapted for new caption text. If at the same time `WordWrap = False`, the label expands horizontally and if `WordWrap = True` vertically.
Alignment	Determines the horizontal alignment of the text (left justified, centered or right justified).
BackStyle	Defines the type of background: *0: Transparent*: the background is transparent. *1: Non-transparent*: the background is marked in a color defined by `BackColor`.
Caption	Caption defines the text. An "&" in front of a character defines a hotkey when at the same time the UseMnemonic property is set to True. If the user activates **Alt** + hotkey, then the next control in the tabulator order receives the focus.
WordWrap	Determines with `True` that the text wraps at the right border, if it does not fit onto one line. If additionally `AutoSize=True`, the label height is automatically adjusted.

Table 5.4 *The most important properties of the label*

The most important events

Event	Meaning
Click	The user has clicked on the label.
DblClick	The user has double-clicked on the label.
Change	The text has been changed (the user cannot change the text from the program).

Table 5.5 *The most important label events*

5.3.2   The text box

The text box is a text input field, where single-line and multi-line text can be displayed. The text box supports the clipboard with the usual key combinations **CTRL+C**, **CTRL+X**, **CTRL+V**. Of course the usual editing functions (delete, insert, etc.) are also integrated.

The most important property is Text. This is where the input field text is stored. In the text box you can normally manage up to 64 KB of text. Howver, there is a trick that allows you to manage even more MBs (see "Tips and tricks"). Using MultiLine you can set up the text box to allow multiple line text. In this case it frequently makes sense to use scrollbars which can be set up using the ScrollBars property. If you want to access the current selection, you can get the selected text using the SelText property. Using SelStart and SelLength you can redefine the selection. If you are going to enter a password in the text box you can specify the character in PasswordChar, and this then appears instead of the characters which have been entered. In the Text property you also then have access to the input.

Missing properties

Unfortunately the text box does not allow automatic selection on receiving the focus. But you can program this property yourself, as described in "Tips and tricks".

Frequently input in a text box has to be restricted in a particular way. So a text box which allows only number values or date values makes a lot of sense. Unfortunately in the first instance the text box does not allow this. If you look yourself in properties, the DataFormat property is valid only, if the text box is linked to an ADO recordset, in order to display the content of a data source (e.g. a database table). You will find fundamentals for restriction of input in the "Tips and tricks" section overleaf.

The most important properties

Property	Meaning
Text	Contains the text. This property is restricted to 64 KB because of a bug, although the text box can store more MB without any problems.
MultiLine	Defines with True that several lines are possible.
Alignment	Defines how the text is aligned.
ScrollBars	Defines the availability of scrollbars with MultiLine = True.
MaxLength	Defines the maximum possible number of input characters. 0 stands for as many characters as you want.
PasswordChar	Defines a password character that appears instead of the characters that have been entered. The text can be reached furthermore using the Text property.
SelStart	The index at the start of a possible selection. The index begins at 0. Only available at run-time.

Property	Meaning
SelLength	The number of characters in a possible selection. Only available at run-time.
SelText	The text in a possible selection. Only available at run-time.
HideSelection	Defines with True that marked text is highlighted when the control no longer has the focus.

Table 5.6 *The most important properties of the text box*

The most important events

Event	Meaning
Change	The text has been changed.
GotFocus	The user has placed the cursor in the text box.
LostFocus	The user has left the text box.
KeyPress	The user has pressed a key. Via the argument KeyAscii you can ascertain which key has been pressed. If you set KeyAscii on 0, then the key press is ignored.
Validate	The user has left the text box. You can validate the input and cancel Exit. There is more on this in Chapter 6.
Click	The user has clicked on the text box.

Table 5.7 *The most important Text box events*

Tips and tricks

Fill multiple line text boxes from the program

If you want to manage several lines in a text box, set up the MultiLine property to True. If you now want to fill the text box from the program, attach the constant vbCrLf (Carriage Return / Line Feed) to each string that represents a line.

Automatic Selection

In order to achieve automatic text selection on receiving the focus, program the following lines in the GotFocus event of the text box:

```
Private Sub txtTest_GotFocus()
 txtTest.SelStart = 0
 txtTest.SelLength = Len(txtTest.Text)
End Sub
```

Only allow numbers

If for example you only want to allow numbers as input, you program in the KeyPress event. As you can also change the transferred KeyAscii value, you can set this for all invalid entries to 0, meaning that the input is ignored.

```
Private Sub txtTest_KeyPress(KeyAscii As Integer)
 Select Case KeyAscii
   Case 48 To 57, 8, Asc("-"), Asc("+")
      ' Do nothing
   Case Else
      ' Reject key
      Beep
      KeyAscii = 0
 End Select
End Sub
```

This example is far from perfect however, because for example several + and –
signs are allowed and the clipboard is not taken into account.

Enable Undo

You can enable a simple Undo merely by sending the relevant Windows message
to the text box:

```
Const EM_UNDO = &HC7
SendMessage txtTest.hwnd, EM_UNDO, 0, 0
```

User irritation

If you do not wish to bother the user with nonsense error messages and annoying confirmation dialogs, simply use the following source code:

```
Private Sub txtTest_KeyPress(KeyAscii As Integer)
 KeyAscii = KeyAscii + 1
End Sub
```

5.3.3   The Command button

The Command button is a simple button that the user can activate. The most important property is Caption, the text. The only interesting event is the Click
event. Click is called whenever the button has been activated, including operation via the keyboard.

If you want to display a picture on the button, you have to set the style of the
button to graphic in the Style property and load the picture into the Picture
property. Normally this is sufficient and the picture is usually suitably converted
when the button is activated or deactivated. Alternatively you can specify pictures in the DisabledPicture and DownPicture properties for the deactivated
or activated status. You can show pictures and text at the same time. If you do
not want any text with the picture you have to delete the text in Caption. You
can get a default button, which you can also activate with (ø), without having the
focus, if you set Default on True. This is similar for the Cancel property. If
you enter True here, the button can also be activated with **Esc**.

The most important properties

Property	Meaning
Caption	Contains text.
Default	Defines with True that you can also select the button if it does not have the focus using (↵).
Cancel	Defines with True whether you can also select the switch with **Esc.**
Style	Defines whether the button appears normal (only with lettering) or graphically (with image and optional text).
Picture	Defines the standard picture that is visible on the button when the picture is in the graphic style.
DisabledPicture	Defines the picture that is visible in the window when the window is in the graphic style and is deactivated.
DownPicture	Defines the picture that is visible on the button when the button is in the graphic style and is activated.

Table 5.8 *The most important properties of the Command button*

The most important events

Event	Meaning
Click	The switch has been activated. Click is also called on operating the keyboard.
GotFocus	The window has received the focus.
LostFocus	The window has lost the focus.

Table 5.9 *The most important command button events*

5.3.4 CheckBox and OptionButton

The user can click on the CheckBox and the OptionButton to change the on/off value. If option buttons are arranged in a group (e.g. a frame), then only one option button can be turned on in the group (as was the case with old radios, which is why the option buttons are also called *RadioButtons*).

As is the case with the Label you can also set up a shortkey by simply placing an "&" in front of a character in the text.

The most important property for both controls is Value. You have to take care here: with the OptionButton Value has the value True when switched on and False when switched off. The CheckBox however uses the values 1 and vbChecked (switched on), 0 and vbUnchecked (switched off) and 2 and vbGrayed (interim status). You can only turn on the interim status from the program. As you probably already know from different options when installing applications, the interim status represents neither on nor off.

It is interesting that using the property Style you can make a toggle from both controls.

If you arrange option buttons in a container control (for example a frame), then you have to take care that you install the already existing option buttons into the container using cut and paste. If you simply drag existing option buttons into a container, then group radio toggle will not function for this group.

The most important properties

Property	Meaning
Caption	Text. An "&" before a character defines a shortkey.
Value	Defines the status. OptionButton: True = On, False = Off. Check-box: 1 = On, 0 = Off, 2 = interim status.
Style	Defines whether the control appears in standard or graphic view. Graphically displayed option buttons and CheckBoxes look like buttons. You can also allocate to a picture instead of text these controls using the properties Picture, DownPicture and DisabledPicture, which is shown on the button. Using the property MaskColor you can determine which color in the image is marked transparent, if at the same time UseMaskColor is True.

Table 5.10 *The most important properties of the CheckBox and Option-Button*

The most important events

Event	Meaning
Click	Called when the user clicks on the control.

Table 5.11 *The most important events of the CheckBox and OptionButton*

5.3.5 The List box

The List box displays a series of items in a list, from which the user can select one or several items. In addition it is possible to store a Longint value with each item. A List box enables three different types to be shown which are defined using the `MultiSelect` property (Table 5.12).

MultiSelect	List box type
0 (None)	Simple List box – the user can select only one entry at any one time.
1 (Simple)	Simple multiple choice List box – the user can select several entries at the same time. Individual entries are selected or deselected by a simple choice of click or space bar.
2 (Extended)	Extended multiple choice List box – the user can select several items at once. Using ($\uparrow$) + Cursor and ($\uparrow$) + click you can select or deselect a list of items. Using **Ctrl** + click individual items are selected or deselected.

Table 5.12 *The different types of List box*

Setting and reading entries

Using the `AddItem` method you can attach a string to the current list:

```
Listbox.AddItem Item [,Index]
```

If you specify the optional Index, you can add an item in the middle as well as at the beginning of the list:

```
' Addition of a new entry at the beginning
lstDemo.AddItem "Test input", 0
```

The individual items are accessible via the `List` property, where you transfer the index items you want. The list index starts at 0. *Listbox*.`List`(*Index*) = *Value* replaces the entry to the *Index* with a new entry.

> **Tip** Although the number of entries in the List box is limited only by the available memory and you can add 100,000 items for example using `AddItem`, the query properties are unfortunately limited to integer values (up to 32767). If for example you want to run a query on the number of items, `ListCount` results in the value −31072 and List(99999) returns an overflow. It is a pity, but it is not very often that you need more than 32767 entries. If nevertheless you do need to store more items, I recommend Windows API. The List box can be controlled completely using SendMessage with the LB messages. So `SendMessage(lstDemo.hWnd, LB_GETCOUNT, 0, 0)` returns the correct number.

Define the selected item

When List box is first started using presetting at this stage no item has been selected. With a single choice List box the selected item can be set using the set `ListIndex` property:

```
Listbox.ListIndex = Index
```

Each of the items to be selected in the multiple choice List boxes has to be set using `Selected` Listing:

```
Listbox.Selected(Index) = True
```

Determine the selected entry

With a single choice List box the `ListIndex` property returns the Index containing the item selected by the user. If no item is currently selected the result is a –1. In order to ascertain the text of the selected item, you can simply evaluate the `Text` property:

```
Dim strItem As String
strItem = lstSource.Text
```

With multiple choice List boxes you have to run through the whole list, and in so doing you can check the selection of the items using `Selected`. The following example copies all selected items from the multiple choice List box *lstSource* to *lstDest*:

```
Dim intIndex As Integer
For intIndex = 0 To lstSource.ListCount - 1
   If lstSource.Selected(intIndex) Then
      lstResult.AddItem lstSource.List(intIndex)
   End If
Next
```

Sorting additional Long values in ItemData

`ItemData` is a property which gives access to a Longint field, which is stored with every List string. You can use this field freely. For example when reading data sets to a List box, you can file an ID number stored in the data set in `ItemData`:

```
While rstAddress.EOF = False
  lstAddress.AddItem rstAddress.Fields("last name").Value
  lstAddress.ItemData(lstAddress.NewIndex) = _
    rstAddress.Fields("Id").Value
Next
```

When selecting an item with the help of this ID, you can search the data set in the table and for example issue the remaining data of the data set.

The most important properties

Property	Meaning
Columns	Defines how many columns the List box has. Unfortunately the columns are not valid for one entry. Instead, the list box breaks the list into several columns.
ItemData(*Index*)	Specifies access to the Longint value *Index*.
List(*Index*)	Specifies access to the String *Index*.
ListCount	Returns the number of stored elements. Take care: with more than **32767** items ListCount returns an incorrect negative value.
ListIndex	Returns the Index of the current selected item.
MultiSelect	Sets the multiple choice mode (see above).
NewIndex	Returns the index of the last element which was added. Also functions when the list is automatically sorted.
Selected(*Index*)	Returns True when the element on Index is selected; is required in the MultiSelect mode in order to establish which items are selected.
Sorted	With True the List box is automatically sorted.
Style	Determines whether the List box appears in standard mode or with the items as check boxes. The user can select several items at the same time in a List box with check boxes, even when MultiSelect is False.
TopIndex	Determines the item to be shown at the very top of the list.

Table 5.13 *The most important properties of the List box*

The most important methods

Method	Meaning
AddItem (*Item* [, *Index*])	Adds an item to a list. If you specify the index, the entry is added to this index. The preceding item and all following items are pushed one place downwards. If you do not specify the index, the new item is added to the bottom of the list.
Clear	Deletes the list.
RemoveItem(*Index*)	Deletes the item in the *Index*.

Table 5.14 *The most important List box methods*

The most important events

Event	Meaning
Click	Called, when an item is selected.
DblClick	Called, when you double-click on an item.

Table 5.15   *The most important List box events*

Tips and tricks

Fast Search

Do you want to search in a List box or Combo box for a value? Just leave the search to Windows. Windows can search the memory, and you cannot. So send a message to the List box or Combo box requesting a search for the transferred value and an answer as to the index where the item has been found. Logically SendMessage returns −1 if nothing has been found. You can search for an exact item (LB_FINDSTRINGEXACT) and for a search item, which ends with (LB_FINDSTRING):

```
' Fast Exact Search
lstDemo.ListIndex = SendMessage(lstDemo.hwnd, _
   LB_FINDSTRINGEXACT, 0, ByVal txtFind.Text)
' Fast Initial Search
lstDemo.ListIndex = SendMessage(lstDemo.hwnd, _
  LB_FINDSTRING, 0, ByVal txtFind.Text)
```

On the book's Internet page you will find examples of Fast Search in the List box and Combo box.

Fast Fill

Because filling the Combo box using the API function SendMessage with the message LB_ADDSTRING is faster than using the AddItem method, this should also be the case for the List box. During a test I unexpectedly obtained the opposite result: filling with 10,000 figures only took me approximately 0.7 seconds with AddItem and with SendMessage approximately 0.9 seconds. If you want to try it yourself:

```
' Fill using SendMessage
SendMessage lstDemo.hwnd, LB_ADDSTRING, 0, _
   ByVal "Item x"
```

Tip With the Combo box filling runs much more quickly using SendMessage.

5.3.6   The Combo box

The Combo box is very similar to the List box. The first clear difference is that at first the list is invisible. Programming is done exactly as with the List box, in many cases you can simply interchange a List box for a Combo box. One essential difference is that the Combo box has a text field with style 0 where the user can enter text independently from the list. You evaluate this text field using the Text property. The other essential difference is that the Combo box does not allow multiple choice.

The most important properties (additional to or altered to those in the List box)

Property	Meaning
Style	Defines the style: 0: normal Combo box with the possibility of input into text box; 1: simple Combo box without text box and without Dropdown list. Nevertheless you can run through the list using the cursor keys; 2: normal Combo box without the possibility of input into text box.

Table 5.16   *The most important properties of the Combo box (only the additional ones compared with the List box)*

The most important events (additional to those in the List box)

Event	Meaning
Change	Called when the text is changed in the editing field.

Table 5.17   *The most important events of the Combo box (only the additional ones compared with the List box)*

Tips and tricks

Fast Filling and Fast Search

In principle the same tips apply for the Combo box as for the List box, only here you use the CB_constants in place of the LB_constants. Fast Filling works for the Combo box, which is not the case for the List box. Certainly the Combo box needs considerably longer when filling with AddItem than the List box. For the List box it appears that AddItem is considerably better implemented than for the Combo box. Filling with 10,000 figures for the Combo box needed approximately 6.9 seconds using AddItem and using SendMessage only 3.6 seconds. Here once more is the code for Fast Filling:

```
SendMessage cboDemo.hwnd, CB_ADDSTRING, 0, _
    ByVal "item x"
```

5.3.7   VScrollBar, HScrollBar

The scroll bars implemented in the HScrollBar and VScrollBar controls enable scrolling of screens or values to be set. You can only scroll in VB by shifting a container control such as the Picture control above the scrollbar control in the upper and left position.

Programming the Scrollbar control is really easy. In Min and Max you define the range. In SmallChange and LargeChange you set the number of units by which the value is to be changed whenever the user activates the arrow and clicks between the sliding box and the arrow. In Value you finally interpret the set value.

The most important properties

Property	Meaning
Value	Contains the current value that can be used to control other actions.
Min, Max	Defines the Value achieved on reaching the upper or lower border of the scrollbar.
SmallChange	Defines the number of units by which the moving box is moved when you click on the arrows.
LargeChange	Defines the number of units by which the sliding box is moved when you click on the area between the sliding box and the arrow.

Table 5.18   *The most important properties of the Scrollbar controls*

The most important events

Event	Meaning
Change	Called after the sliding box setting has been changed.
Scroll	Called whenever the sliding box setting is changed. In Scroll you are able to respond immediately to every change, however this only works for actions requiring little computing power.

Table 5.19   *The most important events of the Scrollbar controls*

5.3.8   FileListBox, DirListBox and DriveListBox

Unfortunately Visual Basic still has no control that shows files, folders and drives as in Explorer. If you want to offer the user a file, folder or drive selection, you have to firstly fall back on the old FileListBox, DirListBox and DriveListBox controls. If you want to let the user select a file, it is better to use the Windows standard dialog. The control `CommonDialog` used for this is described from page179 in this chapter. Before you deal with the following controls, you should know that it is possible to integrate a file/folder selection dialog into your application in a way similar to Explorer. To do this you use certain API functions in a rather complicated way.

File, folder and drive list fields make drives, folders and directories visible in List boxes. The treatment of list fields corresponds to that of normal List boxes. User selection is ascertained for example using `List` and `ListIndex`.

FileListBox

The FileListBox displays folder files. In the `Path` property you set which folder contents will be displayed. In the properties `Pattern`, `Archive`, `ReadOnly` etc. you can define which files are to be displayed.

The FileListBox as a rule is combined with the DriveListBox using the `Path` property, and in so doing the latter is reciprocally assigned on amendment:

```
Private Sub dirDemo_Change()
 filDemo.Path = dirDemo.Path
End Sub
```

The most important properties

Property	Meaning
Path	Defines the search path for the files. Path can only be reached during program execution and updates the List with any amendment.
Pattern	Defines the mask (*.* etc.). The display is restricted according to this mask.
Archive; Hidden; ReadOnly; System	The significance of the file attributes limits the file display.
FileName	Contains the selected file names.

Table 5.20   *The most important properties of the FileListBox*

DirListBox

The DirListBox displays all folders of a higher folder or drive in the hierarchy. In the `Path` property you set the higher folder and drive.

The directory list box as a rule is combined with the DriveListBox using the `Drive` and `Path` properties:

```
Private Sub drvDemo_Change()
 dirDemo.Path = drvDemo.Drive
End Sub
```

The most important properties

Property	Meaning
Path	Defines the search path.
Click	Responds to a user Click on an element (DblClick does not exist!).
Change	Responds to a Click and to a change in the list (via Path)

Table 5.21   *The most important properties of the DirListBox*

DriveListBox

The DriveListBox is a joy in its simplicity when it comes to programming. In principle only the `Drive` property is of interest via which the drive is set and evaluated.

The most important property

Property	Meaning
Drive	Defines the selected drive.

Table 5.22   *The most important property of the DriveListBox*

5.3.9   The Shape control

The Shape control is a very simple control for representing simple geometric figures. The Shape control cannot respond to events.

The most important properties

Property	Meaning
Shape	Defines the appearance (circle, rectangle, etc.).
FillStyle	Defines the filling style (solid, stripes, etc.).
FillColor	Defines the filling color.

Table 5.23   *The most important properties of the Shape control*

Tips and tricks

Draw using graphics methods

Do not overlook the considerably better options you have with self-draw using the graphics methods and the GDI functions when using Shape control.

5.3.10   The Line control

The Line control is not really worth mentioning. It is a simple line whose width, color and type (continuous, chain, etc.) only can be changed. Please note that a change to the BorderStyle property only becomes effective if you set Value 1 in BorderWidth because of the Windows GDI restrictions. A tip: the same applies as for the Shape control.

5.3.11   The PictureBox and Image control

You can use the Image control like the PictureBox control to produce pictures. But in addition you can produce graphics using graphics methods and API functions on the PictureBox control. The Image control needs considerably fewer resources because there is no graphics output. One advantage of the Image control as opposed to the PictureBox control is the possibility of using Stretch = True to set preferences so that the loaded picture always fits into the maximum area of the control.

You can already allocate to both controls a picture in the form of a BMP, ICO, WMF, GIF or JPG file in design mode. If the picture is allocated in design, then it is stored in the EXE file. You also have the possibility of loading and allocating a picture with the LoadPicture function at run-time:

```
Set picBlueMan.Picture = _
   LoadPicture(App.Path & "\BlueMan.bmp")
```

The PictureBox control is best suited to the output of graphics and therefore has the usual graphics methods. In Chapter 8 you will find more information on the output of graphics. With the Print method you can also issue texts in a picture field.

You can combine two variants, for example in Picture you can allocate a picture and draw on this picture. You get the complete picture via the Image property but then only when AutoRedraw is True.

The most important properties

Property	Meaning
AutoRedraw (PictureBox)	AutoRedraw defines whether drawings are reproduced in the working memory and therefore always available or whether in the Paint event. In Chapter 8 you will find more information about this property.
AutoSize (PictureBox)	If you set AutoSize to True, the size of the control is automatically adapted to the size of a loaded bitmap.
Image (PictureBox)	Image refers to the whole visible picture, therefore to any possible underlying picture, the entire area and all drawings which have been implemented on the area. Image only functions then when AutoRedraw is True.
Picture	Picture refers to a loaded picture. Using the LoadPicture function you can load images and with SavePicture store them.
Stretch (Image)	Defines whether a bitmap adapts to the size of the control or the reverse, whether the control adapts to the size of the bitmap.

Table 5.24 *The most important properties of the PictureBox and the Image control*

The most important methods of the PictureBox control

Method	Meaning
Circle, Cls, Line, PaintPicture, Print, PSet	Using these graphics methods you can draw on the control. You will find more on this in Chapter 8.

Table 5.25 *The most important methods of the PictureBox control*

Tips and tricks

Temporary drawing using graphics

The PictureBox is frequently used for drawing. In so doing the problem often arises of how to draw a temporary picture across a surface which already has a drawing, without having to redraw the whole basic drawing. The solution to this problem is very simple, even if rather heavy on resources: Set AutoRedraw to True, draw the basic drawing and allocate the contents of Image to the Picture property:

```
Set picBlueMan.Picture = picBlueMan.Image
```

The basic drawing is now permanently filed, can be drawn over and restored using the Cls method.

5.3.12   The Timer

The Timer is a control which triggers the `Timer` event at regular intervals and in using its event procedure you can set up time-controlled runs.

> **Warning** The `Timer` event is not always triggered if the program is set in the background or if the user shifts the window. This event is not triggered at all if a modal form is opened. Windows timers possess even less priority than a new screen output or loading and storing files and for this reason also cannot be called for a longer period of time. So writing time-critical process control becomes difficult with Visual Basic, though not impossible with a few precautionary measures. I control the production equipment of a chemical factory using a timer with a Visual Basic 4 application. Up to now the inhabitants of the town concerned have only had to close their doors and windows once (but not because of this factory, something which I only found out when I was already in the Bahamas...).

The most important properties

Property	Meaning
Interval	The interval for triggering the Timer event in milliseconds (0 to 65535). At interval 0 (presetting) the Timer is not in operation.
Enabled	Determines whether the Timer is switched on or not.

Table 5.26   *The most important properties of the Timer control*

The most important events

Event	Meaning
Timer	This event is always called whenever the time specified in `Interval` has elapsed.

Table 5.27   *The most important events of the Timer control*

5.3.13   Arrays and frames

All the same types of control can be combined in a control array. You can produce such an array by giving the controls the same name. It is easier however to copy and paste an available control using the clipboard. VB asks you if you want to produce a control array. The `Index` property of a control defines the Array Index, which normally starts at 0. The individual controls are then "spoken to" using

object name(Index)

For a control array only one event procedure exists. The control Index is transferred as argument to this procedure and using this you can query or describe for example all the same types of controls in a loop.

A frame is more of a passive control which combines other controls. If other controls are placed on a frame there are several advantages:

→ a frame combines option buttons into one group;

→ all controls placed in a frame in design can be copied to the clipboard using the frame selection;

→ shifting the frame automatically moves the controls held in the frame.

5.4 The ActiveX controls

Integration into the project

If you want to use ActiveX controls you have to integrate them into your project. In the components' dialog, which you can reach via `Project | Components`, you will find in the register `Controls` all ActiveX controls installed on your system. In order to integrate a control, just mark the relevant component and activate `OK`. Of course you have to know how the controls are described.

Many controls however are installed from any application. As a rule you do not know what these controls do and how they are programmed because the related documentation is missing. If you want to use controls other than those supplied with VB and you do not have the documentation, only the Object catalog and trial and error will help.

If possible only integrate controls which you are actually going to use, otherwise your application will become very large when creating an installation version.

Run-time and Designtime license

These are stored for every ActiveX component in the registry whether only a Run-time license or a Designtime license also are available. For controls with which you can also develop your own applications, a Designtime license is available. Whenever an application is installed which uses ActiveX controls, these are normally only installed with a Run-time license. Compiled applications can use these controls, but you cannot use them for development. So do not be surprised by a related error message when you try to put on a form a control which has not been supplied with VB.

Transfer on installation

You can incorporate ActiveX components supplied with VB free of charge when you create an installation version of your program. The package and transfer assistant does this automatically for you. If you are using ActiveX components which other programs have installed on your PC, there is a high probability that these cannot be distributed free of charge. You would contravene the manufacturer's copyright if you were to distribute the controls with your installation program. Before distribution you have to find out whether you may distribute these controls or possibly whether you have to acquire a license.

The properties dialog

All ActiveX controls possess a properties dialog, via which you can set the most important properties in a register. There are two reasons for this:

→ Some development environments do not have any special option for setting up ActiveX control properties and only use this dialog.

→ Some properties cannot be displayed in the Properties window, only in the Properties dialog. All array properties belong in this category as for example the properties for the definition of the registers for a register control.

You can open the Properties dialog by selecting the item `User defined` in the Properties window or by right-clicking on the control and the item `Properties`. With some controls, particularly those with dynamic design capability (TabStrip, Toolbar, ImageList, etc.), you have to use the Properties dialog in order to set the definitive properties.

5.4.1   The CommonDialog

The CommonDialog is a control with which you can easily use the Windows standard dialog. A control method determines the type of dialog. Using Properties you set default values and evaluate the user selection. It is true that programming the CommonDialog is in principle the same for the different dialogs, but you have to be careful about some things if you want to avoid errors. For this reason I am describing here first the grass roots of programming and then programming of the individual dialogs.

The grass roots of programming

In order to be able to use CommonDialog, you have to integrate the "Microsoft Common Dialog Control 6.0" components into your project. You open the dialog with one of the Show methods of the CommonDialog control. So `ShowOpen` for example opens the Open File dialog. Irrespective of the type of dialog you still have to set different properties before opening. With the Open file dialog this would be for example the `Filter` property where you specify the file filters which appear in the File Type list of the dialog. But for most dialogs the `Flags` property is very important, and this is described below for the individual dialogs in more detail. Using `Flags` you can "fine-tune" the dialog. Flags is a bitmask. You will find the values which you can write to this bitmask in constants whose name begins with "cdl".

The programming of the CommonDialog control is unfortunately not very intelligent when it comes to the dialog's Cancel button. If you do not set any more preferences, then the dialog will always return the last value of the values set whenever the user activates `Cancel`. Because of this you can no longer decide after the second dialog call whether the user has cancelled. The programmer of the dialog then had the "brilliant" idea that on canceling the dialog produces a run-time error if you set the `CancelError` property to `True`. It would have been better simply to implement the Show methods as a function, which returns `True` or `False`. So you have to tediously evaluate the run-time error.

Open File dialog with evaluation of the Cancel button:

```
cdl.CancelError = True
' Set the flags such that the file must exist;
' the Read Only Checkbox is not permitted.
cdl.Flags = cdlOFNFileMustExist Or cdlOFNHideReadOnly
cdl.Filter = "Textfiles|*.txt|all Files|*.*"
cdl.DefaultExt = ".txt"
cdl.FilterIndex = 1
On Error Resume Next
cdl.ShowOpen
If Err.Number = 0 Then
    ' You can evaluate the dialog here
Else
    ' You can respond to cancel here
End If
```

Take care that in this example error treatment, which should be present in every event procedure, is switched off with On Error Resume Next in order to be able to analyze the error immediately. Using On Error Goto ErrHandler the Error Handler must then be switched on again afterwards. See also Chapter 7 from page 251 onwards as a comparison.

Open File dialog

Before opening a File dialog you should set one or several data filters in the `Filter` property. These data filters appear afterward in the file type list of the dialog and restrict the view of the files accordingly. You define the filter with a String, which looks as follows:

```
"FilterName 1|Mask 1[|FilterName 2|Mask 2][...]"
```

A typical filter for example looks like this:

```
"Text Files|*.txt|All Files|*.*"
```

On opening you can identify the filter which is activated in the `FilterIndex` property. If let us say you identify 2 for the example above, then the "All Files" filter is active.

You should write to the `DefaultExt` property a preset file ending. The dialog uses this if the user specifies only the basic file name without an ending. Always specify the file name with the full stop. You can still describe the `FileName` property using a file name, which should be preset on opening the dialog. In `InitDir` you can set the directory where the dialog starts.

In `Flags` you can then specially set the dialog. `Flags` is a combination (addition) of several constants. You can find the constants for the Open File dialog in Table 5.28.

Flag	Meaning
cdlOFNAllowMultiSelect	Allows selection of several files at the same time. Multiple selection dialogs are not described in this book because of the high programming complexity.
cdlOFNCreatePrompt	If the user selects a file which does not exist, Windows enquires with OK whether the file should be created. If the user does not want to create the file, the user can only leave the dialog with Cancel.
cdlOFNExplorer	As a MultiSelect dialog uses as standard Windows 3.1 for compatibility reasons, you have to switch Explorer on.

Flag	Meaning
cdlOFNFileMustExist	The specified file must exist, otherwise Windows will not let the user out of the dialog with OK.
cdlOFNHideReadOnly	The Read Only checkbox in the dialog is not visible when you identify this Flag.
cdlOFNNoReadOnlyReturn	The user can only select files which are not read only.
cdlOFNPathMustExist	The specified path must exist otherwise Windows will not let the user out of the dialog with OK.
cdlOFNReadOnly	Has the effect that the Read Only checkbox is activated on creating the dialog field. Using this Flag you can evaluate the status of the Read Only checkbox even after opening.
cdlOFNShareAware	The user can also select files when network protective measures would normally prevent this.

Table 5.28 *The Open File Flags*

As standard for Open Dialogs is `cdlOFNFileMustExist` or `cdlOFNHideReadOnly`.

'Must' open dialog – the file exists and hidden Read Only checkbox:

```
cdl.CancelError = True
' Set Flags, that the file
' must exist and the Read Only
' Checkbox is not visible
cdl.Flags = cdlOFNFileMustExist Or cdlOFNHideReadOnly
' Set Filter
cdl.Filter = "Textfiles|*.txt|All Files|*.*"
' Set the preset file ending
cdl.DefaultExt = ".txt"
' Open and evaluate Dialog
On Error Resume Next
cdl.ShowOpen
If Err.Number = 0 Then
   On Error Goto ErrHandler
   MsgBox cdl.FileName
Else
   On Error Goto ErrHandler
   MsgBox "Cancel or Error"
End If
```

The Store File dialog

The Store File dialog is programmed in principle in the same way as the Open File dialog. There are differences however when it comes to the Flags. You will find useful settings in Table 5.29.

Flag	Meaning
cdlOFNCreatePrompt	If the user selects a file which still does not exist, then Windows enquires with OK whether the file should be created. If the user does not want to create the file he can leave the dialog using Cancel.
cdlOFNHideReadOnly	The Read Only checkbox in the dialog is not visible when you specify this Flag.
cdlOFNNoReadOnlyReturn	The user can only select files which are not Read Only.
cdlOFNOverwritePrompt	If the selected file already exists, Windows asks whether the file is to be overwritten when the dialog is closed with OK. If the user does not want to overwrite the file he can leave the dialog with Cancel.
cdlOFNPathMustExist	The specified path must exist otherwise Windows will not let the user out of the dialog with OK.
cdlOFNShareAware	The user can also select files when network protective measures would normally prevent this.

Table 5.29 *The Store File dialog Flags*

Open File dialog with Read Only checkbox

If you allow the Read Only checkbox in the dialog using the Flags property you can evaluate after calling the dialog whether the user wants to open the file as Read Only. To do this you must compare Flags with the Flag cdlOFNReadOnly:

```
If (cdl.Flags And cdlOFNReadOnly) = cdlOFNReadOnly Then
    MsgBox "Open Read Only"
Else
    MsgBox "Do not open Read Only"
End If
```

When doing this remember the brackets: evaluation will not work without them!

Color Selection dialog

You start the Color Selection dialog with the `ShowColor` method. In the `Color` property specify the color which will be activated on call. You will also get the selected color in this property after calling. Using the Flags property you can fine-tune the dialog. To do this, use the Flags shown in Table 5.30.

Flag	Meaning
`cdlCCFullOpen`	The dialog appears in its full size with the field for fine-tuning the color. Without this field you cannot enlarge the dialog yourself if you have not specified `cdlCCPreventFullOpen`.
`cdlCCPreventFullOpen`	The user cannot enlarge the color setting area.
`cdlCCRGBInit`	The color set up in `Color` is used as the start setting.

Table 5.30 *The Color Selection dialog Flags*

Tip If you want to set a color as a presetting you must set Flags at least to `cdlCCRGBInit`. Otherwise black is always used as the presetting. You will create a fully opened Color Selection dialog using a preset color as shown in the following example:

```
On Error Resume Next
cdl.Color = vbRed ' Presetting
cdl.CancelError = True
cdl.Flags = cdlCCFullOpen Or cdlCCRGBInit
cdl.ShowColor
If Err.Number = 0 Then
    ' Evaluate Color
    Me.BackColor = cdl.Color
End If
```

Write Selection dialog

The Write Selection dialog is in principle very easy to program. Unfortunately Microsoft failed to provide the Write Selection dialog with a `Font` property which is compatible with the `Font` property used with many other controls. Instead you have to laboriously select the font from individual font properties.

Using `ShowFont` you open the Font Selection dialog. Before opening you can preset the type of font in font properties. The font color is managed in the `Color` property. In the `Min` and `Max` properties you can set the minimum and maximum font size if the Flag `cdlCFLimitSize` is set. The `Flags` property also serves as for other dialogs to fine-tune the dialog. Table 5.31 describes the appropriate Flags for Font Selection dialog.

Flag	Meaning
`cdlCFEffects`	Using this flag colors and the attributes scored through and underscored can be selected.
`cdlCFForceFontExists`	Prevents selection of a font which is unavailable.
`cdlCFLimitSize`	Using this flag you can set the font size only in the specified Min and Max range.
`cdlCFScreenFonts`	The dialog only displays screen fonts.
`cdlCFPrinterFonts`	The dialog only shows printer fonts.
`cdlCFBoth`	The dialog shows all fonts.
`cdlCFAnsiOnly`	The dialog only shows ANSI fonts (no DOS or graphic fonts such as Symbol or Wingdings).
`cdlCFFixedPitchOnly`	The dialog only shows non-proportional fonts e.g. Courier.

Table 5.31   *The Flags of the Font Selection dialog*

The usual setting for many applications is: `cdlCFBoth Or cdlCFEffects Or cdlCFForceFontExists`.

Tip In every case you must set `Flags` to at least `cdlCFScreenFonts`, `cdlCFPrinterFonts` or `cdlCFBoth`, otherwise Windows sends an incorrect message that no fonts are installed.

Set font for a Label:

```
cdl.FontName = lblTest.FontName
cdl.FontSize = lblTest.FontSize
cdl.Color = lblTest.ForeColor
cdl.FontBold = lblTest.FontBold
cdl.FontItalic = lblTest.FontItalic
cdl.FontStrikethru = lblTest.FontStrikethru
cdl.FontUnderline = lblTest.FontUnderline
cdl.Min = 0
cdl.Max = 128
' Set flags so that printer and
' Screen fonts are displayed,
' Font attributes (scored through, color etc.)
```

```
' are allowed and the selected
' Font type must exist.
cdl.Flags = cdlCFBoth Or cdlCFEffects Or _
            cdlCFForceFontExist
' Display dialog
cdl.CancelError = True
On Error Resume Next
cdl.ShowFont
If Err.Number = 0 Then
    On Error Goto ErrHandler
    ' Set Font
    lblTest.FontName = cdl.FontName
    lblTest.FontSize = cdl.FontSize
    lblTest.ForeColor = cdl.Color
    lblTest.FontBold = cdl.FontBold
    lblTest.FontItalic = cdl.FontItalic
    lblTest.FontStrikethru = cdl.FontStrikethru
    lblTest.FontUnderline = cdl.FontUnderline
End If
```

The Printer dialog and the Printer Settings dialog

The printer dialog serves to select the printer to be used and other different settings, for example pages and the number of copies to be printed. As long as you do not have to evaluate the selected printer, evaluation of the values set by the user presents only moderate difficulties. Printer selection however is really quite difficult to evaluate if you are not printing with GDI functions. If the Printer-Default property is False, the printer dialog returns the HDC (handle for the device context) of the selected printer in the property of the same name. Using this device context you can then call the GDI functions, which are very laborious to program to print. However if you want to print with the Printer object of Visual Basic, you will not be able to start anything with the HDC property. In this case you have to set the PrinterDefault property to True. Selecting the printer now has the effect that Windows changes the standard printer to the selected printer. This is advantageous for you in that you can print with the Printer object without a lot of effort on the programming side. The serious disadvantage to the programmer however is that without his knowledge, the standard printer readjusts and then prints other applications as well on this printer. This dialog does not offer a practicable solution. One conceivable solution to this problem would be to somehow find out, using API functions, which printer is hidden behind the device context, then ascertain this via the Printers listing and allocate to the Printer object. Unfortunately I have never managed to do this. Microsoft could have simply returned the printer name in a dialog property.

Another conceivable solution buffers the standard printer before opening the dialog and resets this after printing. However, to do this you must use API functions.

Via the printer settings dialog you access the basic settings of a printer (for example paper size, alignment, etc.).

The printer dialog is opened with ShowPrinter. Using the Min and Max properties you restrict the permissible page range. In FromPage and ToPage you set and read the page range. The Copies property manages the number of copies to be printed. In Flags the dialog is fine-tuned once again. Table 5.32 lists the most important of the (many) Flags available.

Flag	Meaning
cdlPDPrintSetup	Displays the Setup dialog instead of the normal printer dialog.
cdlPDNoSelection	Deactivates the OptionButton High-lighting in the print range field.
cdlPDNoPageNums	Deactivates the OptionButton Pages and Fields From and To.
cdlPDDisablePrintToFile	Deactivates the Checkbox Print to File.
cdlPDHidePrintToFile	Makes the Checkbox Print to File invisible.
cdlPDReturnDC	This Flag effects the return of the device context handle in the hDC property, when PrinterDefault is False.
cdlPDAllPages	With this flag you set the OptionButton All Pages as a presetting and evaluate this after opening the dialog.
cdlPDSelection	With this flag you set the OptionButton Highlighting and evaluate this after opening the dialog.
cdlPDPageNums	With this flag you set the OptionButton Pages as a presetting and evaluate this after opening the dialog.
cdlPDCollate	Presetting and evaluation of the checkbox Sort.
cdlPDPrintToFile	Presetting and evaluation of the checkbox Output to File.

Table 5.32 *The Flags of the Printer dialog*

Tip If you allow the page area to have the fields `From` and `To` (by not identifying the flag `cdlPD-NoPageNums`), you have to write a value greater than 0 to the properties `Min` and `Max`. If you write nothing or 0 to these properties, the OptionButton `Pages` and the fields `From` and `To` are deactivated.

A summary of the most important properties

Property	Meaning
CancelError	If you verify `CancelError` with `True`, an error with number 32755 is produced when the user activates the `Cancel` button. You have to use `CancelError` to be able to ascertain a Cancel in the dialog.
Color	The Color Selection dialog manages the set color as an RGB value in this property.
Copies	In `Copies` you enter the value for the Printer dialog, which appears in the "Copies" field.
DialogTitle	Defines the title of the dialog. If you enter nothing here, the dialog with the standard title appears.
FileTitle	`FileTitle` supplies the file name for a file dialog without specifying the path.
Filter	Specifies the file filters (for example "All files | *.* | EXE Files | *.exe") for a File dialog.
Flags	`Flags` defines special settings for individual dialogs. `Flags` is a bitfile, which is made up from several flag constants. Via this property different settings are evaluated after opening (as for example the status of the Read Only checkbox for Open File dialogs).
FontName; Font-Size; FontBold; etc.	These properties define the font for a font selection dialog.
FromPage; ToPage	These properties define the values for the Printer dialog, which appear in the "Pages: From .. To ..".
HelpCommand	Defines the type of Help (Context, HelpOnHelp, Key, etc.) for a Help dialog.

Property	Meaning
Helpfile	In `Helpfile` you specify the Help file if the dialog is going to display Help. To do this you still have to set `HelpKey`.
HelpKey	This is where you specify the key value of the Help page, which will display the dialog when the user activates the Help key.
InitDir	In `InitDir` you identify the folder with which the file dialog will start. If you do not identify anything here, the dialog uses the current folder.
PrinterDefault	`PrinterDefault` defines for the Printer dialog that all printer changes which the user identifies in the dialog are written to the Registry and so are permanently stored. `PrinterDefault` enables the user to select the printer and then use the selected printer using `Printer` object.

Table 5.33 *The most important properties of the CommonDialog control*

A summary of the most important methods

Method	Meaning
ShowOpen	Opens the dialog for opening a file.
ShowSave	Opens the dialog for saving a file.
ShowColor	Opens the dialog for color selection.
ShowFont	Opens the dialog for font selection.
ShowPrinter	Opens the dialog for the printer setting.
ShowHelp	Calls Windows Help.

Table 5.34 *The most important methods of the CommonDialog control*

5.4.2 ProgressBar

The ProgressBar control is used for longer lasting processes, to show the user how far the process has progressed. To do this set the properties Min to the lower and Max to the upper threshold and in the course of the process the property Value to the value that is to be displayed:

```
Dim lngIndex As Long
ProgressBar1.Min = 0
ProgressBar1.Max = 1000000
For lngIndex = 1 To 1000000
   ProgressBar1.Value = lngIndex
Next
```

In the `Orientation` property you can set whether the progress bar is horizontally or vertically aligned, in `Scrolling` property you define whether the progress bar is displayed as segmented or smooth.

Tips and tricks

Only update the display when necessary

On setting Value, the progress display implicitly calls `Refresh`, which is why there is no need to explicitly call `Refresh` and `DoEvents`, if in so doing you only want to force the progress display into number-crunching loops. The implicit use of `Refresh` is unfortunately only half-heartedly implemented, since for every change of `Value`, `Refresh` is called. Consequently updating takes a relatively long time (try the above example!). So if you do not want to slow down your program unnecessarily, do not update `Value` at every amendment, but only at intervals of so many progress stages, so that for instance an update will show a progress bar with a bar display.

Example: Progress bar with 12 bars (the number of bars adjusts itself to the width)

```
Dim lngIndex As Long
ProgressBar1.Min = 0
ProgressBar1.Max = 1000000
For lngIndex = 1 To 1000000
    If lngIndex Mod (1000000 / 12) = 0 Then
        ProgressBar1.Value = lngIndex
    End If
Next
```

5.4.3   StatusBar

To set up status bars, use the StatusBar control which you integrate into your project using the components "Microsoft Windows Common Controls 6.0". Set `Style` to `sbrNormal` if you need several panels in the status line. If you only need one panel, set `Style` to `sbrSimple`, which makes subsequent writing to the panel easier. With several panels you have to set the individual panels in the Properties dialog of the control. For each panel you can issue data other than text using its `Style` property, e.g. the current time or the status of **CapsLock**. Using `AutoSize` you can set whether the panel is not automatically adapted (*None*) or is automatically adapted to the maximum possible width (*Spring*) or width of the contents (*Content*).

If you create a simple StatusBar, using `SimpleText` you can write a string to the panel:

```
sbrStatus.SimpeText = "Hello user, how are you?"
```

If there are several panels in the StatusBar, you access the individual panels using the `Panels` listing:

```
sbrStatus.Panels(1).Text = "Hello user, " & _
          " how are you?"
sbrStatus.Panels(2).Text = "Today is " & _
          WeekdayName(Weekday(Now, vbSunday), , vbSunday)
```

5.4.4　ImageList

The ImageList control is a container for bitmaps or icons, which is normally used together with other controls (Toolbar, TreeView, ListView). Integrate "Microsoft Windows Common Controls 6.0" components into your project to use this control which is invisible in run-time.

If for example you want to equip the Toolbar buttons with pictures, load the images you need into an ImageList control, link the Toolbar with the ImageList control and specify either the index or the key for the images to be displayed for the individual switches.

You can load the images either via the Properties dialog of the ImageList control or also during run-time. Before loading set the size of the images to be displayed in the first register (16*16, 32*32, 48*48 or user-defined). In the list all bitmaps are always the same size. The control automatically sizes pictures that are too big or too small. If the control already contains pictures, you can no longer change the size.

In the `Pictures` register you can add individual images in design. You should give each image a key. Using this key it is really easy to identify the image in the linked control afterwards.

In the `Color` register you can set which bitmap color is to be transparent (*MaskColor*) and which color will then be used as the background color (*Back-Color*). These settings are then only used if in the register `General` the option `Use Mask Color` is switched on. If you use icons with a transparent background, you can dispense with these settings.

Programming

During run-time you gain access to images via the `ListImages` property, which is a listing of `ListImage` objects. The most important methods of this listing are `Clear`, `Add` and `Remove`. The `Add` method expects the index as the first argument, when the picture is to be added to a particular position, the key as second argument and the image as third argument. You read in the image either using the `LoadPicture` function from a file:

```
ilsDemo.ListImages.Add , "Exit", _
    LoadPicture("c:\icons\exit.ico")
ilsDemo.ListImages.Add , "Filter1", _
    LoadPicture("c:\icons\Filter1.ico")
ilsDemo.ListImages.Add , "Filter2", _
    LoadPicture("c:\icons\Filter2.ico")
```

or you take it from the `Picture` property of another control. The `Picture` property of the objects stored in the listing refers to the loaded pictures. You can then access an image using the index of the picture or the key:

```
Set picDemo.Picture = ilsDemo.ListImages("Exit").Picture
Set picDemo.Picture = ilsDemo.ListImages(0).Picture
```

Tips and tricks

Add as many pictures as possible

If you want to add pictures in design, consider before linking the image list control with the other controls which pictures you need and load all these pictures before making the link. In design the image list control does not allow you to add or remove pictures if it is linked to another control. If after allocating and setting up the pictures you want to display you separate a toolbar from the image list control, in order to be able to adapt the image list control, all your picture settings in the toolbar will be deleted and you will have to start all over again.

Load pictures at run-time

If you load the pictures at run-time though, you do not have to remove the link with the other control:

```
' Load pictures into the ImageList control
ilsDemo.ListImages.Add , "Exit", _
    LoadPicture("c:\icons\exit.ico")
ilsDemo.ListImages.Add , "Filter", _
    LoadPicture("c:\icons\Filter.ico")
' Allocate pictures to the individual buttons
' of a toolbar
tbrDemo.Buttons(1).Image = "Exit"
tbrDemo.Buttons(2).Image = "Filter"
```

5.4.5 Toolbar

With the `Toolbar` control it is really easy to produce symbol bars. The `Toolbar` control is contained like the ImageList in the component "Microsoft Windows Common Controls 6.0".

You set the definitive properties in design in the Properties dialog of the control. However before you begin setting the toolbar, you should consider which pictures you need. That is to say before setting the toolbar buttons these must be loaded into an ImageList control. You will find pictures suited to the toolbar in the Visual Basic folder in the sub-folder `Common\Graphics\Bitmaps\Tlbr_95` and `\Offctlbr`.

The `Style` property of the toolbar determines whether this will appear in the "Old Look" or in the new 3 D Look.

In the `buttons` register you define the buttons which are to appear in your icon bar. Using `add button` you add new buttons. Using `Style` you define the type of button for each. You can define a normal button (*Default*) or an on/off button (*Check*) as a simple button. Setting 2 (*Button Group*) arranges all buttons which have this style and are not separated by a separator in a group as on/off buttons. These buttons then behave like grouped option buttons: in any one group only one button can be turned on, as was the case with the old radios. You can create several groups by placing a separator between the groups. Setting 3 (*Separator*) creates a narrow empty surface for optical separation of buttons and divides groups from one another. With 4 (*Placeholders*) you can define a currently unused item (no button created), which you can use during run-time as a button or separator with one of the other values.

Give each button a key (in `Key`), then you can use it better in the `ButtonClick` event of the toolbox.

If you want to place pictures on the buttons, you allocate an `ImageList` control to the `ImageList` property. In any case load all the required pictures before allocation into the `ImageList` control. For each button the `Image` property now defines the index or key of the picture that is going to be used.

In the `ButtonClick` event you can respond to the activation of a button. The transferred object parameter `Button` defines the activated button, which can be identified via `Button.Index` or better `Button.Key`.

The toolbar has other properties, for example the possibility that the user can adapt the toolbar (double-click) and save and load the toolbar (`SaveToolbar`, `RestoreToolbar`). These are not described here.

Tips and tricks

Subsequent addition of pictures

As I frequently forget a button and so the picture required, I use the following trick to avoid the troublesome reallocation of pictures after disconnecting the image list control: save the form and open it in an editor. Copy all lines of the form description concerning toolbar buttons to the clipboard. Close the editor and disconnect the toolbar in VB from the image list control. Afterwards load the other pictures into the ImageList control, connect these again and save the form. At this stage you should still not set up any new buttons. First open the form file again in an editor and replace all lines concerning buttons with the contents of the clipboard. Perhaps somewhat complicated but possibly better than the irritating reallocation of pictures.

5.5 The windowless controls

As already stated above, the windowless controls do not possess a handle and therefore consume considerably fewer resources than the normal control (which, for example, leads to visibly faster form creation). In order to be able to use the windowless controls, you first have to install these. To do this copy the files from the folder `Common\Tools\Vb\Winless` on the Visual Basic Installations CD to the Windows systems directory. Afterwards you have to register the controls: start a DOS window, change to the systems directory and execute here the command `Regsvr32 Mswless.Ocx`. In order to carry out the necessary licensing, execute immediately in the DOS window the file `Mswless.Reg`. In this way the windowless controls are installed and registered.

In Visual Basic you integrate these controls via the `Project | Components` menu by activating in the register `Controls` the `Microsoft Windowless Controls 6.0`.

The controls WLText, WLFrame, WLCommand, WLCheck, WLOption, WLCombo, WLList, WLHScroll and WLVScroll, apart from a few details (for example the missing DDE support), are compatible with the standard controls. If you are missing some controls, for example the Label or Image control, this is because these controls already have no Windows handle.

Windowless controls are used for forms which contain a lot of controls and are slow to open using normal controls, for ActiveX documents which will be made available on the Internet or intranet, and for self-created ActiveX controls which are going to be windowless.

5.6 Dynamic creation of controls

If you want to create controls dynamically at run-time, you can choose between two variants. The first variant uses the `Load` procedure, to recreate a control based on a currently available control. The second variant uses the `Add` method from the `Controls` listing. Both variants have advantages and disadvantages. Variant 1 requires that a control of the type to be created should already be present on the form. This control should be created so that it is invisible and must contain in the `Index` property a value (ideally 0), as newly added controls turn into a control array. The advantage of Variant 1 is that you can respond to events relatively easily via the events' procedure of the base control. The disadvantage is that you cannot create controls which are not already in existence on the form.

With Variant 2 you can produce controls without there being a base control on the form already. These controls are also not created in a control array. The disadvantage of this variant is that you cannot really respond to events in these controls.

Variant 1

Create for example a text box on a form, whose index you set to 0, and set `Visible` to `False`. Now you can create text boxes at run-time based on this text box:

```
Dim intIndex As Integer
For intIndex = 1 To 10
    Load txtDynamic(intIndex)
    With txtDynamic(intIndex)
        .Left = 100
        .Height = 315
        .Width = 1500
        .Top = 100 + ((intIndex - 1) * (.Height + 50))
        .Visible = True
    End With
Next
```

Please note that you always have to set the `Visible` property of the dynamically created controls to `True`, even if the base control is visible.

If you want to respond to events, simply define an event procedure for the base control and query the index there:

```
Private Sub txtDynamic_LostFocus(Index As Integer)
 MsgBox "TextBox Number " & Index & " has been left."
End Sub
```

Using `Load`, you can remove again dynamically created controls with `Unload`:

```
Dim intIndex As Integer
For intIndex = 1 To 10
   Unload txtDynamic(intIndex)
Next
```

Variant 2

For Variant 2 use the `Add` method from the controls listing:

```
Controls.Add control class, control name
```

The control class is specified via *library name.class name*. For standard controls it is the VB library (so for example *VB.text box* for a text box). You can find out the library and class name in the object catalog or simply create a control on a form, save this and look for the class name in the form file using an editor. The control name must be unambiguous, as the following example demonstrates:

```
Dim intIndex As Integer
For intIndex = 1 To 10
  With Me.Controls.Add("VB.TextBox", _
          "txtDynamic" & intIndex)
     .Left = 4000
     .Height = 315
     .Width = 1500
     .Top = 100 + ((intIndex - 1) * (.Height + 50))
     .Visible = True
  End With
Next
```

If you want to evaluate the events of controls created in this way, you have to declare a global variable of the type of control using `With Events` and evaluate events for this variable:

```
Private WithEvents txtDynamic1 As text box
Private WithEvents txtDynamic2 As text box

Private Sub cmdCreateControls_Click()
 Set txtDynamic1 = Me.Controls.Add("VB.TextBox", _
"txtDynamic1")
 txtDynamic1.Left = 3000
 txtDynamic1.Top = 100
 txtDynamic1.Width = 1500
 txtDynamic1.Height = 315
 txtDynamic1.Visible = True
```

```
  Set txtDynamic2 = Me.Controls.Add("VB.TextBox", _
                    "txtDynamic_2")
  txtDynamic2.Left = 3000
  txtDynamic2.Top = 415 + 50
  txtDynamic2.Width = 1500
  txtDynamic2.Height = 315
  txtDynamic2.Visible = True
End Sub


Private Sub txtDynamic1_LostFocus()
  MsgBox "TextBox 1 left"
End Sub


Private Sub txtDynamic2_LostFocus()
  MsgBox "TextBox 2 left"
End Sub
```

This procedure however contradicts the fundamental idea that if you need to know in advance how many controls you have to create (because you have to declare the correct number of variables) there is no need to dynamically create controls at all. One conceivable solution (and I still have not tried it out) would be the management of control variables in a dynamic array or sub-classing of controls. When sub-classing you intercept the control during creation and bind this to a Windows procedure, which Windows then calls as a normal Windows procedure such as in C++. In this Windows procedure you can dispense with all messages which Windows sends to the control and thus you can respond to all events. Sub-classing is however a laborious and delicate matter.

Look on the Internet at `Search.Microsoft.Com/Us/Dev/Default.Asp` for *Visual Basic Subclassing* to obtain further information.

You can delete dynamically created controls using the `Remove` method:

```
Me.Controls.Remove "txtDynamic1"
```

5.7 Working with forms

The concept *form* is the description in VBA of a Windows window. In this window besides the controls you already know you can set up menus as well. Of course you can also allocate several forms to a project.

5.7.1 Create forms

The Start form

A VB application starts normally with a form (alternatively you can also start a VB application with a procedure *Main* in a standard module). You specify the Start form in the project properties in the General register. The first of the forms integrated into the project has already been entered. The form, as with every other form, is produced automatically, so there is no need to worry about anything else.

Integrating more forms

Under the Project menu you can add more forms to the project. In the Add dialog of the form you can also select different templates besides the forms already available. These templates are saved in the Template\Forms in the VB folder. Most templates are normal form files. By default there is also a form which starts an assistant (the data form assistant). You can of course also copy your own forms as templates to this folder.

Select the index Form if you only want to integrate an empty form into the project.

The tabulator order

You determine the tabulator order of the individual controls of a form using the TabIndex property of the controls. On designing the controls, TabIndex of the development environment is automatically set to the next highest value, which generally upsets the tabulator order. Unfortunately you have to adjust the TAB position by hand, as the development environment knows no way of automatically doing this (as, for example, in Access). Using the TabStop property you can determine whether a control can be started with the TAB key.

Keyboard shortcut

Usually controls can be activated by pressing the **ALT** key in connection with a letter which is shown as underlined in the control text. In Visual Basic you simply put an "&" in front of the character in the text. In order to start a control without its own annotation (e.g. a text box or a list box) you define the keyboard shortcut in a label, which serves as text. The label still has to have a TabIndex, which is lower by 1 than the TabIndex of the control to be started. If a label keyboard shortcut is activated, this then simply activates the next control in the tabulator order.

Layers

A form has three layers (levels). All graphic outputs appear on the lowest layer and these are issued to the form. Graphic elements and labels are drawn on the middle layer. The upper layer contains all other controls (text boxes, buttons, checkboxes, etc.). An element on an upper layer always covers one underneath. You can however change the position of an element on its layer using the ZOrder method (Argument 0 = bring forward; 1 = move backwards) or in the development environment with the menu items Format | Sequence, but in so doing it is only possible to move forwards or backwards.

Setting a form

The most important property of a form has to be BorderStyle. This is where you can set whether the form has a border, allows a change in size, and whether the title bar is shown as normal or reduced. You can find the relevant settings for the most important properties below. Please note that if you allow a change in scale you also have to respond to a change in size (in the Resize event). The reduction, enlargement and positioning of individual controls that is then necessary is often so laborious that it is better not to allow any size change.

The ControlBox property determines whether the form has the system menu icon (top left) and the Close button (top right) or not. If you turn off Control-Box, the minimize and maximize buttons from the title bar disappear. If ControlBox is True and BorderStyle is set a variable border or on *1 - static simple*, you can turn the minimize and maximize buttons on and off separately using MinButton and MaxButton properties.

If the form has the system menu icon, you should determine in the Icon property the icon that you want to display. You will find some icons in the Visual Studio folder in the sub-folder Common\Graphics. Unfortunately Microsoft does not supply an icon editor with Visual Basic. If you also have Delphi as well as Visual Basic, you can use the Delphi picture editor (Imageedit.Exe) to create icons.

Using the StartUpPosition property you can fix where the form will appear on the screen. The settings *1 - center of window* or *2 - center of screen* are certainly the most customary. *1 - center of window* centrally displays a form in its owner window when it is opened using its owner form (see from page 200). The setting *3 - Windows standard* is only rarely appropriate. This is where Windows decides where the form appears. With *0 - manual* you can determine the position yourself using the Top and Left properties.

5.7.2 Using forms in the program code

Naming and the automatic production of forms

The name of a form only describes in the first place the form class. If you come from other programming languages (such as Delphi) you will probably wonder why you can also use this name in the program code to work with the form (for example you can display the form with *Form name*.Show). If you are not wondering you had perhaps better not read the rest of this section.

For every form, Visual Basic generates program code in the background in a virtual standard module, which looks something like the following:

```
Public Form name As New Form_Name
```

Thus VB declares a global variable, which has the same name as the class, which is not problematic in VBA. Such a declaration means that the compiler produces program code additionally for every instruction that the declared variable uses, which checks whether the object has already been created.

```
frmTest.Show
```

becomes for example

```
If frmTest Is Nothing Then
    Set frmTest = New frmTest
End If
frmTest.Show
```

That is the explanation for why you do not have to create forms yourself in VB (but can as you will see from page 205).

Opening and closing a form

You can open a form in the program code at any point using its Show method. If a form is already opened and only placed in the background, the form is merely brought into the foreground. The Show method has two optional arguments:

```
Form name.Show [Modal] [, OwnerForm]
```

In the *Modal* argument you identify with the constants vbModeless and vbModal whether you want to open the form modally or not. If you do not want to open the form modally, you can omit the *Modal* argument. vbModeless is the presetting. After opening a modeless form you might work the following program code further. The user can change to another form with the mouse or with **Ctrl F6**. The individual windows of the VB development environment are examples of modeless forms. If you open the form modally, it is linked to the user. Windows waits until the form is closed by the user or in the program code to work on further program code. The user cannot edit other forms in the project before the form is closed. Normally opening modally is the safe way, because the user is then compelled to close the form if he wants to edit another form. The user cannot therefore effect changes in other parts of the application, which might possibly cause side effects in the opened form (e.g. delete a customer from whom you have just taken an order). Modeless forms also have the disadvantage that the program code, which follows the opening of the form, is executed directly after opening. If you force inputs and you want to evaluate these directly after opening, you must open the form modally.

The second argument of the Show method specifies the form, which "owns" the opened form. This argument has three effects:

→ A form which is modeless and opened in this way always remains visible in relation to the owner form and does not disappear in the background as modeless forms opened in the usual way when the owner form is activated.

→ If the owner form is closed, all forms are closed automatically with it. This is of course only true if a form has been opened modelessly (otherwise the owner form cannot be closed at all). In so doing you can make sure that no form remains in the memory, when for example the main form of the application (as owner form) is closed.

→ The last effect concerns the StartUpPosition property of a form. If you specify here *1 - Window Center*, the form is always opened in the center of the owner form. This argument is also interesting for forms opened modally.

As *OwnerForm* you normally identify the form from where you are opening the other form. To do this use the Me operator:

```
frmLogin.Show vbModal, Me
```

If you want to cause minimal acceleration when opening a form, you can perhaps do this on starting the application by using Load *Form* into the memory. You should take care in so doing that every loaded form reduces the memory available. However, with today's computers advance loading this is no longer necessary, even for big forms.

In the program code you close a form using Hide method or with Unload Me. Hide simply makes the form invisible. To every user it looks as if the form has been closed. In the program however you can access all properties of the form and in so doing the contents of controls. But do not forget to unload the form afterwards. The Unload instruction unloads a form completely from the memory. Normally Unload is the preferred method, because you can then be sure that when the form is next opened, it will be freshly initialized. The following example demonstrates this procedure on a Login form, which is opened modally and evaluated afterwards:

```
frmLogin.Show vbModal, Me
```

```
If frmLogin.txtPassword.Text = "Nitty Gritty" Then
   ' Login was successful; do something else ...
Else
   ' Login was unsuccessful
End If
' Unload form again
Unload frmLogin
```

In the Login form only the Hide method can be used if the form is going to be closed in the program code:

```
Private Sub cmdOK_Click()
   Me.Hide
End Sub
```

Incidentally if a user closes a form using **Alt F4** or with the Close button top right in the title bar, the form is completely unloaded from the memory. There is no problem in evaluating form inputs, as in the example above, because the program on access loads the form once more into the memory.

The Me operator

The Me operator is located within a form module for the current entity of the form. If you want to access properties or methods of the form or have to specify the form with instructions (as with Unload), use the Me operator. If you access properties or methods within the form module, the Compiler places Me implicitly in front of the property or method. So here you do not have to specify Me (I often do however, to make the program code legible). By the way never use the form name instead of Me. In principle it still works, but it has two disadvantages: if you change the form name, you have to match the program code. You will see that this disadvantage is not all that bad. It is worse when you create forms dynamically (see from page 205). You have to address these forms using Me, because the form name stands for a completely different form (as I explained at the beginning of this section).

5.7.3   Initialize and terminate forms

When opening forms it is often necessary to initialize them. If the form is to initialize itself, use the Load event. This event is always called whenever a form is loaded into the memory. You can use the Initialize event less to do this and it is only called for the *first* loading of a form. If the form is going to be initialized from outside, you normally have to add a new method with arguments to the form. To do this, simply create a public procedure with the necessary arguments to initialize in the form module. You then have to call these arguments before opening the form. Unfortunately VB 6 does not have a constructor (but this will be possible in VB.NET).

If you want to execute program code when you close the form, use the `Unload` or the `QueryUnload` event. Both events are called when unloading a form (not if the form is hidden only with the `Hide` method) and both have a *Cancel* argument whereby you can cancel Unload (`Cancel = True`). `QueryUnload` is always called in front of `Unload`. The difference between `QueryUnload` and `Unload` is that you can cancel Windows exit with `QueryUnload`[4], but not with `Unload` (although `Unload` is also called on Windows exit). So to be safe use `QueryUnload`.

In the examples in the book there is a project (*Load and QueryUnload Demo*) which uses both these events in order to read a text file at the start of an application and to save the text file on closing after running a query.

5.7.4   Object-oriented definition of forms

Forms wherever possible should run on their own and therefore be independent of other forms. This requires that you equip the forms with additional properties and possibly also methods that you can access from the user-side. Using the example of a universally applicable Login form I would like to clarify this procedure: on activating the OK button the Login form will check a password and signal to the user whether login has been successful or whether the `Cancel` button has been activated (Fig. 5.1).

Figure 5.1   *The Login form*

To do this, the form has to be told the password from the user-side that has to be checked. This is simply done using an Init method. So that the caller can recognize on the user-side whether login has been successful, an *OK* property is implemented, which can only be read from the user-side:

```
Option Explicit

' Private variables for the password
' to be set in Init and the
' property OK
```

---

4. When shutting down, Windows sends a close message to all windows which are open. The window closes and at the same time calls the Unload events. If the Cancel argument is set to True in QueryUnload, this cancels Close Windows.

```
Private mstrPassword As String
Private mblnOK As Boolean

' New Only Read property
Public Property Get OK() As Boolean
   OK = mblnOK
End Property

' Init Method
Public Sub Init(ByVal Password As String)
 mstrPassword = Password
End Sub

Private Sub cmdCancel_Click()
 ' Value of the OK property set on False in order to
 ' identify failed log in.
 mblnOK = False
 ' Hide form only to make
 ' subsequent access possible
 Me.Hide
End Sub

Private Sub cmdOK_Click()
 ' Check for correct password
 If txtPassword.Text = mstrpassword Then
    ' Set value of OK property on True,
    ' to identify correct log in.
    mblnOK = True
    ' Hide form only to make _
    ' subsequent access possible
    Me.Hide
 Else
    MsgBox "Invalid password. Please try " & _
           "once again!", , "Log in"
    txtPassword.SetFocus
 End If
End Sub
```

When using the Login form the caller has to call the Init method after loading the form and after the modal display evaluate the OK property. After this the form has to be unloaded again because it cannot unload itself without deleting the OK property:

```
Private Sub cmdLogin_Click()
 ' Initialize Login Form
 frmLogin.Init "42"
 ' Open Login Form
 frmLogin.Show vbModal
 ' Evaluate whether OK has been activated
 If frmLogin.OK = True Then
    MsgBox "Login OK"
 Else
    MsgBox "Login failed"
 End If
End Sub
```

5.7.5   Dynamically created forms

Whenever you need several entities from a form these always have to be created dynamically. Just to give one example: the forms, which Word used as individual documents, are also created dynamically. You create a form as a normal object (in the chapter on object-oriented programming I explain this procedure in more detail). Declare a local variable of the form type, create an entity for the form class and allocate this to the variable:

```
Dim frm As frmDocument
Set frm = New frmDocument
```

Then you can work quite normally with the form:

```
frmDocument.Show vbModeless
```

Incidentally the form remains loaded if the variable leaves the scope (when the procedure is finished).

5.7.6   The most important properties, methods and events

The most important properties

Property	Meaning
AutoRedraw	AutoRedraw determines whether drawings are created in the working memory so they are always available or whether they are drawn in the Paint event. In Chapter 8 you will find more on this property.
BackColor	The background color.

Property	Meaning
BorderStyle	Determines the form's border: *0 – None*: form has no border and no title bar; *1 – Fixed Simple*: simple border. The user cannot change the size of the form. Contrary to *3 – Fixed dialog* can contain maximize and minimize button; *2 – Changeable*: normal border. The user can change the size of the form; *3 – Fixed dialog*: setting with fixed border, which cannot be changed. The title line cannot contain the maximize and minimize button. *4 – Fixed Tool window*: setting with reduced title bar. The user cannot change the size of the window. The title line cannot contain the maximize and minimize button; *5 – Changeable Tool window*: like *4 – Fixed Tool window*, only the user can change the size of the window.
Caption	Form's caption in the Title bar.
ControlBox	Determines whether the window has a system menu field and close button in the Title bar.
Enabled	Determines whether the form can respond to events triggered by the user.
Icon	Determines the form's symbol.
KeyPreview	If you set KeyPreview to True, when you press a key Windows firstly calls KeyPress, KeyDown and KeyUp event of the form before these events are called for the active control. So you can set up global treatment of the keyboard for the form.
MaxButton MinButton	Determines whether the title line contains the minimize and maximize buttons (provided that the form's border allows this).
Moveable	Determines whether the user can shift the form on the screen.
Picture	You can allocate a picture from a picture file to this property, which can then be used as a background picture for the form. To do this you can use the Load Picture function at run-time.

Property	Meaning
StartUpPosition	Determines where the form appears on the screen: *0 – manual*: the form appears in the position defined by Left and Top; *1– Window center*: the form appears in the center of the owner form to which the form (via the *owner form* argument of the show method) is allocated; *2 – screen center*: the form appears in the center of the screen. *3 – Windows standard*: the form appears on the spot which Windows provides as standard for the next form.
WindowState	Determines whether the form on normal opening (i.e. in the size defined by Width and Height) appears minimized or maximized on the screen.

Table 5.35 *The most important properties of the form*

The most important methods

Method	Meaning
Hide	Using the Hide method you can hide a form. But the form remains loaded in the working memory, so that you can access all inputs in the form and all values in the properties.
Show [*Modal*] [, *Owner form*]	Using the Show method you open a form. In the Modal argument modal you specify whether the form is to be opened modally (vbModal) or modelessly (vbModeless, Default). The argument *OwnerForm* specifies the form, that is the owner of the opened form. You will find information on this on page 200.

Table 5.36 *The most important methods of the form*

The most important events

Event	Meaning
Activate	This event is called whenever a form is completely visible on the screen. This is only true however for the application. If the user changes to another application and back again, Activate is not called. Activate is used in preference for modeless forms (only here Activate is called more often than once).
Deactivate	This event is called whenever the user changes to a different form within the application.
Initialize	Initialize is only called for standard forms before initial loading of the form. You can undertake initialization processes here that will only be implemented on initial loading.

Event	Meaning
KeyPress, KeyUp, KeyDown	If KeyPreview is set to True, keystrokes are always sent first of all to these events in the form. So you can set up global treatment of the keyboard for the form.
Load	Load is called when the form is loaded into the memory. This event is usually preferred when it comes to initialization.
Paint	You use the Paint event when you want to issue your own graphics on the form. If the AutoRedraw property is set to False, Windows calls this event whenever the window is being redrawn. This is where you carry out all drawing operations. When AutoRedraw is set to True, Paint is not called. This makes sense too, because you can then draw in any event you like (for example in Load).
Resize	The Resize event is always called whenever the size of the form is changed. When you allow a size change (via Border-Style), you have to use this event to match controls in position and size to the new size.
Terminate	Terminate is called whenever the form is finally removed from the memory. A form that has only been unloaded is not finally removed. It is not until the last unloading (when the application is ended) that Terminate is called.
Unload, Query-Unload	These events are called whenever the form is unloaded. Using the *Cancel* argument you can cancel Unload. Unlike the Unload event you can also cancel Windows exit in the QueryUnload event.

Table 5.37 *The most important events of the form*

5.7.7   Tips and tricks

Add-in for the tabulator order

In the Visual Basic examples you will find an Add-in which enables simpler setting of the tabulator order by window. This Add-in is normally found in the folder C:\Program Files\Microsoft Visual Studio\Msdn98\98vs\1031\ Samples\Vb98\Taborder. Open the project Taborder.Vbp and compile the DLL file, and the Add-in will automatically be registered. Via the Add-In-Manager in the ADD-IN menu you can then integrate this Add-in into the development environment.

Correct matching of the control size in Resize

When you allow a size change as a rule you must match the controls in size and position using the Resize event. In so doing however, you must bear in mind the current size of the internal area of the form. The Height and Width properties give you the size including the border width and height of the Title bar, whose dimensions you do not know. The trick is to use the ScaleHeight and Scale-Width properties instead. If you have not set the scaling mode to *user defined*, these properties return the size of the internal area.

Match a text box and two buttons (buttons always below, and text box on the maximum possible size with small border):

```
Private Sub Form_Resize()
 ' Demonstrates, how you correctly
 ' respond to Resize
 ' Firstly force minimum size
 If Me.Height < 2500 Then Me.Height = 2500
 If Me.Width < 3500 Then Me.Width = 3500
 ' Then position the controls
 ' For positioning ScaleWidth and
 ' ScaleHeight are used, which both
 ' define the size of the available internal area
 ' of the form
 txtDemo.Left = 100
 txtDemo.Top = 100
 txtDemo.Width = Me.ScaleWidth - 200
 txtDemo.Height = Me.ScaleHeight - 300 - cmdEnd.Height
 cmdEnd.Top = Me.ScaleHeight - cmdEnd.Height - 100
 cmdSave.Top = cmdEnd.Top
End Sub
```

Make forms into real pop-up forms

If you want to create forms which are always visible via the forms of other applications, you have to use the Windows API function SetWindowPos, as the following example shows:

```
' On loading form make it into
' real pop-up form
Private Declare Function SetWindowPos _
    Lib "user32" (ByVal hwnd As Long, _
    ByVal hWndInsertAfter As Long, _
    ByVal x As Long, ByVal y As Long, _
```

```
        ByVal cx As Long, ByVal cy As Long, _
        ByVal wFlags As Long) As Long
Private Const SWP_NOMOVE = 2

Private Const SWP_NOSIZE = 1

Private Const HWND_TOPMOST = -1


Private Sub Form_Load()
 SetWindowPos Me.hwnd, HWND_TOPMOST, 0, 0, 0, 0, _
SWP_NOMOVE Or SWP_NOSIZE
End Sub
```

5.8 Create menus

You can set up a normal (pulldown) menu on a form and work with pop-up menus. Pulldown menus are the menus positioned in the upper window area or in a menu list. Pop-up menus usually appear at the current mouse position whenever the user presses the right mouse button.

The rectangular box is described as a menu, which contains one or several menu items. Such an item can implement an action or open other menus (sub-menus).

5.8.1 Pulldown menus

Pulldown menus are set up using the menu editor (Tools | Menu editor). You can set the properties for each menu item displayed in Table 5.38.

Property	Meaning
Caption	Defines the item that appears in the menu.
Name	Defines the name of the menu, via which you can access the menu later.
Index	The index for an optional menu array, which is used like a control array.
Checked	Defines whether the menu item appears ticked in the menu. This property is often only set in run-time.
Enabled	Defines whether the menu item can be selected or not. This property is often only set in run-time.
Visible	Defines whether the menu item is visible. Likewise this property is often only set in run-time.

Property	Meaning
Shortcut	Defines an optional shortcut combination that can be called using the menu command at any time in the program without having to open the menu.
HelpContextId	Contains the number for an optional context-sensitive help facility.
WindowList	Only valid for MDI applications. When WindowList is activated, the menu contains in run-time a list of opened MDI child windows via which you can toggle a particular window.
NegotiatePosition	Defines the position of a Toplevel menu (the menu that appears in the menu line) in the menu line: 0 = normal, from left to right, 1 = left, 2 = center, 3 = right.

Table 5.38 *The properties of a menu*

In the lower list of the menu editor all menus are displayed in a hierarchy. Using the arrow keys you can shift individual menu items. Sub-menus are shown shifted to the right. Each menu can have other sub-menus, which can be moved around on the level using the arrow keys. You can define up to four menu levels.

Access to a menu

You can access a menu like any other object using the name. This access is interesting whenever you deactivate individual items according to context or make them invisible or you want to change the caption. In design you cannot set properties using the properties window, but have to use the menu editor.

Menus have as their only event the Click event, which is called whenever the user activates the menu. The Click event is only called for menu items at the end of the menu hierarchy.

5.8.2   Pop-up menus

Pop-up menus are produced and treated in the first instance like a pulldown menu using the menu editor in the form. Set the visibility of the Toplevel menu to False when you have programmed the menu events. By simply calling PopupMenu, *MenuName* the menu is then displayed at the current position of the mouse. To do this use the MouseUp event of the object for which the pop-up menu is valid:

```
Private Sub Form_MouseUp(Button As Integer, _
    Shift As Integer, X As Single, Y As Single)
  If Button = 2 Then
    PopUpMenu mnuContext
```

```
      End If
End Sub
```

5.8.3   Tips and tricks

Copy menus

Unfortunately the menu editor does not allow copying of a menu from one form to another. Of course there are tools which allow you to copy menus and so save you a lot of time. However you can simply open the form file in a text editor and copy the lines from `Begin Menu` to `End` for each individual Toplevel menu to the clipboard and then to another form.

Dividing lines between menu items

You can produce dividing lines simply using an item in the menu that contains a hyphen as text. The name of this item is really unimportant, I always call these items *T1, T2,* etc.

Dynamic menus

You can create menus which in run-time are filled with other items by adding an empty item to the menu whose property `Index` is set to 0. In run-time you can then create new items with `Load` *MenuName*(*NewIndex*). Just leave the first empty item out of the equation, to make programming easier.

Load all file names from C:\ to the file menu:

```
Dim strFilename As String, intCount As Integer
strFilename = Dir("c:\*.*")
Do While strFilename > ""
   intCount = intCount + 1
   Load mnuFileList(intCount)
   mnuFileList(intCount).Visible = True
   mnuFileList(intCount).Caption = strFilename
   strFilename = Dir()
 Loop
```

Pop-up menus on forms which have been opened modally from a pop-up menu

When you use a pop-up menu to open a form modally and this form also has a pop-up menu, then the pop-up menu will not function on the opened form. Microsoft describes this as a bug in Knowledgebase Article Q167839.

Opening a modal form in the pop-up menu:

```
Private Sub mnuContextOpenFormWithoutTrick_Click()
  ' Using this call the pop-up menu does not function in
  ' frmDemo2 unfortunately, because pop-up menus
  ' cannot be called recursively. The pop-up menu call
```

```
' however is not closed here.
 frmDemo2.Show vbModal
End Sub
```

The solution works with a timer, which is placed on the first form. Set `Enabled` to `False` and `Interval` to 1. Instead of opening the form directly, turn on the timer, which then opens the form and deactivates it again. In so doing the `Click` event and so the pop-up menu are worked through before opening the form:

```
Private Sub mnuContextOpenFormWithTrick_Click()
 ' With this call the pop-up menus functions in
 ' frmDemo2. Before the timer opens the form
 ' modally, this procedure and thus the
 ' pop-up menu are closed
 tmrPopupBug Workaround.Enabled = True
End Sub
Private Sub tmrPopupBug Workaround_Timer()
 tmrPopupBug Workaround.Enabled = False
 frmDemo2.Show vbModal
End Sub
```

Part III

Go ahead!

Techniques of program development

6

6.1 Calculations and numerical comparisons with variants

The data type for properties is `Variant`. When a value is assigned, this has no special significance, since the property usually does not permit an invalid value. If, however, you allow for numerical values in the properties of controls or for the values in table fields or for other variants, or if you wish to compare these values with other numerical values, you must take a few factors into account.

Testing for numerical values in calculations and comparisons with numbers

Before a calculation or comparison, you must check whether the value stored in the property or table field or variant is numeric, since otherwise a run-time error 13 ("Type mismatch") may arise:

```
txtDemo1.Text = "TEST"
' this comparison generates error no. 13,
' "Type mismatch"
If txtDemo1.Text = 10 Then
    ' ...
End If
' This line generates the same error
txtDemo2.Text = txtDemo1.Text + 10
```

It would be better to use:

```
If IsNumeric(txtDemo1.Text) Then
    If CLng(txtDemo1.Text) = 10 Then
    ...
End If
```

Conversion with numeric comparisons

When comparing numerical values in variants, you must take account of the fact that VBA does not compare the numerical values in the variants, but undertakes a text comparison. In a text comparison, the individual characters are compared with each other from left to right. As soon as a character in the ANSI sequence is found to be larger than the character of the other value in the same position, this value is the "larger" one:

```
txtDemo1.Text = 1000
txtDemo2.Text = 9
If txtDemo1.Text > txtDemo2.Text Then
    . . .
```

This comparison will not be true, since in a text comparison, "1000" is smaller than "9"!

Conversion with additions

On addition of numerical values in variants, you should note that the addition is not a numerical addition but rather a text addition if you also assign the result to a variant:

```
txtDemo1.Text = 100
txtDemo2.Text = 100
txtDemo3.Text = txtDemo1.Text + txtDemo2.Text
```

After the addition, the value contained in *txtDemo3.Text* is "100100"!

As soon as a purely numerical type occurs in the calculation, the calculation is correct again. However, the calculation will also be incorrect if the result is assigned to a numerical data type:

```
Dim lngI As Long
txtDemo1.Text = 100
txtDemo2.Text = 100
lngI = txtDemo1.Text + txtDemo2.Text
```

Following this addition, the value in lngI is 100100!

Solution

In order to avoid errors, you should always explicitly convert `Variant` data types before calculations or comparisons into a data type that corresponds to the value to be stored in the `Variant`:

```
Dim i As Long
txtDemo1.Text = 100
txtDemo2.Text = 100
i = CLng(txtDemo1.Text) + CLng(txtDemo2.Text)


txtDemo1.Text = 1000
txtDemo2.Text = 9
If CLng(txtDemo1.Text) > CLng(txtDemo2.Text) Then
  ' ...
```

6.2 Checking input

For the checking of input, VB 6 at last offers assistance in the form of properties and events. Each control that can be given the input focus possesses a property CausesValidation and an event Validate. In the Validate event, you can undertake validations. This event is always called if the user wishes to leave a control and change to a control whose CausesValidation property has been set to True. If you discern that the user has input an incorrect value, then simply set the Cancel argument of the Validate event to True, so that the input cursor remains in the current control. Using this technique, you can attain validation of the individual inputs directly on leaving the control. The fact that you can additionally set CausesValidation to False also has its purpose. In order to enable the user to abort, set this property for the Cancel button to False. An abort will then have the effect that no Validate event is called, because no validation needs to be carried out.

Form with two text boxes, in which only numbers should be input, and an OK and a Cancel button:

```
Private Sub txtNumber1_Validate(Cancel As Boolean)
  If Not IsNumeric(txtNumber1.Text) Then
    MsgBox "Please enter a number" & _
           "in the field 'Number1'"
    Cancel = True
  End If
End Sub


Private Sub txtNumber2_Validate(Cancel As Boolean)
  If Not IsNumeric(txtNumber2.Text) Then
    MsgBox "Please enter a number" & _
           "in the field 'Number2'"
    Cancel = True
  End If
End Sub
```

```
Private Sub cmdOK_Click()
 ' Evaluate the input
 ' ...
 Unload Me
End Sub

Private Sub cmdCancel_Click()
 Unload Me
End Sub
```

This is all of value only if you wish to validate immediately after leaving a control. If you only wish to validate when the user presses your OK button, it would be better to check the input in the Click event of this button. Sensibly, the whole thing no longer functions if `CausesValidation` is set to `True` for only one button (the OK button).

If you wish to enable correct input even if the user does not close the form with a button, using the `ValidateControls` method you can ensure that the control which last had the focus is checked. This is only seldom necessary since you would normally place an OK button on the form and for this, `CausesValidation` would be `True`.

6.3 Simulate keyboard input

With `SendKeys`, you can send text and all the keyboard keys (including special keys) to the current window. The syntax is well explained in the online Help program and will therefore not be described in detail here. Using `SendKeys`, you can "remotely control" any applications through simulation of keyboard input.

```
SendKeys Text [,Pause]
```

In the argument *Text*, you can input any desired text or special key codes. Normal keys are included in {}; (↑), **Ctrl** and **Alt** are represented by the symbols +, ^ and %, which are not inserted in {}. Pause defines with True that all keys sent will be processed before the ensuing program code is worked through. If you enter `False` here, program execution is continued immediately following sending of the keys.

Closing the active window with **ALT+F4**:

```
SendKeys "%{F4}", True
```

6.4 Changing the mouse pointer

You can change the cursor shape of the mouse pointer with the property `MousePointer` for every object individually:

```
Object.MousePointer = n
```

Should the mouse pointer be above this object, the icon defined by *n* is used as the mouse pointer. Setting of the mouse pointer that is global for the application can be achieved using the `Screen` object:

```
Screen.MousePointer = n
```

Outside the screen area of the program, the mouse cursor is again displayed as normal.

A variety of values is possible for *n*, each standing for a different cursor shape. Frequently used values are: `vbNormal` (standard cursor) and `vbHourglass` (the hour glass). In the property `MouseIcon`, you can also store an icon for the mouse pointer, which can be used by setting the value of `vbCustom` in Mouse-Pointer.

6.5 Defining color values

If you are one of those people who like to make everything colorful (and do not like to leave it to the user to decide what color his application should have), you can set colors for almost all the controls and forms. A color value is a `Long` value, in which the first byte stands for the red portion, the second for the green portion and the third for the blue portion. If you wish to assign colors, you need make no complex calculations. VBA has a few constants for colors, such as `vbBlue`, `vbRed`, `vbYellow`, etc. You can determine special colors with the `RGB` function. Here you specify the individual color portions as values between 0 and 255. Certain color constants have a special significance and if you set these colors, such as `vbButtonText` and `vbWindowText`, Visual Basic uses the colors set in the system controls. These constants can be found in the object catalog under the entry `SystemColorConstants`.

If the user is to select a color, use the standard color selection dialog. I have already described in Chapter 5 how this is done.

6.6 Using the window API

The Windows API (application interface) is just one of many APIs, even though it is the most important of these. Windows and some other applications frequently make some of their functionality available to other applications for external use via their API, i.e. through functions or objects in one or more DLL files. The application that wishes to use the API need only link in the requisite functions from these DLLs (if it is a classic DLL), or it can refer to the class library (if it is a COM-DLL, as with Word and Excel). The application can then use the functions or objects as though they were its own.

The Windows API consists of several DLL files (which sometimes also possess the ending .EXE, but are nevertheless DLL files). The most important of these are the GDI32 (functions for graphical output), Kernel32 (memory administration, access to data media, process administration, etc.) and User32 (for working with windows, menus and sending messages, etc.).

Why API functions?

Why do you need to use the Windows API at all? The answer is simple: for professional applications, you simply cannot avoid using the Windows API. On the one hand, it offers functions of far greater functional power than you will get with VB and VBA. For instance with Visual Basic itself, you have no simple possibility for reading and writing data from and to INI files or for reading or writing a particular key in the Windows registry. And just try drawing a polygon (in the simplest case a triangle) using VB methods or integrating an Explorer-style directory window into a form. This is all no problem with Windows API functions (you only need to know how it works). A further reason for using Windows API functions is that most VB controls do not give access to the full range of functionality offered in Windows. The developers of Visual Basic have quite simply missed out several functions. Most of the Windows controls into which text can be input, for example, possess an Undo function, while ListBoxes and Combo-Boxes offer functions for rapid searching for a particular entry. You can only call these functions in VB via an API function (in this case SendMessage).

The performance of API functions can be a further reason for using them. Calling them directly is often significantly faster than an equivalent call of a VB(A) function or method. The graphics method Circle is a good example of this. This method is heavily overloaded with optional arguments. Depending on which of the optional arguments is set, Circle either calls the API function Ellipse, Chord, Arc or Pie. When Circle is called, the necessary case discrimination according to the arguments entered and evaluation of the optional arguments naturally costs time. Directly calling the right API function is significantly faster.

How do I find the right function?

Finding the right function is often a difficult task. Visual Basic actually leaves you in the lurch with this task. You do have the possibility with the API Viewer of integrating declaration of most API functions into your project, although this still does not tell you which function you can use for which purpose. Something that I find baffling is that Microsoft does not supply any API documentation with Visual Basic. Most of the existing API documentation (even that from Microsoft) relates to its use with C. Unfortunately, though, this is not of much use to VB programmers, since translation of the data types from C to VB can be very difficult and some of the API functions can only be used with C or similar languages. If you own a copy of Delphi, you can use the documentation supplied with that language, as it is significantly nearer to Visual Basic than the C documentation.

The solution, however, comes in the form of the API bible "Visual Basic Programmer's Guide to the Win32 API" by Dan Appleman. It gives the API functions arranged by category and – apart from the basics of API programming – described in great detail. The Help text with the book is also very usable as a reference.

API or COM?

Most Windows functions are still exported via classical DLL files and the binding-in of these functions is usually no problem. However, new applications often export their functionality by means of COM[1] classes. Winword, Excel and co are the best examples of this. But Windows, too, is parting company from the old API. More recent functions are already implemented in COM classes or COM interfaces (the difference between an interface and a class being, in this instance, unimportant and an interface is also a class). You will, for example, not find any DLL function in Windows API that can create a link to a file. To achieve this, you must use the COM interface IShellLink. Using these COM interfaces is no simple matter in Visual Basic, unfortunately, because usually the type library is missing. This type library, which gives information about the methods and properties of the interface, you must acquire or write yourself. In the specialist literature about Visual Basic and on the Internet, you can find type libraries for the most important interfaces. There is a type library among the examples on the website and an example for the use of IShellLink.

6.6.1   Linking in Visual Basic

Visual Basic needs to know from which DLL an API function should be read and must also know the declaration of this function. To this end, make the function known using a Declare statement in a module. The declaration of most Windows API functions can be found in the file WIN32API.TXT supplied with VB. You can look through this text file using the accessory program API Viewer also supplied with VB, and this can be linked into the development environment as an add-in. For DLL files from external manufacturers, you will have to take the declarations from the manufacturer's documentation.

---

1. The component object model is Microsoft's answer to CORBA. COM defines a standard for the implementation of interfaces of objects in binary code. Applications that have mastered the COM standard use (compiled) COM objects with relatively little difficulty.

Declaration of the function or procedure must be carried out in the declaration section of a module or form. You can link a procedure as follows:

```
[{Private | Public}] Declare Sub Name Lib _
    "DLL Name" [Alias "Alias "] [(Argument list)]
```

For a function, the following applies:

```
[{Private | Public}] Declare Function Name Lib _
    "DLL Name" [Alias "Alias "] [(Argument list)] _
    As Data type
```

Name is the name under which you wish to use the DLL function in your program code. If you do not cite the argument *Alias*, then the function name specified under *Name* must correspond to the original name of the DLL function.

DLL Name is the name of the DLL file. If the DLL file is stored in the Windows system directory or in the current directory, you do not need to, nor should you, enter a path[2].

If you write the name of the DLL function in the argument *Alias*, you can give any other valid function name in *Name*. You will then use this name in the program, but when it uses it, VB will call the function designated by *Alias*.

The use of an alias is called for if:

→ the name of the function in the DLL begins with an underline, which is not allowed in VB;

→ the name of the function has already been used for a designator in the program or in VB;

→ the function in the DLL possesses arguments with variable data types and is to be imported in VB with the possible different data types;

→ importation is to take place in 32-bit Windows functions with strings as arguments.

Linking the function GetWindowsDirectoryA with Alias:

```
Declare Function GetWindowsDirectory Lib "kernel32" _
    Alias_"GetWindowsDirectoryA" ( _
    ByVal lpBuffer As String, ByVal nSize As Long) _
    As Long
```

---

2. You should never use fixed paths in your program, since you cannot assume that a given path is also available to the user.

Private and Public

If you put neither `Private` nor `Public` in front of the declaration, the declaration is always public, i.e. it applies throughout the entire project. You can only undertake the public declaration of an API function in standard modules and only once in the entire project. With the keyword `Private`, you can cause the declaration to apply only in the module concerned. Since `Private` declarations can also occur several times, the use of `Private` is particularly important for modules that are to be used for several projects. I use exclusively `Private` declarations so that I do not experience problems when I link pre-prepared forms, class modules or standard modules into a project.

6.6.2   The passing and return of simple data types

The passing of simple data types is not too difficult. You must only translate the data types of DLLs which are mostly written in C into VBA data types. Because you will usually have a suitable declaration for the API function, I shall forgo making a comparison of the data types here.

6.6.3   Passing and return of strings

Ansi and Unicode strings

In Windows 95, 98 (99, 2000 etc.) and in NT from Version 4.0 and above, all string functions, except those belonging to the component object model, are implemented in two or three variants. The ANSI variant supports ANSI strings, which use one byte per character. The Unicode variant supports Unicode strings, which require two bytes for storing a character. Thus, almost all the characters of all the world's languages can be represented in the character set. In the interests of compatibility with ANSI, the first 256 characters are the same in Unicode and ANSI, so that the characters used in our own language use only the first byte of a Unicode character. The ANSI variant of an API function can be recognized from an attached "A" (for *ANSI*), and the Unicode variant from a "W" (for *Wide String*).

Unicode is currently only supported by Windows NT from Version 4.0 and above. Windows 95 also offers the normal (i.e. not belonging to the component object model) string functions in ANSI and Unicode variants, whereas Unicode support is not yet implemented.

Visual Basic already administers strings internally in their Unicode version, although when calling API functions, it currently still makes an ANSI copy automatically, so that API calls will also function within Windows 95.

In describing string functions, I shall consider only the use of ANSI strings here.

The passing of strings

The standard method of passing strings to DLL functions is as pointers to a zero-terminated (ending with the character 0) character sequence. In order that you can pass a string to the DLL function, you must declare the argument in the declaration of the API function *By Value*. But just a moment: By Value? In this context, By Value is exactly right, because the *Value* of a string variable is a pointer to an actual string. Were you to declare By Reference, then VB would pass the address of the string variables and not that of the string. Indeed, VB keeps in the string variables only the address of the string stored entirely elsewhere in the memory. Otherwise the dynamic administration of strings would not be possible.

The return of strings

Functions that return strings (and usually zero-terminated strings) as their function return value can only be imported into VBA with some difficulty. This is also the reason why most functions which return strings do so in an argument of the argument list. This argument is also declared with `ByVal`. The reason for this is the same as for the arguments which serve only in the passing of strings.

You must pass to these functions a string variable that is defined to be sufficiently large. For this purpose, either use a fixed string or, better still, fill a dynamic string with arbitrary characters. You must rid the returned string from its terminating 0 character. The removal of the 0 character is generally assisted by the API function, which as a rule returns the number of characters read (without the 0 character) as the function value.

Warning The return string variable must either be a fixed string variable or, if dynamic, it must be set to a particular length before reading with Space$(n) or `String$`(n, " "). If a dynamic variable that is too small or empty is passed, then the consequence, as a rule, is that a general storage protection violation results from this, since the API function writes to the memory from the start address of the variable and thus into a storage space not belonging to the program (and therefore not protected).

Finding the Windows directory

```
Declare Function GetWindowsDirectory Lib "kernel32" Alias _
    "GetWindowsDirectoryA" (ByVal lpBuffer As String, _
    ByVal nSize As Long) As Long
```

```
Private Sub cmdGetWinDir_Click()
 Dim strResult As String, lngCount As Long
 ' dimension string to be sufficiently large
 strResult = Space$(260)
 ' call API function
 lngCount = GetWindowsDirectory(strResult, 260)
 ' remove the final 0 character
 strResult = Left$(strResult, lngCount)
 ' output the test string
 MsgBox strResult
End Sub
```

6.6.4   Arguments without data type

Some DLL functions have arguments whose data type is not defined. A function of this kind can be called with different data types in this argument. VB offers two possibilities for declaring these functions: declaration with As Any and declaration with several alias functions having different suitable data types.

On declaration using As Any, when calling you can decide which data type will be passed. The API function SendMessage, for example, can be called dependent upon the third argument, with a pointer to a string or a Long value as the fourth argument:

```
Private Declare Function SendMessage Lib "user32" _
   Alias "SendMessageA" (ByVal hwnd As Long, _
   ByVal wMsg As Long, ByVal wParam As Long, _
   lParam As Any) As Long
```

When functions of this type are called, the arguments must be modified according to the data type. Table 6.1 shows how you should make the modification.

Argument	Input
Null pointer	ByVal 0&
Null value	0&
String	ByVal *String value*
Long value	ByVal *Value*&
Pointer to variable	*Variable*

Table 6.1   *The passing of certain data types in an As Any declaration*

For the above example, then, the following applies:

```
' on passing a string
SendMessage(..., ByVal Str)
' on passing a Long value
SendMessage(..., ByVal LongVal&)
```

Example: call Undo in a TextBox (this can indeed be done, and not only in Text-Boxes) and seek an entry (very rapidly) in a ListBox (why is this not implemented as a method in the ListBox?):

```
Private Declare Function SendMessage Lib "user32" _
    Alias "SendMessageA" (ByVal hwnd As Long, _
    ByVal wMsg As Long, ByVal wParam As Long, _
    lParam As Any) As Long
Private Const EM_UNDO = &HC7
Private Const LB_FINDSTRING = &H18F

Private Sub TestSendMessage()
 ' call Undo
 SendMessage txtFirstName.hwnd, EM_UNDO, _
            ByVal 0&, ByVal 0&

 Dim strFind As String
 strFind = "Zaphod"

 ' quickly search for the first entry
 ' beginning with "Zaphod"
 lstNames.ListIndex = SendMessage( _
    lstNames.hwnd, LB_FINDSTRING, -1, ByVal strFind)
End Sub
```

The second, and possibly better, option is to declare the relevant function with as many aliases as there are possible data types:

```
Declare Function SendMessageL ... , _
    lParam As Long) As Long
Declare Function SendMessageS ... , _
    ByVal lParam As String) As Long
```

6.6.5 Passing arrays

In the event that the DLL function demands an array, as a rule you must pass a pointer to the array. To do this, simply pass the first element of the array. The API function also expects the number of elements stored in the array. For instance, the GDI function `Polygon` for drawing a polygon expects an array made up of `POINTAPI` elements. Every `POINTAPI` element defines a point on the polygon. The following example draws a triangle:

```
Private Type POINTAPI
 x As Long
 y As Long
End Type


Private Declare Function Polygon Lib "gdi32" ( _
    ByVal hdc As Long, lpPoint As POINTAPI, _
    ByVal nCount As Long) As Long


Private Sub cmdPolygon_Click()
 ' draw triangle
 Dim audtPoints(1 To 3) As POINTAPI
 ' set scaling mode to pixels,
 ' since GDI functions always calculate in pixels
 Me.ScaleMode = vbPixels
 ' define fill style, fill color and
 ' drawing color
 Me.FillColor = vbRed
 Me.FillStyle = vbDiagonalCross
 Me.ForeColor = vbBlue
 ' set the polygon points
 audtPoints(1).x = Me.ScaleWidth / 2
 audtPoints(1).y = 0
 audtPoints(2).x = 0
 audtPoints(2).y = Me.ScaleHeight
 audtPoints(3).x = Me.ScaleWidth
 audtPoints(3).y = Me.ScaleHeight
 ' call the polygon function with the first array
 ' element and the number of elements
 Polygon Me.hdc, audtPoints(1), 3
End Sub
```

Note: graphic functions always expect a *handle* to the *device context* (HDC) of the object on which drawing is to take place. You can read this handle from the hdc property of the object.

It is important with API functions which receive an array passed to them that the size of the array is defined. In the case of the Polygon function, this is the argument *nCount*, which in our example is set to 3. Note that the scaling mode must be set to vbPixels if, when drawing, you refer to the object on which you are drawing, since GDI functions always calculate in pixels. In this connection you should also always use the ScaleWidth and ScaleHeight property instead of Width and Height, since ScaleWidth and ScaleHeight always use the scaling mode (Width and Height always calculate in twips).

6.6.6   Passing null pointers

You can pass null pointers (pointers to Null) to some DLL functions. The function FindWindow, for example, returns the handle of a window. If in the second argument of this function you pass the window title, you can leave out the first argument, the class name. Then you must pass a null pointer. Declare arguments of this type with the data type String and pass the constant vbNullString if you wish to pass a zero pointer.

Search for the window with the title "Microsoft Word – Chapter06.doc":

```
Private Declare Function FindWindow Lib "user32" _
  Alias "FindWindowA" (ByVal lpClassName As String, _
  ByVal lpWindowName As String) As Long
Private Sub cmdGetWordWindow_Click()
 Dim hwndHandle As Long
 hwndHandle = FindWindow(vbNullString, _
    "Microsoft Word - Chapter06.doc")
 ' ...
End Sub
```

6.6.7   Large, whole-number arguments

Windows API functions sometimes work with 64-bit sized integer values. If you pass a value of this type or wish to use a corresponding function return, simply take the data type Currency. This 64-bit data type has a fixed decimal point, but because it is fixed, no decimal place is stored. Currency therefore behaves in memory as though it were a large integer value. You need only to multiply by 10,000 to obtain the integer value.

A very good application for this technique is the API function QueryPerformanceCounter, which together with QueryPerformanceFrequency provides a highly precise time measure (which otherwise would only be obtained by direct BIOS access):

```
Private Declare Function QueryPerformanceCounter Lib _
    "kernel32" (ByRef lpPerformanceCount As Currency) _
    As Long
Private Declare Function QueryPerformanceFrequency Lib _
    "kernel32" (ByRef lpFrequency As Currency) As Long

Private mcurFrequency

Private Sub Form_Load()
 ' find the frequency
 QueryPerformanceFrequency mcurFrequency
End Sub

Private Sub cmdTest_Click()
 Dim curStart As Currency, curEnd As Currency
 Dim curTime As Currency, intIndex As Integer
 ' start
 QueryPerformanceCounter curStart

 ' execute action
 For intIndex = 1 To 30000
     ' ...
 Next

 ' Stop
 QueryPerformanceCounter curEnd

 ' evaluate
 If mcurFrequency = 0 Then
     ' timer does not have high resolution
     curTime = 0
 Else
     curTime = (curEnd - curStart) / mcurFrequency
 End If

 ' output can take place directly with the currency
 ' decimal place in seconds
 MsgBox "The action would take " & curTime & " seconds."
End Sub
```

6

GO AHEAD!

The declaration from the API catalog, by contrast, uses the data type LARGE_INTEGER, which is made up as follows:

```
Type LARGE_INTEGER
 lowpart As Long
 highpart As Long
End Type
```

If you use this data type, you will have to solve the problem of putting together the low part and the high part of the 64-bit number so that the value is correct (which could well be fun...).

6.6.8   Callback functions

Some of the API functions expect a function address as an argument in order to be able to call this function in a Callback. The Windows API function EnumWindows is an example of this. For the realization of this call, Visual Basic offers you an AddressOf operator, which passes the address of a VB function to an API function.

The function that you wish to pass to the API function must be declared in a standard module (not a class or form module!) and, in relation to the declaration, exactly match up to the requirements of the API function (data types of the arguments, passing "By Value" or "By Reference"). If the declaration is not correct, you run the risk of generating a program or Windows crash. When calling the API function, state the address of the Callback function with the aid of the AddressOf operator:

```
AddressOf functionname
```

The best example of Callback functions is the API function EnumWindows, which goes through all the loaded windows (including the invisible ones) and passes the handle of each window to a Callback function:

```
Declare Function EnumWindows Lib "user32" ( _
   ByVal lpEnumFunc As Long, _
   ByVal lParam As Any) As Long

Declare Function GetWindowText Lib "user32" _
   Alias "GetWindowTextA" (ByVal hwnd As Long, _
   ByVal lpString As String, _
   ByVal cch As Long) As Long

' The Callback function. When this function is called
' EnumWindows passes the Handle of the
```

```vb
' individual window in hwnd. lpData is an argument
' that can be passed to EnumWindows on the call
' and which EnumWindows simply passes on.
' In this example, lpData is used to pass on a
' pointer to a ListBox, which is to be filled with
' the window texts.
Public Function EnumWindowsProc(ByVal hwnd As Long, _
   ByVal lpData As ListBox) As Long
 Dim lngTextLen As Long, strBuffer As String * 255
 lngTextLen = GetWindowText(hwnd, strBuffer, _
    Len(strBuffer) + 1)
 If lngTextLen > 0 Then
    ' store window text in list string
    lpData.AddItem Left$(strBuffer, lngTextLen)
    ' store window Handle in ItemData
    lpData.ItemData(lpData.NewIndex) = hwnd
 End If
 EnumWindowsProc = True
End Function

Sub FillWindowList(lstList As ListBox)
 lstList.Clear
 EnumWindows AddressOf EnumWindowsProc, lstList
End Sub
```

6.7 Saving initialization data

You have several possibilities for placing initialization data on the user's system. Either you store the data in an INI file (which has the advantage of being very easy to edit) or in a random access file (which is markedly more involved and has the disadvantage that this file cannot be edited) or in the Windows Registry. Use of the Windows Registry has the advantage that the data from Windows are generally stored user-specifically. Every user of the computer can administer his or her own options for the individual applications separately, provided each user has unique login details. Use of an INI file has the advantage that you can supply this very simply with your application and that the data can be easily edited in this file. If you use an INI file, you may even be able to dispense with the dialogue box in which the user can set the initialization data. I do not intend to describe INI files here for reasons of space, since storage in the Registry is up to date and, what is more, simpler.

There is no need to concern yourself with storing data in the Registry. Every application can now do that. If you ever use a tool such as `Regmon` (from the website www.sysinternals.com) to monitor Registry access by an application, you will notice that the storage of a couple of initialization data is no problem at all. Every application of larger size frequently writes to and reads a great deal of data to and from the Registry. But note that you should not place large amounts of data in the Registry. It is intended as a place for initialization data and system data and not as a database. You should also not place any important data in the Registry. It is usually not secured and the data will be lost on a reinstallation of Windows, if not before.

VBA offers two functions that write string values into the Registry or read them from it. Access is very simple with this function. `SaveSetting` writes a string into the Registry:

```
SaveSetting AppName, Section, Key, Setting
```

`GetSetting` reads a string from:

```
strResult = GetSetting(AppName, Section, Key [,Default])
```

Both functions use the key `HKEY_CURRENT_USER\ Software\VB and VBA Program Settings\` and within it a sub-key that corresponds to your input in the argument *AppName* as a group for the settings in your application. Within this group, for each section given in the argument *Section*, further sub-keys are created. The argument *Key* defines the key to which or from which the value is written or read. Thus these functions behave in a similar way to the functions of an INI file, with the difference that they give the application name in place of the INI file name.

Store the contents of the TextBox in the Registry

```
SaveSetting "Nitty-Gritty Reg-Demo", "System", _
          "Name", txtName.Text
```

Read the contents of a TextBox from the Registry:

```
txtName.Text = GetSetting("Nitty-Gritty Reg-Demo", _
          "System", "Name", "")
```

`SaveSetting` in this example creates the entries represented in Figure 6.1.

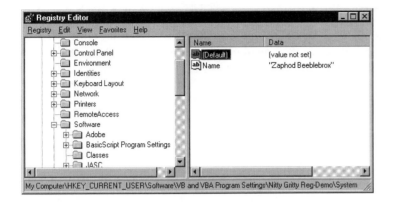

Figure 6.1 *The key created by SaveSetting with the values in the Registry*

> **Tip** In the argument *AppName*, you should use an absolutely unambiguous identifier, ideally with your initials as a prefix. If you use simple identifiers, you take the risk that your settings will be over-written by others, even in applications written using VBA.

Direct access to the Registry

Naturally enough, direct access to the Registry is also possible. However, to do this, you must use certain Windows-API functions. Since their use is not altogether simple, I shall dispense here with a description of these and draw your attention to the examples within this book. You will find there a file called REG-PROCS.BAS, in which the API functions are encapsulated in VB functions that are significantly simpler to call.

6.8 Refresh and DoEvents

With the `Refresh` method, you can force updating of a control or a form if your program is so intensively utilized within a procedure or function that automatic updating is not performed. The VBA procedure `DoEvents`, on the other hand, has the effect that your program gives Windows time to process the message queue, so that in the case of processor-intensive actions in your application, user inputs are still possible. The two sections that follow describe how you should proceed to implement these techniques.

6.8.1   Updating the screen

You will frequently find yourself in the situation that an output from your program does not appear as wanted – or at once – on the screen. If, for example, you update the labeling of a control within a loop, output will generally occur only after the loop has ended.

Update a label within a loop:

```
Dim lngIndex As Long
For lngIndex = 1 To 100000
    lblInfo.Caption = "Cycle " & lngIndex
Next
```

This *problem* results from a great *strength* of Windows, which is that Windows is a multi-tasking system. Tasks are carried out according to their priority, piece by piece. Apart from the example above, in which the calculation has a higher priority than refreshing the window, you will meet this situation in many other cases. Display of a non-modal form can be interrupted – after, say, Windows has constructed a part of the window –for just as long as the program code following the opening needs to finish running.

You can, however, force updating of the screen with the Refresh method:

```
Dim lngIndex As Long
For lngIndex = 1 To 100000
    lblInfo.Caption = "Cycle " & lngIndex
    Refresh
Next
```

Note that the loop will now run significantly more slowly. In my case, the loop without Refresh took about 6 seconds to complete, while with Refresh, it ran through in about 55 seconds. You should possibly carry out the Refresh at intervals, so as to accelerate execution:

```
' Refresh only once every 100 cycles
Dim lngIndex As Long
For lngIndex = 1 To 100000
    lblInfo.Caption = "Cycle  " & lngIndex
    If lngIndex Mod 100 = 0 Then
       Refresh
    End If
Next
```

In my case, this led to the loop being executed in 22 seconds. A refresh for every 10th cycle, however, did not lead to a significant acceleration. You should therefore experiment in each case.

> **Tip** Note that some controls, such as the ProgressBar, carry out a Refresh implicitly. A further implicit Refresh would not make any sense in this case and would simply slow down the program further.

6.8.2   Enable interruption of processor-intensive actions

In the case of processor-intensive actions that take up a great deal of time (e.g. printing several hundred pages of text), you will probably want to give the user the option of stopping the action. In principle, programming this feature is very simple. During the action, you check a global variable that is set by the interrupt switch. Unfortunately, in the case of processor-intensive actions, your application does not react to user actions if you do not build any DoEvents into the action. The program in Figure 6.2, for example, calculates prime numbers.

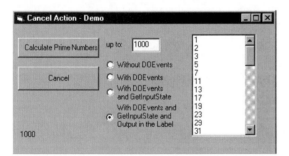

Figure 6.2   *Example program to illustrate interruption of an action taking a relatively long time*

The code for the prime numbers function looks as follows:

```
Public Function GetPrimeNumbers(lngLastNumber As Long) _
              As Long()
 'Calculates all the prime numbers from 1 to lngLastNumber
 gysnCancel = False
 Dim lngCount As Long, lngNumber1 As Long
 Dim lngNumber2 As Long, ysnNoPrimeNumber As Boolean
 Dim lngNumbers() As Long
 lngCount = 0
```

```
For lngNumber1 = 1 To lngLastNumber
   ysnNoPrimeNumber = False
   For lngNumber2 = lngNumber1 - 1 To 2 Step -1
      If lngNumber1 Mod lngNumber2 = 0 Then
         ysnNoPrimeNumber = True
         Exit For
      End If
      DoEvents
      If gysnCancel Then
         GetPrimeNumbers = alngNumbers
         Exit Function
      End IF
   Next
   If ysnNoPrimeNumber = False Then
      lngCount = lngCount + 1
      ReDim Preserve alngNumbers(1 To lngCount)
      alngNumbers(lngCount) = lngNumber1
   End If
 Next
 GetPrimeNumbers = alngNumbers
End Function
```

gysnCancel is a Boolean variable, which is declared in a VB module.

The Start button initiates the calculation and causes the results to be written in a ListBox:

```
Private Sub cmdStart_Click()
 Dim alngNumbers() As Long
 lstNumbers.Clear
 alngNumbers = GetPrimeNumbers(Val(txtLastNumber.Text))
 Dim i As Long
 For i = 1 To UBound(alngNumbers)
    lstNumbers.AddItem alngNumbers(i)
 Next
End Sub
```

The Cancel button simply sets *gysnCancel*:

```
Private Sub cmdCancel_Click()
 gysnCancel = True
End Sub
```

Try the whole thing without `DoEvents` and you will see that the user cannot interrupt the calculation. Unfortunately, `DoEvents` requires some time, and this extends the action to a not insignificant degree. On my computer, the calculation of 1,000 numbers without `DoEvents` took 0.13 seconds, while with DoEvents it took 100.5 seconds! You can, of course, enhance the performance by calling `DoEvents` less often (e.g. only every 100 times round the external loop), although then the program will be slower to react to action by the user.

Avoiding the recursive call

The possibility of controlling this aspect with `DoEvents` also means that the procedure which is just being processed can be repeatedly called *during* its processing. Should this occur, it can lead to the error "Invalid procedure call or argument". You must ensure that the procedure cannot be called repeatedly during its processing. To do this, use a static local variable, and this will be the first thing to be checked in the procedure:

```
Static sblnRunning As Boolean
If sblnRunning Then Exit Sub ' check status variable
sblnRunning = True          ' set status variable
. . .
For lngNumber1 = 1 To lngLastNumber
   . . .
Next
ysnRunning = False          ' set status variable back
again
```

Tips and tricks

The trick using GetInputState

Using the API function `GetInputState` is a good "trick" for preventing performance being hindered too much by certain actions, as discussed above, while nevertheless giving the user the possibility of interrupting the action. `GetInputState` returns a value `<>` of 0 if the mouse or keyboard is operated. In this event only will `DoEvents` be called, to give the operating system time to process this user input. In contrast to `DoEvents`, calling the API function requires very little time. The program code for the prime numbers function then looks as follows (extract only):

```
Public Function GetPrimeNumbers(lngLastNumber As Long) _
      As Long()
 . . .

      If GetInputState <> 0 Then
         DoEvents
      End If
```

```
      If gysnCancel Then
         GetPrimeNumbers = alngNumbers
         Exit Function
      End If
   ...
End Function
```

Calculation of 1,000 numbers takes only 0.26 seconds. This is only twice as long as without the interrupt facility, but a good compromise.

6.9 OLE Drag&Drop

Visual Basic now possesses two types of Drag&Drop. The older standard Drag&Drop, in which you could only exchange data between VB applications, and the new OLE Drag&Drop, with which you can implement Drag&Drop between different OLE-capable applications. Thus you can, for instance, pull a text from Word into a text field or vice versa. This section describes the more universal and more efficient OLE Drag&Drop.

If you want to integrate OLE Drag&Drop into your application, in the simplest case, you can set the properties OLEDragMode and OLEDropMode to *Automatic*. Now, the user can pull an object into the relevant control and move the contents of the control into another application. Provided the control can show the data of the dragged object, this is indicated to the user by the OLE icon when the mouse pointer lies over the control. Only a few controls support automatic dropping (pictures, images, RichText controls, DBGrids, TextBoxes, MaskedEdBoxes). Other controls, such as CheckBox, ComboBox and ListBox, only support automatic dragging from the control. Yet other controls support no automatic mode at all. For these controls, and naturally for all others, you can quickly program OLE Drag&Drop yourself. To this end, most of the controls and some of the methods and events are at your disposal.

Method	Purpose
OLEDrag	Starts manual dragging if OLEDragMode is set to *Manual*.

Table 6.2 *The method for starting an OLE drag action*

Event	Purpose
OLEDragDrop	A source object has been placed on a control.
OLEDragOver	A source object is moved over a control.
OLEGiveFeed -back	Gives the user individually adapted feedback in the form of a drag symbol.

Table 6.3 *The events for OLE Drag&Drop*

Starting manually

If OLEDragMode has been set to *Manual*, you can start an OLE Drag&Drop operation with the OLEDrag method of the control. After OLEDrag has been called, the OLEStartDrag event of the control starts. The parameter Data of the event procedure points to a DataObject whose method SetData you can use to make the data available. The parameter *AllowedEffects* determines which *effects* are allowed. With the allowed effects, the source specifies whether the data are copied to the target or merely shifted onto the target, or if the target can decide whether copying or shifting will take place. Table 6.4 shows the possible constants.

Effect	Purpose
vbDropEffectNone	The target cannot accept the data.
vbDropEffectCopy	A drop operation leads to the copying of data from the source to the target. The original data are not altered by the drag operation.
vbDropEffectMove	The drop operation leads to data being moved from the source to the target. The source should remove the data in its domain (in the OLECompleteDrag event) after completion of the moving.

Table 6.4 *The effects of OLE Drag&Drop operations*

You will normally call OLEDrag in the Mouse_Down of the source element:

```
Private Sub txtSource_MouseDown(Button As Integer, _
    Shift As Integer, X As Single, Y As Single)
  If Button = vbLeftButton Then
    ' start OLE Drag&Drop operation
    txtSource.OLEDrag
  End If
End Sub
```

Immediately afterwards, the `OLEStartDrag` event takes place in which you set the data and define the allowed effects. The following example allows copying and moving:

```
Private Sub txtSource_OLEStartDrag( _
    Data As DataObject, AllowedEffects As Long)
 ' supply the data to the data object
 Data.SetData txtSource.Text, vbCFText
 ' define the allowed effects
 AllowedEffects = vbDropEffectCopy Or vbDropEffectMove
End Sub
```

If the data are dropped on the target, it accepts the data and sets *Effects* to `vbDropEffectCopy` if it has been decided there that copying should take place, or `vbDropEffectMove` if it has been decided in the target that moving should take place. How this is programmed can be seen in the next section, in the example on manual placement. The source must then only check in the event `OLECompleteDrag` whether the data should be moved, i.e. deleted in the source:

```
Private Sub txtSource_OLECompleteDrag(Effect As Long)
 ' check whether the target has decided
 ' moving should take place
 If (Effect And vbDropEffectMove) = vbDropEffectMove Then
    ' delete text
    txtSource.Text = ""
 End If
End Sub
```

Manual placement

If `OLEDropMode` for an OLE Drag&Drop-capable control is set to *Manual*, the event `OLEDragDrop` is called if the user drops dragged data on the control in question. The parameter *Data* of the event procedure points to the data. In order to discover which format the OLE data have, you can use the method `GetFormat` of this object. You pass a constant to this method that says what format you want to test for. If the method returns `True`, the data of the object do possess the format being sought. You have several constants available for the different formats (Table 6.5).

Constant	Format
vbCFText	Text
vbCFBitmap	Bitmap
vbCFMetafile	Metafile (.WMF)

Constant	Format
vbCFEMetafile	Extended Metafile files (.EMF)
vbCFDIB	Device-independent bitmap (.DIB)
vbCFPalette	Color palette
vbCFFiles	List of files
vbCFRTF	Rich Text Format (.RTF files)

Table 6.5 *The formats of OLE Drag&Drop data*

Using the GetData method of the Data object, to which you must also pass the format, you can then read the data. The target can now still decide whether the data should be copied or moved, given that the allowed effects permit it. Normally the Shift key (*Move*) and the Ctrl key (*Copy*) and a combination of both keys (*Link*, only with files) are used:

```
Private Sub txtDest_OLEDragDrop(Data As DataObject, _
    Effect As Long, Button As Integer, _
    Shift As Integer, X As Single, Y As Single)
' Data has been dropped
' Check whether the data fits
If Data.GetFormat(vbCFText) Then
    ' Check whether CTRL (Copy) or
    ' SHIFT (Move) has been pressed
    Select Case Shift
      Case 0, vbShiftMask
        ' Initialize Move
        Effect = vbDropEffectMove
      Case vbCtrlMask
        ' Specify that only copying will take place
        Effect = vbDropEffectCopy
      Case vbShiftMask Or vbCtrlMask
        ' If linking is to take place, the value
        ' 4 must be set (it has no meaning
        ' for this example)
        Effect = 4
    End Select
    ' Read data
    txtDest.Text = Data.GetData(vbCFText)
Else
    ' Data type does not fit, terminate Drag&Drop
    ' operation
    Effect = vbDropEffectNone
End If
End Sub
```

Adapt the mouse pointer

The target should communicate to the user via the mouse pointer what it intends to do with the data. To do this, use the `OLEDragOver` event. The source code looks exactly as for the `OLEDragDrop` event, except that you do not write the data here:

```
Private Sub txtDest_OLEDragOver(Data As DataObject, _
    Effect As Long, Button As Integer, _
    Shift As Integer, X As Single, Y As Single, _
    State As Integer)
 ' The user moves the mouse with OLE data
 ' over the target
 ' Check whether the data type fits
 If Data.GetFormat(vbCFText) Then
    ' Check whether Ctrl (Copy) or
    ' SHIFT (Move) has been activated
    Select Case Shift
      Case 0, vbShiftMask
        ' Initiate the move
        Effect = vbDropEffectMove
      Case vbCtrlMask
        ' Specify that only copying will take place
        Effect = vbDropEffectCopy
      Case vbShiftMask Or vbCtrlMask
        Effect = 4
    End Select
 Else
    ' Data type does not fit
    Effect = vbDropEffectNone
 End If
End Sub
```

Further OLE Drag&Drop techniques

With OLE Drag&Drop, as well as normal data, you can also drag file names, e.g. from Explorer into a ListBox in your application. This technique is very simple. If, however, you wish to drag data that are not supported as standard (you can find the data types in Table 6.5), you will need a little more expertise. On the website for the book, you will find an example concerning OLE Drag&Drop, which also takes these variants into account.

6.10 MDI and Explorer applications

6.10.1 The VB Application Wizard

When creating a new project, you can choose the VB Application Wizard as an option. This assistant creates the basic framework of an application in SDI (single document interface), MDI (multiple document interface) or Explorer style, as required. SDI applications are ones that consist of several individual windows independent of each other. Every normal application that you wish to create in VB is an SDI application. MDI and Explorer applications are described in the next sections.

Optionally, you can add to your application various menus, resource files, a splash screen (a screen that appears only when the program starts), an information window, an option dialog, a login dialog (e.g. for database login), forms for accessing a database and a web browser screen (that uses the ActiveX control of Internet Explorer). The basic framework created in this way provides an excellent base for your applications.

6.10.2 MDI applications

MDI applications consist of an MDI main form (also called an MDI parent) and one or more subsidiary MDI forms (also called MDI child windows). MDI forms are windows in which other windows (the MDI child windows) can move about, although without being able to protrude beyond the edge of the MDI form. An example of an MDI application is Winword. Winword itself is the MDI main form, and all opened documents are MDI child windows. The MDI main form therefore represents a type of work surface.

The MDI interface defines certain conventions:

→ MDI child windows can only move within the MDI main form.
→ On reduction to icon size, they are represented within the MDI main form.
→ If MDI child windows have a menu, the one belonging to the active MDI child window is displayed in the menu bar of the MDI parent.
→ Per application, there can be only one MDI parent.

Advantages of an MDI application

Without much trouble, you can integrate a `Window` menu item into your menu.

The menu of the MDI main form can relate to the currently active MDI child form. In this way, therefore, you can implement global menu points that apply for all child forms (for example, see the menu points `Copy` and `Insert` in Winword).

A child form can have a menu of its own, which is automatically displayed in the menu of the MDI form when this child form is displayed.

An example of a simple MDI application is represented in Figure 6.3.

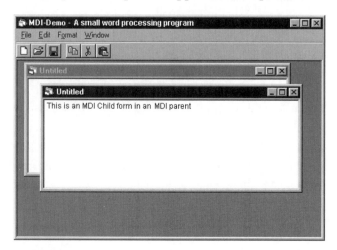

Figure 6.3 *Simple MDI application with two MDI child windows*

Programming an MDI application

First of all a tip: the Application Wizard provides you, apart from SDI and Explorer applications frameworks, with wonderful MDI applications frameworks. A little unfortunate in this is the fact that the wizard does not set up the MDI form as the start object but a procedure Sub Main, which is defined in a module and does nothing other than create and display the MDI form. This process is probably nearer to the Windows standard and would also have advantages if the Wizard were not to declare[3] the form variable with New, but might make your project untransparent. It would be better to set up the MDI form as the start object for your project.

An MDI application consists of an MDI form, which is simultaneously the start object of the application, and one or more normal forms. These normal forms are usually used as MDI child forms, in that their property MDIChild is set to True (an MDI application can also contain normal forms that are not defined as child forms and these are then generally opened modally). A simple MDI application has only one MDI child form, which during run-time is only used as a basis class

---

3. "Dim frm As New frmMain" leads only to VB checking, as with a normal form every time the form is accessed, whether an object already exists, and creating it if necessary. It is only in this way that access to a form that has not previously been loaded using Load can work. "Dim frm As frmMain: Set frm = New frmMain" would be significantly more effective, since the checking process is left out here.

for creating several objects. For example, a word processing program needs the same fundamental form for every document, but in several objects for the individual opened documents. You can also use several different MDI child forms if necessary.

By way of example, we could take a simple MDI application with only one child form. You can find the complete example in the sample files associated with the book.

With the menu item `Add | MDI Form`, you add an MDI form to your project. You should set this form as the Startup form in the Project Properties. Your project should contain yet another form, to which you add, for example, a Rich Text control, in order to create a small word processing program. Set the property `MDI-Child` of this form to `True`.

On the MDI form create a menu with, for example, the menu items `File | New`, `File | Open`, `File | Save` and `Window`.

In `File | New`, you must now simply create a new instance of the MDI child form:

```
Public Sub mnuNew_Click()
 Dim frm As frmMDIChild
 Set frm = New frmMDIChild
 frm.Caption = "Unnamed"
 frm.Show
End Sub
```

`File | Open` works in a similar way, except that you should first ascertain the file to be opened using a `CommonDialog` control (which is placed on the MDI form) and open this with the `LoadFile` method of the RichText control of the MDI child form:

```
Public Sub mnuOpen_Click()
    cdlFileName.DefaultExt = ".rtf"
    cdlFileName.DialogTitle = "Open"
    cdlFileName.Flags = cdlOFNFileMustExist _
                    Or cdlOFNHideReadOnly
    cdlFileName.Filter = "RTF files " & _
            "(*.rtf)|*.rtf|All files" & _
            "(*.*)|*.*"
    cdlFileName.ShowOpen
    If cdlFileName.FileName > "" Then
        ' if not cancelled,
        ' create new child form
        Dim frm As frmMDIChild
        Set frm = New frmMDIChild
        ' open file
```

```
        frm.rtf.LoadFile cdlFileName.FileName, _
                          rtfRTF
        ' save current file name
        frm.gstrFilename = cdlFileName.FileName
        ' label file as saved
        frm.gysnChanged = False
        ' use the file name without path
        ' as caption
        frm.Caption = ExtractFileName( _
                      cdlFileName.FileName)
        ' ExtractFilename is a separate function!
        frm.Show
    End If
End Sub
```

In order to implement a File | Save menu item, you can follow one of two routes. Either you integrate this menu item into the MDI form's menu or you create a menu in the MDI child form, which will then be automatically displayed in the menu of the MDI form.

With the first method, you can use the property ActiveForm of the MDI form in order to gain access to the active MDI child form. You should be aware that ActiveForm applies for your action only if there is an MDI child form in the foreground (it may be that no MDI child form has been opened or that a normal form is in the foreground). To solve this problem, you can ensure that the menu item concerned is activated (enabled) only if an MDI child form is in the foreground. This must be decided in Form_Activate for the MDI child form, although this is a little difficult since it is possible for several MDI child forms to be open at once. Another solution would be initially to check ActiveForm for Nothing and then, if your project contains other forms, to check for a valid MDI child form.

```
Private Sub mnuSave_Click()
' check for Nothing
If Not (ActiveForm Is Nothing) Then
  ' check for the correct form
  If TypeOf ActiveForm Is frmMDIChild Then
    ' save
    ' ...
  Else
    MsgBox "This form cannot be saved"
  End If
Else
  MsgBox "Save not possible, " & _
         "if no form is activated"
End If
End Sub
```

Much simpler, though, is the second route. You simply integrate the Save menu item into the (possibly new) menu of the MDI child form. This procedure is also significantly more object-oriented, since the logic for saving is given to the object itself. This menu of the child form will now automatically be displayed in the menu of the MDI form.

What does now cause difficulties is the fact that the menu of the child form entirely replaces the menu of the MDI form when the child form is activated. The menu items File | New, File | Open and Window are missing. Somehow it must be possible to manage that the menu of the child form is displayed so that the menu of the MDI form is merely extended. The property NegotiatePosition of the individual menus in the MDI form probably has something to do with it. Unfortunately, all my attempts produced no result. Since Microsoft itself in the online documentation on NegotiatePosition explains it only sparingly and not in relation to MDI forms, and in its MDI examples goes the other route, explained in the next section, I think that NegotiatePosition simply does not function with MDI applications.

The other route is to create the menu of the MDI form completely in the MDI child form. However, so that we are not forced to program the logic anew, in the menu items that are actually menu items of the MDI form, only the event procedures of the MDI form menu items are called (and these are therefore declared as Public in the examples above).

The menu item File | New in the MDI child form:

```
Private Sub mnuNew_Click()
  ' call of the new sub in the MDI parent
  frmMDIParent.mnuNew_Click
End Sub
```

A window menu item

To give the user the possibility of activating an MDI child form quickly, you can set up a WINDOW menu item, whose property WindowList you set to True. In this menu, the MDI form automatically enters all the opened MDI child forms in the lower area, together with their captions.

You have the possibility of arranging and integrating windows with separate menu items, such as Tile horizontally, Tile vertically, Cascade and Arrange icons. In the event procedures, simply call the Arrange method of the MDI form and pass the constants vbCascade (arrange cascaded), vbTile-Horizontal, vbTileVertical and vbArrangeIcons (arrange windows that are displayed as icons).

If you use the display technique described above, the complete window menu can only be sensibly implemented in the MDI child form unless you solve the problem with `NegotiatePosition` (in which case, please mail me the solution).

```
Private Sub mnuCascade_Click()
 frmMDIParent.Arrange vbCascade
End Sub
```

Tips and tricks

Controls on the MDI form

If you try to place a control on an MDI form (e.g. a button), the MDI form usually rejects it. To overcome this, simply place a `PictureBox` control on the form. Within this `Picture` element, you can now place other controls without difficulty.

6.10.3   Explorer applications

Explorer applications use windows that are similar to those of Explorer. Explorer windows are programmed as a combination of a ListView and a TreeView control. Leave the creation of the basic framework of an Explorer application to the VB Application Wizard. Starting from this basis, you can then readily adapt the application produced to your own particular requirements.

Error handling and debugging

Debugging is an important part of program development. Visual Basic supports you with its very good integrated debugger when debugging run-time errors and much worse logical errors. This debugger benefits from the fact that Basic was once an interpretive language. In test mode the interpreter simply executes a program, unlike other languages where debugging information is compiled into an EXE file. This is also to your advantage because you can immediately amend the program code on testing.

Even if you still test and debug often, run-time errors can always occur. Unfortunately you still have to handle these in Visual Basic 6 so your program will not crash. An untreated run-time error in Visual Basic programs leads to a simple error message with an OK button resulting in your application closing after confirmation of this message. This will probably all change in VB.NET, since VB.NET has a completely different way of handling errors (similar to that of Delphi).

7.1 Handling of run-time errors

It is true that a program written in VBA already has generic error handling. However this simply displays the error that has occurred in a message box and then exits the application as if you had called End. This hard Exit is only appropriate in a very few cases. Which user is pleased, for example, when the application virtually crashes when they cannot edit the database table because another user locks this. Other programming languages, Delphi for example, generate an "exception" whenever a run-time error occurs. This as a rule results in the error being displayed, you leave only the procedure where the error has occurred and the application does not close.

In VBA you have to integrate error handling into every event procedure at least so that your application's operation is stable. That it is sufficient to define error handling in the event procedure is connected with the fact that exclusively event procedures are always the first procedures in the call path. Errors in procedures called at a subordinate level are passed on to the higher level procedure.

To be able to respond to possible run-time errors, for example if a file you want to open is not there, you have to write your own error handling. The instruction On Error turns on such error handling. You have to call On Error before the error occurs and in the procedure where you expect the error to arise and it is valid as long as the program stays within the procedure. VBA differentiates between general and in-line error handling.

7.1.1   General error handling

General error handling should at least be implemented in every event procedure and looks more or less as follows:

```
Private Sub cmd_OK_Click()
 ' Switch on own error handling
 On Error Goto ErrHandler

 ... ' The source code of the procedure

' After error handling, the mark
Exit_: ' to which program jumps
 Exit Sub

' The mark, to which program jumps with error
ErrHandler:

 ' Error handling, here by simple display
 MsgBox "Unexpected error number " & Err.Number & _
        ": " & Err.Description, vbCritical
  ' After handling jump to exit mark
 Resume Exit_
End Sub
```

Note: You can of course name both jump tags as you like. The "Exit_" tag has an underscore because Exit is a keyword and so cannot be used as a tag.

The otherwise tricky unstructured Goto application is unfortunately necessary (and also appropriate, as a run-time error by its very nature is likewise unstructured). To forestall a frequently asked question (in my seminars): no, global error handling, as for example in Delphi using its application object, is still impossible. The only thing that you can do is analyze errors by calling global functions.

Expected and unexpected errors

The example above handles only unexpected errors. In practice however you will be expecting particular errors. You can identify the errors using the global

`Err` object and its `Number` property. Every error (usually) has an unambiguous number. You can try to learn all these numbers by rote and to handle possible errors in the relevant procedure. In practice you are presented with the problem that very many errors are always possible and every object used can produce its own error numbers. My solution to the problem looks like this. I simulate in the first instance all the most likely errors (e.g. I delete a file that is going to be opened, provide a file to be saved with write protection, etc.). I then set a break-point in the handling process for unexpected errors and analyze the number when an error arises. These errors are handled, all other errors are issued to a message box with the prefix "Unexpected error". Handling of the most common errors when trying to open a text file looks for example as follows:

```
Private Sub cmdOpen_Click()
 Dim strRow As String, strFilename As String
 On Error GoTo ErrHandler
 strFilename = "c:\Test.txt"
 Open strFilename For Input As #1
 While Not EOF(1)
   Line Input #1, strRow
   Debug.Print strRow
 Wend
 Close #1

Exit_:
 Exit Sub

ErrHandler:
 Select Case Err.Number
  Case 53    ' File not found
    MsgBox "File '" & strFilename & _
          "' does not exist.", vbExclamation
  Case 76    ' Path not found
    MsgBox "the folder '" & strFilename & _
          "' does not exist.", vbExclamation
  Case 55    '  File already open
    MsgBox "The file '" & strFilename & _
          "' is already open.", vbExclamation
  Case Else ' Unexpected error
    Debug.Print Err.Number, Err.Description
    MsgBox "Unexpected error: " & _
          Err.Description, vbCritical
 End Select
 Resume Exit_
End Sub
```

Tip Do not make too much work for yourself when handling possible run-time errors. In new versions of VB or used components, the error numbers can be different and then your error handling will no longer work correctly. In addition the important ActiveX data objects for data access (where in fact most errors occur) often deliver one and the same number for quite different errors. Meaningful handling of such errors is almost impossible for the user. As such I only respond to a few errors which I assume are going to occur most frequently. I output all other errors as "Unexpected errors".

Responding to certain errors

Errors require a response from the program. For example if on opening a file the file cannot be found, you can give the user the possibility of searching for the file in the Open File dialog. To do this you have to implement error handling somewhat differently. Within error handling you correct the error and return to the line where the error has occurred with Resume. In so doing however, take care that within error handling no other error can be produced, otherwise you will get continuous execution.

```
Private Sub cmdOpen_Click()
 ... (as above)
ErrHandler:
 Select Case Err.Number
    Case 53, 76 ' File or path not found
       strFilename = InputBox("The file '" & _
       strFilename & "' was not found. " & _
       "Enter correct file name:", _
       "File not found", strFilename)
       If strFilename > "" Then ' not cancelled
          Resume ' try again
       End If
    Case 55    ' File already open
       MsgBox "The file '" & strFilename & _
             "' is already open.", vbExclamation
    Case Else ' Unexpected errors
       Debug.Print Err.Number, Err.Description
       MsgBox "Unexpected error: " & _
             Err.Description, vbCritical
 End Select
 Resume Exit_
End Sub
```

You can also ignore an error that has occurred in error handling with `Resume Next` (instead of `Resume` *Exit_*). The program then continues on the next line in the source text. This procedure is however only appropriate in exceptional cases.

Testing error handling

The instruction

```
Error errornumber
```

produces a run-time error. In this way you can test error handling, but it is always better to simply simulate an expected error.

Unexpected errors and the call path

When an error arises within active error handling or in a procedure that does not have (with `On Error`) activated error handling, VBA searches along the call path for activated error handling. Assuming that the search path looks as follows:

1   An expression calls procedure A

2   A calls procedure B

3   B calls procedure C

Call path A, B, C executes C. If an error occurs, VBA now goes backwards in the sequence C, B, A in search of any activated error handling. This process is only of interest to you because it shows you that at the beginning of the call path there is always an event procedure. Here at least you have to implement error handling.

7.1.2   In-line error handling

If it is possible that a procedure may produce one and the same error many times, for example if two files have to be opened, it is difficult to differentiate in general error handling which action has triggered the error. For this and other special cases in-line error handling is available. You start it in front of the line where you expect the error to occur using `On Error Resume Next`. This amounts to the same as "If there is an error just continue on the next line". Immediately behind the line you analyze the error. You have to remember here that error numbers can also be negative.

```
' Turn on in-line error handling
On Error Resume Next
' Try to open a file
Open strFilename1 For Input As #1
' analyze error
```

```
If Err.Number <> 0 Then
    Select Case Err.Number
      Case 53, 76  ' File or path not found
        MsgBox "The file '" & strFilename1 & _
               "' was not found.", vbExclamation
        Exit Sub
      Case 55  '  File already open
        MsgBox "The file '" & strFilename1 & _
               "' is already open.", vbExclamation
        Exit Sub
      Case Else ' Unexpected error
        MsgBox "Unexpected error: " & _
               Err.Description, vbCritical
        Exit Sub
    End Select
End If
' Turn on general error handling again.
On Error GoTo ErrHandler
```

Since in this variant you cannot use `Resume` to jump to the error-triggering line (`On Error Resume Next` triggers internal error handling), responding to individual errors, as described in more detail above for general error handling, becomes very difficult. It would be conceivable to use here `Goto` *Mark*, but who wants to use `Goto`? (I never want to, but you will probably find in my examples somewhere a `Goto` *Mark*, much to my shame). It would be easier not to carry out explicit handling but note a value in a variable before the error-triggering line, which in general error handling provides statements about the error location.

Warning It is still absolutely vital that after explicit handling you turn general error handling on again, otherwise you will not see subsequent errors (which in many cases has given me hours of unnecessary error searching). Go carefully when it comes to this type of error handling.

In-line error handling is appropriate for simple actions such as opening standard dialog, where in fact only the error that the user has cancelled can occur:

```
cdl.CancelError = True
On Error Resume Next
cdl.ShowOpen
If Err.Number = 0 Then
    ' User has not cancelled
    On Error Goto ErrHandler
    ' Do something with the file
End If
On Error Goto ErrHandler
```

Tips and tricks

Output of line numbers for debugging purposes

It is precisely when the product is already running at the customer that you need as much information as possible on unexpected errors that have occurred. There is no problem with the procedure name output (unfortunately hard-coded, because seemingly it is impossible to select the name of the current procedure). In many cases however output of the line numbers for the error lines is appropriate. Some of the tools available on the market do just that. You can however also output error numbers: give each line a line number and use the (for Visual Basic 6) undocumented variable Erl for ascertaining the error number.

```
Private Sub cmdError_Click()
 On Error GoTo ErrHandler

1: Dim i As Integer
2: i = 1
3: i = i + 1
4: i = i / 0
5: i = i + 1 _
   * 2
6: i = i - 1

Exit_:
 Screen.MousePointer = vbNormal
 On Error Resume Next
 Exit Sub

ErrHandler:
```

```
Screen.MousePointer = vbNormal
MsgBox "unexpected error " & _
       (Err.Number And &HFFFF&) & _
       " in procedure 'cmdError_Click' in line " & _
       Erl & ": " & Err.Description, vbCritical
Resume Exit_
End Sub
```

Error handling for each procedure

If possible write an error handling system for each procedure and function. If an error arises in the customer's EXE file, you need as much information as possible for debugging the error. The name of the procedure (that you output in the error message) is then very important information. This is particularly true when you do not get an error (because the error has something to do with the configuration of the computer).

7.2 Using debugging tools

7.2.1 Stopping the program

If you want to use the debugging tools of the development environment, you have to stop the program at the place where it is suspected that the error occurs. If a run-time error occurs, the development environment offers you a dialog either to end the program or to debug. If you choose here the Debug button, the development environment goes over into the debugging mode and displays the error-triggering line.

For debugging logical and other errors you can explicitly stop the program with the Stop instruction in the program code, a set breakpoint, a conditional watch expression or (for example with continuous loops) by pressing **Ctrl PAUSE**.

After stopping the program you can:

→ change the program code in run-time without leaving the program;
→ work the program step-wise further with **F8** and (↑) **F8**;
→ execute the program anew or further with **F9** from a point to be specified;
→ check in the Immediate window and in the watch window expressions, procedure and function calls;

→ check in the Locals window local variables and parameters;

→ let the program continue to execute from the current point with **F5**.

The development environment marks the program line with a frame as the next line to be executed.

Breakpoints

You set or delete stopping points by placing the cursor on the relevant line and pressing **F9** or by clicking with the mouse on the gray column on the left. VB stops the program when the breakpoint is reached. Alternatively you can accommodate the Stop instruction in the program code. This instruction has the advantage that you can really easily set conditional breakpoints. So for example you can stop whenever a string variable is empty:

```
If gstrDataBaseName = "" Then Stop
```

> **Warning** Always remove Stop instructions before you compile the project into an EXE file. When Stop occurs, VB generates a run-time error in the EXE file.

Options for stopping run-time errors

If no error handling has been set up in the procedure or function which triggers a run-time error (see from page 251), the development environment always stops the program execution at the place concerned. If however error handling is available, the development environment does not stop as standard, but activates error handling. If you also want the development environment to stop in program code when handling errors for run-time errors, you can toggle the appropriate option. To do this select the index tab Next in the development environment options (Tools | Options). The possible settings here are as follows.

Break on All Errors

Visual Basic interrupts the program execution at every error, even if the error is being handled.

Break in class Module

With every error that has not been handled occurring in a class module, Visual Basic switches to the stop mode. There is no interruption with handled errors in normal and form modules. This setting could be interesting for the development of ActiveX components, however I have never needed it.

Break on Unhandled Errors

When handled errors occur Visual Basic does not change to the stop mode. Only when there is no error handling active in the procedure or function in which the error has occurred is the program execution interrupted.

These options are certainly good to use sometimes, but are often really annoying.

7.2.2　Execution of certain code parts

For testing the program code you can execute the code after reaching the breakpoint with **F8** in single step or with (↑) **F8** in procedural steps. With procedural steps, you do not carry out procedural calls in individual steps. Therefore you can carry out a procedure call as a whole and not branch into the procedure itself.

If you want to jump over or execute again program parts after they have been changed for example, place the cursor on the line to be executed next and press **F9**.

7.2.3　The tooltips

If you rest the mouse pointer for a while on a variable, a property or an argument, Visual Basic then displays the value of this element in a tooltip. As a result you are able to easily check variables, properties and arguments.

> **Tip** Tooltips will only function if the syntax of the program code is correct. If in the meantime you have changed a program that you have stopped and you are wondering why no tooltips are being displayed, check that the syntax of the changes you have made is correct. Usually you have to quit a line that has just been changed so that the interpreter compiles the line and can then display tooltips again.

7.2.4   Checking code and data in the Immediate window

In the Immediate window (**Ctrl G**) you can test all the expressions possible in VBA and execute functions and procedures in test mode. This window evaluates every valid expression that can be implemented, as well as those that contain a procedure or function call. To do this just activate (ø) on an instruction in the Immediate window.

Test expressions with the print instruction:

```
Print expression
```

`Print` can be abbreviated with a question mark:

```
? expression
```

> **Tip** After VB 6 it has been possible also to use the Immediate window if the project has not started. This possibility is particularly ideal for testing functions and procedures you have written yourself. You just have to be aware that the function or procedure to be tested needs to be declared with `Public` in a standard module and the program code of the project has to be error-free when it comes to compiler errors. This is because VB compiles the project completely using such a test (unless you have switched on the VB option `Compile as required,` something you should not really do).

You can test simple variables or function calls like this:

```
? strFilename
? MsgBox("Test", vbQuestion Or vbYesNo)
```

During run-time with the `Debug` object and its only method `Print` you can have the results of a printout of the program during run-time as output in the Immediate window:

```
Debug.Print [Printout1] [; Printout2] [...]
```

You build in the debug instruction at the point in the program code you have to check. The result is automatically displayed in the Immediate window only.

> **Tip** `Debug.Print` can be left in the program code if you produce an EXE file, but then the instructions are executed in the EXE file (even if without any result). You can try it out for instance by leaving `Debug.Print MsgBox(Debug)` in the program code. In order not to waste processor time unnecessarily, you should therefore remove all `Debug.Print` instructions.

Allocation of values to variables and properties

Likewise in the Immediate window you can set variables and properties to new values using an instruction:

```
lngMaxCount = 50
frmMain.Visible = False
```

After allocation you can carry on executing the program code with the amended data. This is helpful if you want to execute program parts but have to re-initialize some variables beforehand.

7.2.5   The Locals window

In the Locals window (`View | Locals Window`) Visual Basic displays all local variables and parameters of the current procedure or function. The Locals window simply enables you to monitor variables and arguments.

Watch expressions

As a rule you monitor the value of simple variables while you go through the program in individual stages using a monitor expression ("watch"). However, with watch expressions too you can set a conditional breakpoint. Conditional breakpoints also allow you to find complex errors. Visual Basic stops the program at the point where the set condition for your watch expression becomes true.

Via the `Test | Add Watch` menu you add new watch expressions to the watch window. It is often easier to mark the expression or variable in the module window, to click on this marking with the right mouse button and to select in the context menu the command `Add Watch`.

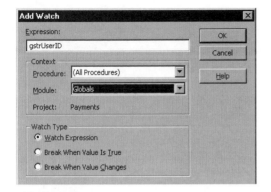

Figure 7.1 *Watch expression dialog with simple watch expression*

The Watch Type setting in the watch expression dialog defines whether you only monitor the dialog or you want to set a conditional breakpoint. Table 7.1 describes the settings that are possible here.

Watch type	Action
Watch Expression	The expression is analyzed and displayed in the watch window.
Break When Value Is True	The program stops if the expression becomes true.
Break When Value Changes	The program stops every time the value of the expression changes.

Table 7.1 *The different types of watch expressions*

If, as in Figure 7.1, you add only simple watches, these values are always shown with the current status in the watch window on debugging.

Using the setting Break When Value Is True you can very easily define conditional breakpoints. Visual Basic stops your program whenever the conditional expression becomes True. You can always make good use of this technique, whenever you want to know when a variable or property accepts a *certain* value. The other option, Break When Value Changes, looks similar. Using this you can find out when a value in a variable or property somehow *changes*. These options are very important if your application incorrectly changes the value of a variable or property without you knowing when and where.

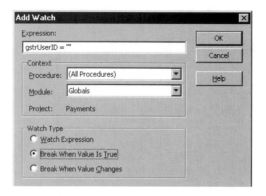

Figure 7.2 *Watch expression dialog with watch expression, which stops the program whenever the variable contains an empty string*

The *context* setting defines on what level the expression is interpreted. The context is important when it comes to standardizing names between local and global variables and to make it possible for the expression to become True at different points in the program (for conditional breakpoints). Table 7.2 describes the context settings.

Context	Action
Procedure	The expression relates to the specified procedure.
Module	The expression refers to the specified form or module.

Table 7.2 *The context settings for watch expression*

7.2.6   The call list

Via **Ctrl L** you can display a window that contains the current procedure calls. In this call list you can retrace all calls that have led to the current point. The last call is always at the top. By double-clicking on one of the calls in the list you access the relevant point in the source code. Using the call list is sometimes appropriate if the source of an error that has occurred could possibly lie somewhere in the call path.

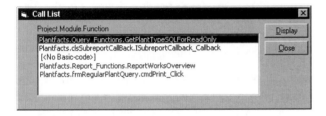

Figure 7.3 *Call list in a complex program*

7.2.7 Tips and tricks

Efficient debugging when error handling is switched on

In larger projects turning on the `Interrupt at every error` option in the debugging options is not very efficient. Normally you will handle a lot of errors and will also wish to have this handling activated when testing the program. You turn on the option `Break on All Errors` only for a short time when error handling shows you an unexpected error that you want to test. Unfortunately the development environment then stops at every error (which in practice ultimately becomes annoying) when you use "in-line error handling" in different procedures or functions, in order for instance to check the validity of expressions. If you want to check whether a dynamic array is filled for example, you have to use the in-line error handling process since `LBound` and `UBound` produce a run-time error for an empty array. A function that checks whether a string array that has been handed over contains elements needs in-line error handling:

```
Private Function IsArrayFilled(ByRef astrArray() _
    As String) As Boolean
 On Error Resume Next
 IsArrayFilled = _
    (UBound(astrArray) > LBound(astrArray))
End Function
```

If you often use such "tricks", it will be no use to you when it comes to the stop options for run-time errors. VB would then always stop even when completely uninteresting run-time errors occur in your in-line error handling.

I use another technique to access the point of error for handled errors in spite of the setting `Interrupt for unhandled errors`. Stop the program using **Ctrl PAUSE** whenever your error handling displays an error. You arrive in the program code that your message box calls to display the error. Have the error displayed perhaps in the Immediate window. Write in the error handling under `Resume Exit_` simply `Resume`. Afterwards using **Ctrl F9** go to the line with the new Resume instruction and carry on executing the program with **F8**. You are now at the line which has caused the error. You can simply leave Resume for further analyses, and this will not disrupt the program.

Execute several instructions in the Immediate window

You can normally enter just one instruction in the Immediate window. Several instructions such as for instance `For-Next` loops, that are normally located on several lines, cannot be tested in this way. However, if you enter the instructions separated with a colon in a line you can also test more complex instructions. In so doing it helps that the implicit variables declaration is working in the Immediate window (OK, here this type of declaration makes sense). In this way you can select for example the forms listing in the Immediate window:

```
For i = 0 To Forms.Count-1: ? Forms(i).Name: _
    ? Forms(i).Caption: Next
```

Graphics and printing

8

8.1 Graphics

Using the (`Line`, `Circle`, etc.) graphics methods it is very easy to produce graphics on a form within a `Picture` control or to print out graphics on the printer. The methodology does not differentiate in principle as for instance you can use the same methods for the printer as on the form.

Another possibility for printing out graphics is to use the Windows GDI functions. Using these functions, which as a rule can be applied without any problem on the above-mentioned objects, you have considerably more flexibility (e.g. you can draw a polygon using the VB graphics methods). In addition, and something which is considerably advantageous, graphics output using the GDI functions is usually noticeably faster. But to describe GDI functions would go beyond the scope of this book, which is why I am merely introducing some of these functions as examples. You will find a detailed description of the GDI functions in the API bible "Visual Basic Programmers Guide to the Win32 API" by Dan Appleman.

Scaling

It is precisely when it comes to printing graphics and text that scaling of the object to be printed is very important. The preset scaling unit *Twips* (1440 twips = 1 inch) is appropriate in only very few cases. Simply set scaling in the `ScaleMode` property of the object on one of the available constants (`vbInch`, `vbMillimeters`, `vbPixels`, etc.). Setting on `vbMillimeters` will probably be the best for our widths. All specified positions always refer to the scaling that is currently set.

CurrentX and CurrentY

For the output coordinates some VB methods use the `CurrentX` and `CurrentY` properties of the object on which the graphics are being printed. These properties define the next output position. `CurrentX` and `CurrentY` are set implicitly to the next value for every graphics output, however they can also be set in the program code. Some other methods though expect output coordinates in arguments.

Line color and type

The `ForeColor` property of the object on which you are drawing defines as a rule the color of the outer line of the graphic. Using the `DrawStyle` property you can set what the line will look like. To do this use the constants listed in Table 8.1.

Constant	Meaning
vbSolid	(presetting) Filled in
vbDash	Dash
vbDot	Dot
vbDashDot	Dash dot
vbDashDotDot	Dash dot dot
vbInvisible	Transparent
vbInsideSolid	Interior filled in

Table 8.1 *Constants of the DrawStyle property*

Fill color and type

Whenever you output graphics with a surface area (rectangles, circles, and with the help of a GDI function, also polygons), you determine with `FillColor` and `FillStyle` before drawing how these surfaces will be filled. The `FillStyle` (*Transparent*) presetting has the effect that the surface will not be filled at all. Set one of the constants shown in Table 8.2 if you want to fill the surface with the color set in `FillColor`.

Tip `FillColor` and `FillStyle` function also when you draw with the GDI functions.

Constant	Meaning
vbFSSolid	Solid filling.
vbFSTransparent	Transparent filling.
vbHorizontalLine	Horizontal dashes.
vbVerticalLine	Vertical dashes.
vbUpwardDiagonal	Diagonal dashes from bottom left to right top.
vbDownwardDiagonal	Diagonal dashes from top left to bottom right.
vbCross	Horizontal and vertical dashes.
vbDiagonalCross	Crosswise diagonal dashes.

Table 8.2 *Constants of the FillStyle property*

The drawing mode

The drawing mode (DrawMode) determines how Visual Basic combines every pixel in the drawing with the background color. In so doing the color value of the pixel is linked bit by bit with different logical operations and the drawing color set accordingly. So, for example, it is possible to mix the background color with the drawing color (vbMergePen). In the (vbCopyPen) presetting the color that is defined in ForeColor is the color used for drawing. It is best that you try for yourself the extremely complex possibilities that this property can produce. Please bear in mind that some tricks such as drawing and "remove drawing" of graphics are possible with this property.

Paint and AutoRedraw

If you want to output graphics on a form, in keeping with the Windows philosophy *as standard* you have to draw in the form's Paint event. If you draw at another point in the program code and AutoRedraw is False, then when this drawing is first covered over it will be destroyed by other windows. Since Windows calls Paint whenever the form is redrawn, all the graphics created in this event are then redrawn if Windows deems this necessary.

However if you set AutoRedraw to True, Windows organizes a diagram of the graphics in the working memory (as a bitmap). If the graphic has to be remade, Windows can simply use the bitmap. The Paint event is then no longer necessary and so there is no need to call it. With AutoRedraw = True you can therefore draw at any point you like in the program code. You should perhaps bear in mind that this means of course that the memory requirements of the application are increased, but today's computers get over this quickly. AutoRedraw provides you with considerably simpler programming to do this, particularly when you are constructing graphics piece by piece.

8.1.1   Output of text

Using the `Print` method you can output text on a form, picture box control or a printer in any of the fonts installed on the system and all available display types (bold, italics etc.).

```
[object.]Print [{Spc(n) | Tab(n)}] _
        [expressionlist][{; | ,}]
```

Positioning the expression

The current position (left, upper point of the text) is defined using the `CurrentX` and `CurrentY` properties of the object that is receiving the output of text. For each text output using `Print`, `CurrentY` is set to the next line and `CurrentX` to the left margin of the object, provided that you do not specify a semicolon or comma behind the instruction. A semicolon behind the instruction has the effect that `CurrentX` and `CurrentY` are positioned directly behind the text output. The following example shows how to work with the semicolon:

```
Me.Print "Hello, ";
Me.Print "this is a line"
Me.Print "and this ";
Me.Print "is a second one."
```

This example produces two lines:

```
Hello, this is a line
and this is a second one.
```

Normally these arguments are sufficient for printing. You can confidently ignore the other arguments of the `Print` method, because you are considerably better off replacing these with other VBA conforming methods. By using a comma behind the instruction for example, you make the next output begin in the next column (14 characters wide). You can achieve column printing that is essentially more flexible and precise by repeated setting of `CurrentX`. If, for example, you want to print in two columns, the program code looks something like this:

```
' Caption line
Me.CurrentY = 10
Me.CurrentX = 10
Me.Print "first name";
Me.CurrentX = 30
Me.Print "last name"
' next line
Me.CurrentX = 10
Me.Print "Ralph";
Me.CurrentX = 30
```

```
Me.Print "Packer"
' next line
Me.CurrentX = 10
Me.Print "Merril";
Me.CurrentX = 30
Me.Print "Overturf"
```

OK, it may look like that after some work, but it is considerably more flexible than if you tackle the problem with individual columns. In addition you can write a procedure that makes your work easier. If you still want to know what the other arguments mean: Spc(*n*) causes the output of n spaces, Tab(*n*) jumps to the specified drawing position. It is better if in place of these arguments you use the Space$ function to output spaces and the column-type printing shown in the above example.

The font

You adjust the font you want to use with the Font property of the object. You can change the font as often as you like. So for example you can print on a form using different font displays:

```
Me.Font.Name = "Times New Roman"
Me.Font.Size = 20
Me.Font.Bold = True
Me.Print "This is a big, bold text"
Me.Font.Size = 12
Me.Font.Bold = False
Me.Font.Italic = True
Me.Print "and this is a small, italic text"
```

Determining the width and height of a text

If you have to determine the width and height of a text output because you have to know whether a word you are going to print will still fit into the current line, you can use the methods TextWidth and TextHeight. You transfer the text you want to print to both methods and receive the text height and width in the scaling units of the object.

Split a long sentence into individual words and print word for word taking account of a right margin:

```
' Print out a text word for word in order
' to be able to word-wrap at the defined right margin
Const LEFT_MARGIN = 10
Const RIGHT_MARGIN = 40
Dim strBrucesErrorHandling As String
str BrucesErrorHandilng = "Bruce McKinney " & _
```

```
"for output of error messages to the client: " & _
"'Put up a dialog box telling users they are " & _
"filthy, unwashed idiots with ugly children. Tell " & _
"them they have just committed error -2147211501 " & _
"(&H80042713). Display the message "I am unworthy,"" & _
"and make them them click OK. Then terminate the program, " & _
"throwing all their wretched, unsaved work into the " & _
"bit bin'"
' Print out this long text word for word
' and in so doing take account of the form's right margin
Dim astrWords() As String, i As Integer
astrWords = Split(strBrucesErrorHandling, " ")
Me.Font.Size = 12
Me.Font.Bold = True
Me.CurrentY = 10
Me.CurrentX = LEFT_MARGIN
Me.Cls
For i = LBound(astrWords) To UBound(astrWords)
    If Me.CurrentX + Me.TextWidth(astrWords(i)) _
        > Me.ScaleWidth - RIGHT_MARGIN Then
      ' Word no longer fits into the line,
      ' therefore wrap
      Me.Print ""
      Me.CurrentX = LEFT_MARGIN
    End If
    ' Re-print word with added space
    Me.Print astrWords(i) & " ";
Next
```

Tip From this example you will see that professional printing using VB methods is a complex undertaking. If you are one of those lucky enough to be blessed with plenty of money, you would be better to buy a professional print component (for example the *Virtual Print Engine*. This is included in the journal basicpro 5/99 as an older but useable version. You can put in a late order on www.basicworld.de.

8.1.2   Drawing lines and rectangles

Using the `Line` method you can draw lines and rectangles.

```
[object.]Line [[Step](x1, y1)] - [Step](x2, y2) _
        [,[color][,B[F]]]
```

The `Line` method draws a line or rectangle from *x1*, *y1* to *x2*, *y2*. Without `Step` the line start and finishing points refer to the upper left corner of the object on which you are drawing. Normally you specify the coordinates as absolutes, then you can omit the `Step`. You therefore draw a simple line accordingly in the following way:

```
Me.Line (10, 10)-(Me.ScaleWidth - 10, 10)
```

You define the color of the line in the argument *Color*:

```
Me.Line (10, 10)-(Me.ScaleWidth - 10, 10), vbRed
```

If you do not specify *Color*, the current drawing color defined in *Object*.`Fore-Color` is used for the line(s).

If you specify argument B, a rectangle is drawn instead of a line if the imaginary line is diagonal. If you specify argument F, the rectangle has a solid filling with the color defined in *Color*. If you do not specify the F argument, the rectangle is filled according to the settings in *Object*.`FillStyle` and *Object*.`FillColor`. So for example you can draw a rectangle with a solid yellow filling with a red border (Fig. 8.1):

```
Me.FillColor = vbYellow
Me.FillStyle = vbFSSolid
Me.Line (10, 10)-(20, 20), vbRed, B
```

You do not normally need the F argument because you can also set the fill style to a solid filling in the `FillStyle` property.

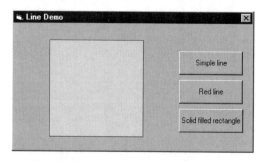

Figure 8.1 *A rectangle drawn using the Line method*

If you want to draw relative to the position defined in `CurrentX` and `CurrentY`, you can use the `Step` arguments. This can be appropriate if at the same time you want to produce text and for example draw a rectangle next to the text.

8.1.3 Drawing dots

Using the `PSet` method you can draw individual dots:

`[object.]PSet [Step](x, y)[,color]`

`PSet` sets a point on the position handed over in *x* and *y*. For `Step` and *Color* the same applies as for `Line`. `PSet` is interesting if you want to draw a grid across a form:

```
Dim intX As Integer, intY As Integer
' draw grid with 2 mm width
For intX = 2 To Me.ScaleWidth Step 2
    For intY = 2 To Me.ScaleHeight Step 2
        Me.PSet (intX, intY), vbBlue
    Next
Next
```

8.1.4 Circle, ellipse, curve and wedge

Using the `Circle` method you can draw circles, ellipses, curves and wedges:

```
[Object.]Circle [Step](x, y), Radius[,[Color] _
                [,[Start] [,[End] [,Aspect]]]]
```

A simple circle is drawn as follows:

```
[Object.]Circle (x, y), Radius, Color
```

x and *y* specify the center. *Start* defines the start angle; *End* the end angle for a wedge. *Aspect* is the relation between radius and height for an ellipse: *Height = Aspect * Radius*. So you draw a flat ellipse like this:

```
' Ellipse with height = 0.5 * width
Me.Circle (1000, 1000), 1000, vbRed, , , 0.5
```

Like all closed objects, you can very nicely fill a circle. The following example results in (quite) a small work of art using circles and ellipses. (Fig. 8.2):

```
' draw a filled circle as background
Me.FillColor = vbRed
Me.FillStyle = vbFSSolid
Me.Circle (30, 30), 20, vbRed
' draw flat, unfilled ellipses over it
Me.FillStyle = vbFSTransparent
Dim sngAspect As Single
For sngAspect = 0 To 1 Step 0.03
Me.Circle (30, 30), 20, vbBlue, , , sngAspect
Next
' draw unfilled circle as a border
Me.Circle (30, 30), 20, vbBlack
```

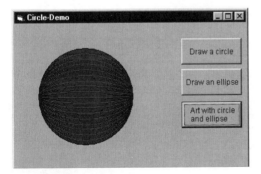

Figure 8.2 *A small work of art with circles and ellipses*

8.1.5   Using a GDI function in the example

You often cannot get very far using the integrated VB graphics methods. It is about time then to think about the application of GDI functions. Since GDI functions are very varied and complex though, at this point I am going to limit myself to the `Polygon` function, which draws any polygon you like. You only need to store the individual points and their x and y coordinates in an array, consisting of POINTAPI elements, and specify this array when you call the function. Since VB also uses GDI functions together with its own graphics methods, you can use the ForeColor, FillStyle and FillMode properties of the object on which you are drawing to fill the polygon with a pattern. The following example draws a filled triangle:

```
' delete old contents
Me.Cls
' draw triangle
Dim audtPoints(1 To 3) As POINTAPI
' set scaling mode to pixels,
' since GDI functions calculate in pixels
Me.ScaleMode = vbPixels
' define fill style, fill color,
' and drawing color
Me.FillColor = vbRed
Me.FillStyle = vbDiagonalCross
Me.ForeColor = vbBlue
' setting of polygon points
' center top
audtPoints(1).x = Me.ScaleWidth / 2
audtPoints(1).y = 0
' bottom left
audtPoints(2).x = 0
audtPoints(2).y = Me.ScaleHeight
' bottom right
audtPoints(3).x = Me.ScaleWidth
audtPoints(3).y = Me.ScaleHeight
' draw
Polygon Me.hdc, audtPoints(1), 3
' when AutoRedraw is True, Refresh
' must be called
Me.Refresh
```

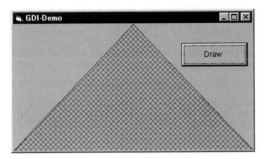

Figure 8.3 *A triangle drawn with the polygon function*

It is important for API functions that receive a transferred array to have an argument that defines the size of the array. In the case of the `polygon` function this is the parameter *nCount*, which is set to 3 in the example. Please remember that the scaling mode must be set on `vbPixels`. In this connection also use the `ScaleWidth` and the `ScaleHeight` properties instead of `Width` and `Height`, since `ScaleWidth` and `ScaleHeight` always use the scaling mode and `Width` and `Height` do not.

Tip Switch the scaling mode over to `vbPixels` whenever you draw with GDI functions. GDI functions calculate in pixels. I often forget that and then wonder why there is no output from the GDI function. In addition whenever you have set `AutoRedraw` to `True` when you have finished drawing, you have to call the `Refresh` method of the object on which you are drawing.

8.2 Printing in VB

You can print text and graphics in VB using the `Printer` object. In principle you print using the same methods as you use for the output of graphics on a form or in a picture box control.

> **Tip** Before you begin you should know that printing with the `Printer` object is a laborious business. In addition some really important features – for instance print preview – are simply not available (and using justifiable means also not feasible). As I said when describing the `Print` method above, for a professional printout it is better to use a bought print component. In tips and tricks I describe how you can get hold of a really good bargain. However for a simple printout the `Printer` object is sufficient.

Selecting the printer

The `Printer` object is preset for the standard printer. Via the separate `Printers` listing you can find out which printers are installed. You can make one of the installed printers into the current printer by allocating it to the `Printer` object. Unfortunately you cannot transfer the name of the printer directly to the `Printers` listing which is why you have to search for the printer in a loop. You accordingly ascertain the printer with the device name "HP LaserJet 5N" in the following way:

```
Dim i As Integer
For i = 0 To Printers.Count - 1
    If Printers(i).DeviceName = "HP LaserJet 5N" Then
        Set Printer = Printers(i)
        Exit For ' End search for a printer
    End If
Next
```

Unfortunately as I described in Chapter 5, you cannot reasonably use the command dialog control to allow the user to select the printer. If however you want to put up with the disadvantage of the changed standard printer, you can use this control. To do this set the `PrinterDefault` property to `True`. You will find an example of this in the description of the CommonDialog control (page 179).

Print

You simply print text using the `Print` method. In Font you set the font and its style (bold, italics, etc.) before printing out. You will find a list of the current fonts supported by the current printer in the `Fonts` listing of the `Printer` object.

Since the print job is not sent to the print manager or printer until after the End-Doc method has been called, the print order is not fixed. For example first of all you can print at the bottom and then at the top. Please remember though that most printer drivers print out at least complete pages, even if printing has not yet finished.

You have to program margins yourself by setting the CurrentX and CurrentY properties to appropriate values. Print begins at CurrentX = 0 and CurrentY = 0 always at the edge of the paper.

You get the height and width of a page using the Width and Height properties.

You can explicitly start a new page via the NewPage method. The current page number is available via the Page property.

In order to send the print to the print manager you have to call the EndDoc method; otherwise your graphics will not be printed out. A simple print then looks like this:

```
Printer.CurrentY = 567 * 2 ' 2 cm upper margin
Printer.CurrentX = 567 * 2 ' 2 cm left margin
Printer.Font.Name = "Times New Roman"
Printer.Font.Bold = True: Printer.Font.Size = 24
Printer.Print "That is a test"
Printer.Font.Bold = False: Printer.Font.Size = 12
Printer.CurrentX = 567 * 2 ' 2 cm left margin
Printer.Print "with the Printer object"
Printer.EndDoc ' send print job
```

If you want to cancel in the middle of printing, you can abort the print job using KillDoc.

The Virtual Print Engine

Not that I want to advertise here, but the *Virtual Print Engine* is a very fast and flexible "engine" for professional printing. With the *Virtual Print Engine*, which you can address either via classic DLLs or an ActiveX control, you can even integrate preview into your project. If you have enough money, buy the current version. If you do not have enough money, buy the 5/99 edition in the basic*pro* journal. Through this you will receive the somewhat limited version 2.4 of the *Virtual Print Engine* with a license for up to 10,000 sold applications on the enclosed CD. You can put in orders for the basic*pro* 5/99 journal at www.basicworld.com.

Working with files and folders

When you want to work with files and folders, you can make use of the VBA functions – which, in this area, are somewhat outmoded – or the new *FileSystemObjects*. FileSystemObjects offer significantly more functionality, spread over several classes. Some programmers think the old VBA functions have not been replaced for so long because the FileSystemObjects contain no classes or methods for reading and writing binary and random access files. In my view, a VB programmer would only very seldom have to read or create binary files. Random-access files (in which data records had earlier been placed) have definitely now been replaced by databases[1]. I think, therefore, that VB programmers can also manage very well without the VBA file and folder functions. I therefore dispense in this book with a description of the VBA functions for reading and writing files. The VBA functions for creating, deleting, renaming and copying folders and files are briefly described in Chapter 4. This chapter concentrates on the FileSystem-Objects. Incidentally, due to the length of the class name, I frequently abbreviate *FileSystemObjects* in the following text to *FSO*, as is customary.

---

1. It is no problem with ADO or ADOX to create a database and to administer data there. ADO is covered in this book and ADOX on the book website.

9.1 Integration of the FileSystemObject

The `FileSystemObject`, which are also installed when Visual Basic is installed, do not actually belong directly to Visual Basic, but to *Microsoft Scripting Runtime Library*, which is also used in VBScript. In order to use the `FileSystemObjects`, you must first create a reference to this class library (Project | References | Microsoft Scripting Runtime). The Microsoft Scripting Runtime Library contains various classes for work with files and folders and the class `Dictionary` (although this has nothing to do with file administration).

When working with the filing system, always start with an object of the class `FileSystemObject`. Some methods of this object return other objects whose classes you will, of course, find in the Scripting Runtime Library. You should therefore first create in your project a `FileSystemObject` object:

```
Dim fso As FileSystemObject
Set fso = New FileSystemObject
```

If you frequently work with files in your application, you would do better to declare the FSO object in a module with `Public` and create it with Form_Load of the startup form. In this way, you will ensure that a new object does not have to be created on every access to the file system. Via methods and listings of the FSO object, you will obtain individual `Drive`, `Folder`, `File` and `Textstream` objects, with which you can then carry on working. These objects possess a large number of properties and methods, of which only the most important will be described in this book. Investigate the classes of the Scripting Runtime Library in the object catalog if appropriate, or look for further methods and properties in Help.

9.2 Working with folders and files

With the aid of certain FSO classes, you can obtain information about the disk drives, folders and files of the filing system.

9.2.1 Read information

Information about drives

The `Drives` property of an FSO object is a listing of `Drive` objects which stand for the drives available on the system in question. Go through this listing if you want to find information about all the drives. With a variety of properties, you can read information about the drives (Table 9.2). Note that, as a rule, you can only read the properties of a `Drive` object if the drive is ready (which you can determine through the `IsReady` property). The following example reads the most important information from all the drives in a system into a ListBox:

```
' create FileSystemObject object
Dim fso As Scripting.FileSystemObject
Dim strDriveType As String
Set fso = New Scripting.FileSystemObject
' go through all drives of system
Dim drv As Scripting.Drive
For Each drv In fso.Drives
  ' determine drive type
  Select Case drv.DriveType
    Case CDRom: strDriveType = "CDRom"
    Case Fixed: strDriveType = "Fixed"
    Case RamDisk: strDriveType = "RamDisk"
    Case Remote: strDriveType = "Remote"
    Case Removable: strDriveType = "Removable"
    Case Unknown: strDriveType = "Unknown"
  End Select
  ' if the drive is ready
  ' (that is, when CD-ROM e.g. CD has been inserted)
  If drv.IsReady Then
      ' also output the size and the free
      ' storage space
      lstFolders.AddItem drv.Path & " " & _
          drv.VolumeName & ", " & _
          "Type: " & strDriveType & ", " & _
          "Size: " & Format(drv.TotalSize / _
              1048576, "0.00") & " MB, " & _
          "Free: " & Format(drv.FreeSpace / _
              1048576, "0.00") & " MB, " & _
          "File system: " & drv.FileSystem & ", " & _
          "Serial number: " & drv.SerialNumber

  Else
      lstFolders.AddItem drv.Path & " " & _
          "Type: " & strDriveType & ", " & _
          "Not ready"
  End If
Next
```

Note: most listings of the FSO objects mysteriously do not allow any access via an integer index and create, in that case, the run-time error "Invalid procedure call or argument". A cycle through a `For Next` loop therefore does not work. Thus I use the `For Each` loop for going through an FSO listing. Incidentally, access through a string index works like all the other listings.

If you wish to address a disk drive specifically, you can use the `GetDrive` method of the FSO object to which you pass a drive letter and which returns a `Drive` object. Thus you can determine whether drive A: is ready:

```
' create FileSystemObject object
Dim fso As Scripting.FileSystemObject
Set fso = New Scripting.FileSystemObject
' get drive A:
Dim drv As Scripting.Drive
Set drv = fso.GetDrive("A:")
' determine whether A: is ready
If drv.IsReady Then
    MsgBox "A: is ready"
Else
    MsgBox "A: is not ready"
End If
```

Information about folders and files

The `GetFolder` method of an FSO object returns a `Folder` object, which you can use to prepare a folder. By way of example, the following program code creates a `Folder` object that represents the master folder of C:

```
Dim fso As FileSystemObject, fol As Folder
Set fso = New FileSystemObject
Set fol = fso.GetFolder("c:\")
```

Every `Folder` object has a `SubFolders` listing, through which you can reach the sub-folders. The individual folder objects possess certain properties with which you can read information about the folder (Table 9.3 and Table 9.4). The following example reads the most important properties of all the sub-folders of C:\ into a ListBox:

```
Dim fso As FileSystemObject, folRoot As Folder
Dim folSub As Folder
Set fso = New FileSystemObject
Set folRoot = fso.GetFolder("c:\")
For Each folSub In folRoot.SubFolders
  lstFolders.AddItem folSub.Name & ": " & _
  "Creates: " & folSub.DateCreated & ", " & _
```

```
    "Last access: " & folSub.DateLastAccessed & ", " & _
    "Last amendment: " & folSub.DateLastModified & ", " & _
    "Type: " & folSub.Type
Next
```

If you give a dot (".") as the folder specification, then you will receive the current folder.

Via the `Files` listing of a `Folder` object, you can gain access to the files in a folder. The `File` objects returned also possess certain properties (Table 9.3).

Read all files on C:\ with the most important information in a ListBox:

```
Dim fso As FileSystemObject, fol As Folder
Dim file As File
Set fso = New FileSystemObject
Set fol = fso.GetFolder("c:\")
For Each file In fol.Files
    lstFiles.AddItem file.Name & _
    ", attribute: " & file.Attributes & _
    ", created:" & file.DateCreated & _
    ", last changed: " & file.DateLastModified & _
    ", last access: " & file.DateLastAccessed
Next
```

Direct information about folder and file names

By using the FSO methods `GetDriveName` (drive without path and file name), `GetParentFolderName` (path name including drive), `GetBaseName` (file name without ending and path), `GetExtensionName` (file extension without dot), you can extract parts of a file or folder specification.

The method `GetAbsolutePathName` finds the absolute path from a relative path specification.

If you have to put together a complete file name from folder and file specifications, assistance is offered by the `BuildPath` method, which saves you having to check whether the folder specification is terminated with a backslash or not:

```
MsgBox fso.BuildPath(App.Path, App.EXEName & ".ini")
```

Find special folders

You can use the `GetSpecialFolder` method to determine the Windows folder, the Windows system folder or the folder for temporary files:

```
Dim folWin As Scripting.Folder
Dim folSystem As Scripting.Folder
Dim folTemp As Scripting.Folder
```

```
Set folWin = fso.GetSpecialFolder(WindowsFolder)
Set folSystem = fso.GetSpecialFolder(SystemFolder)
Set folTemp = fso.GetSpecialFolder(TemporaryFolder)
```

Create temporary name

The FSO method `GetTempName` creates a unique file name for temporary files (e.g. radBo8CC.tmp). With the aid of the `GetSpecialFolder` method, you can find unique and complete file names for temporary files:

```
Dim fso As FileSystemObject, strTempPath As String
Dim strTempFile As String
Set fso = New FileSystemObject
strTempPath = fso.GetSpecialFolder(TemporaryFolder)
strTempFile = fso.GetTempName
MsgBox "Temporary file: " & _
        fso.BuildPath(strTempPath, strTempFile)
```

Determine whether drives, folders or files exist

With the FSO methods `DriveExists`, `FolderExists` and `FileExists`, you can find out in a simple manner whether drives, folders or files exist.

Check whether the drive D:, the folder C:\Temp and the file C:\Command.com exist:

```
Dim fso As FileSystemObject
Set fso = New FileSystemObject
If fso.DriveExists("d:") Then
   MsgBox "Drive d: exists"
Else
   MsgBox "Drive d: does not exist"
End If
If fso.FolderExists("c:\temp") Then
   MsgBox "Folder c:\temp exists"
Else
   MsgBox "Folder c:\temp does not exist"
End If
If fso.FileExists("c:\command.com") Then
   MsgBox "File c:\command.com exists"
Else
   MsgBox "File c:\command.com does not exist"
End If
```

These methods also function with network drives. (Try writing your own FolderExists function that will work in the most diverse of contexts.)

Important properties and methods of the FSO object

Property/Method	Purpose
BuildPath(*Path, Name*)	Puts together a path specification and a folder or file name to make a complete path. The path can be specified as absolute or relative. With Build-Path, you can spare yourself the irritating process of checking whether a backslash has been added onto the path.
Drive	Listing of all available drives. Points towards Drive objects.
DriveExists(*DriveSpec*)	Returns True if the drive given exists.
FileExists(*FileSpec*)	Returns True if the file given exists.
FolderExists(*FolderSpec*)	Returns True if the folder given exists.
GetAbsolutePathName (*Path*)	Determines the absolute path from a relative path specification.
GetBaseName(*Path*)	Returns the base name of a file or folder without an ending or a path.
GetDrive(*DriveSpec*)	Returns a Drive object that stands for the drive passed as drive letter in *DriveSpec*.
GetDriveName(*Path*)	Returns the name of the drive of a path passed as a string in *Path*.
GetExtensionName(*Path*)	Returns the file extension of a file or a folder.
GetFolder(*FolderPath*)	Returns a Folder object that stands for the folder given in *FolderPath*.
GetParentFolderName (*Path*)	Returns the name of the parent folder. You can pass over a file or folder path in *Path*.
GetSpecialFolder (*SpecialFolder*)	Returns a Folder object that represents the Windows (*WindowsFolder*), Windows System (*SystemFolder*) or temporary file folder (*TemporaryFolder*).
GetTempName	Provides a unique name for temporary files. Use this method together with GetSpecialFolder (*TemporaryFolder*).

Table 9.1 *The most important methods and properties of the FSO object*

The properties of the drive class

Property	Purpose
AvailableSpace FreeSpace	Supplies the available (free) storage space in bytes. I was unable to find any difference between these two properties.
DriveLetter	Supplies the drive letter. This is identical, in principle, to the Path property, only that the colon is not added for every drive type.
DriveType	Stands for the drive type with the following (self-explanatory) constants: CDRom, Fixed, RamDisk, Remote, Removable, Unknown.
FileSystem	Returns the type of the file system as a string.
IsReady	Returns True if the drive is available (in the case of removable media).
Path	Returns the drive letter with an attached colon.
RootFolder	Returns a Folder object which represents the master folder of the drive. You can then continue working with this object.
SerialNumber	Returns the serial number of a hard disk drive.
ShareName	Returns the name of the network resource of a particular disk drive.
TotalSize	Returns the overall storage space on the drive in bytes.
VolumeName	Stands for the name of the drive. You can also change the name here.

Table 9.2 *The properties of the drive class*

The shared properties of the folder class and the file class

Property	Purpose
Attributes	Stands for the data attributes of the folder or file. Attributes is a bit pattern that can be made up from the following constants: Alias, Archive, Compressed, Directory, Hidden, Normal, ReadOnly and System.
DateCreated	Returns the date on which the file or folder was created.
DateLastAccessed	Returns the date of the last access to the file or folder.
DateLastModified	Returns the date on which the file or folder was last modified.
Drive	Returns the Drive object on which the folder or file has been placed.
Name	The name of the folder or the file.

Property	Purpose
ParentFolder	Returns a `Folder` object which stands for the parent folder.
Path	The path to the folder or file.
ShortName	The short, 8.3 name of the folder or file.
ShortPath	The short, 8.3 name of the path to the folder or file.
Size	In the case of folders, the `Size` property returns the total size of all files contained in this file and all subordinate files. For files, the file size is given in bytes.
Type	Returns the type of the folder or file as a string.

Table 9.3 *The shared properties of the folder class and the file class*

The special properties of the folder class

Property	Purpose
Files	A listing of all files stored in the folder. Files points to `File` objects.
IsRootFolder	`True` when the folder concerned is the master folder of a disk drive.
SubFolders	`SubFolders` is a listing of all sub-folders and points to `Folder` objects.

Table 9.4 *The special properties of the folder class*

9.2.2   Working with folders and files

Creating folders

The `CreateFolder` method of an FSO creates a folder and returns this as a `Folder` object. Simply enter the complete path name as the argument. The parent folder must already exist – otherwise the run-time error 76 "Path not found" will be generated. If the folder to be created already exists, the FSO generates error 58, "File already exists". You should trap this error when you want to create a folder:

```
Dim fso As FileSystemObject, fol As Folder
Set fso = New FileSystemObject
On Error Resume Next
' Create the new folder Testfolder
' under C:\Foldertest\
Set fol = fso.CreateFolder("C:\Foldertest\Testfolder")
Select Case Err.Number
  Case 0
```

```
      MsgBox "The folder has been successfully created"
   Case 58 ' Folder already exists
      MsgBox "The folder already exists", vbExclamation
   Case 76 ' Path not found
      MsgBox "Folders can only be created " & _
      "under existing folders", vbExclamation
   Case Else
      MsgBox "Unexpected error: " & _
            Err.Description, vbCritical
End Select
```

Alternatively, you can use the `Add` method of the `SubFolder` listing of a `Folder` object to create a sub-folder:

```
Set fol = fol.SubFolders.Add("Testfolder")
```

Rename and move files and folders

When you rename or move folders or files, you should use the `MoveFile` or `MoveFolder` method of an FSO object (whereby you must give the whole path name of the file). Alternatively, you can also use the `Move` method of a `Folder` or a `File` object (whereby you only give the new file or folder name):

```
Dim fso As FileSystemObject
Set fso = New FileSystemObject
' rename file
fso.MoveFile "c:\Temp\Test1.txt", "c:\Temp\Text2.txt"
' move file
fso.MoveFile "c:\Temp\Test2.txt", "c:\Text2.txt"
```

Copying folders and files

You can copy a folder or a file with the FSO methods `CopyFolder` and `Copy-File`, to which you give the complete path name of the source and the target. Alternatively, you can use the `Copy` methods of a `Folder` or `File` object. In the *Overwrite* argument of these methods, you state whether any already existing file of the same name should be overwritten.

Copying a file without overwriting already existing files:

```
Dim fso As FileSystemObject
Set fso = New FileSystemObject
fso.CopyFile "c:\Temp\Test1.txt", _
            "c:\Temp\Test2.txt", False
```

Warning The preset value of an *Overwrite* argument is `True`, so that existing folders or files are overwritten without warning.

Deleting folders and files

Using the FSO methods `DeleteFolder` or `DeleteFile`, or alternatively with the `Delete` method of a `Folder` object or `File` object, you can delete folders and files. In the *Force* argument, you state whether write-protected folders or files should also be deleted. The preset value is `False`.

Warning The Delete methods do not remove items to the Recycle Bin, but erase them permanently. A method that moves files and folders into the Recycle Bin is something that you will seek in vain.

Methods of working with folders and files

Method	Purpose
`CopyFile`(*Source, Destination, [Overwrite]*) `CopyFolder`(*Source, Destination, [Overwrite]*)	Copies a file or folder. With *Overwrite*, you can state whether a possibly existing file should be overwritten. Take care, as the preset value is `True`.
`CreateFolder`(*Path*)	Creates a folder and returns the folder object. The path must be given in full. The parent folder must exist.
`DeleteFile`(*FileSpec, [Force]*) `DeleteFolder`(*FileSpec, [Force]*)	Deletes a file or a folder. If for `Force`, you give `True`, even write-protected files will be deleted. The preset value is `False`.
`MoveFile`(*Source, Destination*) `MoveFolder`(*Source, Destination*)	Moves a file or folder. If you move the item into the same folder, the file or folder is only renamed.

Table 9.5 *Methods of working with folders and files*

9.3 Reading and writing text files

Although the FileSystemObjects are very flexible in other areas, you can only use text files for reading or writing. Binary reading from and writing to files is also desirable, since this is sometimes simply necessary. If you wish to read or write to binary or (the outmoded) random access files, you must use the relevant VBA functions (although these are not described here). Random access files that store individual "data records" consisting of several variables are not of great significance any more, since the storage of data records is much simpler if you use the ActiveX data objects (ADO) supplied with VB. Working with ADO is covered in Chapter 10.

9.3.1 Opening and closing a text file

With the `OpenTextFile` method of an FSO object, you can open a text file for reading, writing or to append it:

```
Set TextStream-Object = fso.OpenTextFile( _
    Filename[, IOMode[, Create[, Format]]])
```

The argument *IOMode* determines how you open the file. You can enter one of the constants explained in Table 9.6. In the argument *Create*, you specify whether the file should be created if it does not already exist, and this also works for opening and reading. The preset is `False`. The argument *Format* determines whether the file should be opened in ANSI or Unicode mode. The constants for this, with their uninspired names, are described in Table 9.7.

Constant	Purpose
ForReading	Open for reading. Preset.
ForWriting	Open for writing.
ForAppending	Open for appending.

Table 9.6 *The constants of the IOMode argument of the OpenTextFile method*

`OpenTextFile` returns a `TextStream` object with which you can work on the file. As an alternative to `OpenTextFile`, you can use the `CreateTextFile` method, which creates and directly opens a new file if you wish to create a new text file.

Constant	Purpose
TristateUseDefault	Opens the file with the system presets.
TristateTrue	Opens the file as a Unicode file.
TristateFalse	Opens the file as an ANSI file. Preset.

Table 9.7 *The constants of the format argument of the OpenTextFile method*

ANSI files use one byte per character. Unicode files consist of the new Unicode characters, which use two bytes to store each character. Thus almost all the characters of all the world's languages can be covered (possibly with the exception of Chinese). In the interests of compatibility with ANSI, the first 256 characters are the same in Unicode and ANSI, and the characters used in our language use only the first byte of a Unicode character. Unicode is currently supported only by Windows NT 4.0.

Warning If you open text files to write to them, any existing files of the same name are overwritten without warning. You should therefore check beforehand using the `FileExists` method of the FSO object whether a file with the same name already exists.

You can simply close a text file with the `Close` method of the TextStream object.

The methods of the FileSystemObject class for opening text files

Method	Purpose
OpenText-File(*FileName* [, *IOMode*] [, *Create*] [, *Format*])	Opens a text file and returns a `TextStream` object. In IOMode, you state how you wish to open the file (Table 9.7). If in *Create* you input `True`, the file is created if it does not yet exist. The preset value is `False`. In the argument Format, you can specify `TristateTrue` if you wish to create a Unicode file (Table 9.7).
CreateText-File(*FileName* [, *Overwrite*] [, *Unicode*])	Creates a new text file and returns a `TextStream` object. If you do not input anything in *Overwrite*, or input `True`, existing files will be overwritten without warning. But beware: the preset value is `True`. In *Unicode* you input `True` if you wish to create a Unicode file (works only in newer Windows operating systems).

Table 9.8 *The methods of the FileSystemObject class for opening text files*

The methods of the TextStream class for closing text files

Method	Purpose
Close	Closes a text file.

Table 9.9 *The methods of the TextStream class for closing text files*

9.3.2 Reading a text file

If you have opened a text file to read from it, you can read from it all in one go (ReadAll), line by line (ReadLine) or character by character (Read). With the property AtEndOfStream, you can determine, when reading line by line or character by character, whether you have reached the end of the file. Depending on the type of programming, reading line by line requires less working storage with large files than reading in the whole thing.

Complete and line by line reading of **Autoexec.bat**:

```
Dim fso As FileSystemObject, tst As TextStream
Dim strFile As String, strRow As String

Set fso = New FileSystemObject

' complete reading into a string variable
Set tst = fso.OpenTextFile("c:\Autoexec.bat", _
        ForReading, False)
strFile = tst.ReadAll
MsgBox strFile
' close the text stream
tst.Close

' reading line by line
Set tst = fso.OpenTextFile("c:\Autoexec.bat", _
        ForReading, False)
While Not tst.AtEndOfStream
  strRow = tst.ReadLine
  MsgBox strRow
Wend
' close the text stream
tst.Close
```

With line by line reading, you can use the SkipLine method to jump over individual lines, although this would probably not be needed.

If you want to read character by character, you can work with the `Read` method. You can check whether you have reached the end of a line by using the `AtEndOfLine` property. This property is `True` if you have reached the end of the line, but before the CRLF[2] terminating the line. If you read several characters, you will be at the end of the line even if the number of characters to be read were to overstep the line. In that case, `Read` only returns the available characters. In order to read in the next line, at the end of a line, you must skip over the current line using the `SkipLine` method. You must, however, test whether you have just reached the end of the file and no further line follows. The following (meaningless) example reads in **Autoexec.bat** character by character:

```
Dim fso As FileSystemObject, tst As TextStream
Dim strFile As String
Set fso = New FileSystemObject
Set tst = fso.OpenTextFile("c:\Autoexec.bat", _
          ForReading, False)
While Not tst.AtEndOfStream
   ' provided not at the end of the file
   While Not tst.AtEndOfLine
      ' provided not at the end of the line:
      ' read in character by character
      ' and attach to the string
      strFile = strFile & tst.Read(1)
   Wend
   If Not tst.AtEndOfStream Then
      ' jump over the rest of the line (CRLF) if
      ' the end of the file has not been reached
      tst.SkipLine
   End If
   ' append CRLF onto the line read in
   strFile = strFile & vbCrLf
Wend
' output contents
MsgBox strFile
' close the TextStream
tst.Close
```

When reading in character by character, you can jump over individual characters with the `Skip` method.

---

2. The carriage return and line feed characters conclude a line in a text file.

Using the `Line` property, you find the current line number, while the `Column` property returns the current column number when reading character by character.

Tip Note that it is often better to read in the entire file with the `ReadAll` method and then to be able to process the string read in using the VBA string functions.

The methods and properties of the TextStream class for reading text files

Method	Purpose
ReadAll	Reads in the entire file and returns a string holding the file contents.
Read(*Character*)	Reads a particular number of characters from the file.
ReadLine	Reads a whole line (concluded with CRLF or at the end of the file). The concluding CRLF is not returned.
AtEndOfLine	Returns True if on reading character by character, the end of a line is reached.
AtEndOfStream	Returns True if the end of the file is reached during reading.

Table 9.10 *The methods and properties of the TextStream class for reading text files*

9.3.3 Writing text files

If you have opened a text file for writing or appending, you can use the `Write` and the `WriteLine` methods to append text to the file. `Write` simply continues writing towards the right, while `WriteLine` creates a line break (CRLF) after writing. Using the `WriteBlankLines` method, you can write several blank lines:

```
Dim fso As FileSystemObject, tst As TextStream
Set fso = New FileSystemObject
' open text file to be written to, if necessary create anew
Set tst = fso.OpenTextFile("c:\Test.txt", _
         ForWriting, True)
' write line with CRLF at end
tst.WriteLine "The answer to the meaning of life " & _
              "is 42"
' write blank lines
tst.WriteBlankLines 2
' write without CRLF at end
```

```
tst.Write "Thanks "
tst.Write "for all the fish"
' close the text stream
tst.Close
```

The methods and properties of the TextStream class for writing text files

Method	Purpose
Write(*Text*)	Writes a string in the text file without a new file being created.
WriteLine(*Text*)	Writes a string in the text file and appends the CRLF character, so that a new line is created.
WriteBlankLines(*Lines*)	Writes the number of blank lines given in *Lines*.

Table 9.11 *The methods and properties of the TextStream class for writing text files*

Database access using ADO

The Microsoft ActiveX data objects have become the standard database access method in almost all Microsoft products. But also other products such as Borland (or Inprise?) Delphi are increasingly backing ADO in newer versions. ADO really simplifies and above all standardizes access to the most diverse data sources. In principle it does not matter whether you access an SQL server database, an Oracle database or just an Access database. With ADO you always use the same objects, methods and properties.

ADO offers a great number of features. Many of these you will probably seldom or never need, but it is good that they exist. However, ADO also has disadvantages. Error handling using ADO objects is often very difficult because the errors generated, at least with Microsoft ADO providers, often tell you very little (for example, does the error tell you anything with "Errors found"?). However this criticism is not meant to give you the impression that ADO would be a bad choice. ADO gives you very simple and flexible technology that allows you to access any data sources you like. Microsoft only needs to add the finishing touches to some areas.

At this point I would like to give you a small word of warning: do not set too much store by ActiveX controls that you bind to ADO data sources that come supplied with Visual Basic. These controls are mostly very unsophisticated and in practice only actually cause problems. It is better if you buy professional controls from outside manufacturers if you want to display your data professionally. This does not apply to standard controls though, which really cause no problems whatsoever when it comes to binding to ADO data sources.

Because ADO possesses very many features, I can only describe here the fundamentals of data access using ADO. It was not in vain that Michael Kofler, for example, wrote a whole book on data access using ADO. If you want to learn more about ADO, I recommend you take a look at the book itself by Michael Kofler entitled "Visual Basic Database Programming".

10.1 What is ADO?

ADO is a class library installed on your system that gives you access to different data sources. ADO combines the advantages of the outdated libraries *DAO* and *RDO* and offers (at last) a common basis for access to almost any data sources you like. Furthermore ADO is not restricted to relational databases like DAO, RDO or ODBC, but can access all other possible data sources such as e-mail or file systems. To do this you simply need to have a compatible *Data Provider* for these data sources. A data provider is based on OLE DB, Microsoft's latest data access technology, and carries out the native[1] access to the data source. The company that manufactures the management software for the data source usually supplies the data provider. With MDAC (see below) Microsoft however already supplies some important data providers. You can download the current provider for Oracle databases, for example, from Oracle on the Internet (as I describe from page 314 onwards).

If there is no native data provider available to you for a relational database, you can use the special data provider for ODBC [2] if you have at least an ODBC driver for these databases. As only ODBC drivers are available at the moment for outdated database systems, this is often the only opportunity for you to access these databases. Figure 10.1 and Figure 10.2 show how a VB program accesses a data source using ADO.

1. The word *native* generally means "innate" or "to do with home". In the computing sense "native" always means direct access to resources.
2. The long-standing "open database connectivity" technology allows access to any data sources provided that a compatible ODBC driver is available. For older database systems it is more probable that an ODBC driver rather than an ADI data provider will be available.

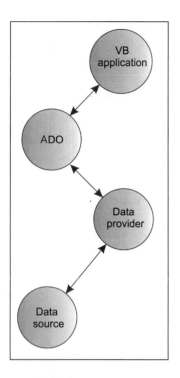

Figure 10.1 *Data access via ADO with a native provider*

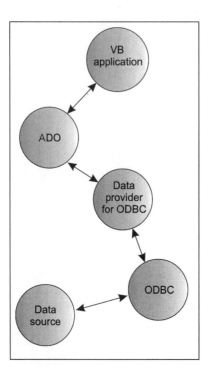
Figure 10.2 *Data access via ADO and ODBC with the ODBC provider*

As ADO and data providers are based on the component object model you can use this technology with all programming systems that support the COM model.

The *Microsoft data access components* (MDAC) contain all the ADO components, several data providers for access to different data sources and updated ODBC drivers. The MDAC version supplied with Visual Basic 6.0 which you have is probably out of date. On the Internet at www.Microsoft.com/data you will find the current version (at the time of writing this book this was Version 2.5). The new version introduces some "bug fixes" together with improved and new providers. In this book I am assuming that you have at least MDAC in Version 2.1 set up on your computer. Please remember to set up the correct language version.

> **Warning** At any rate, after you set up the new MDAC version you should still replace the MDAC_TYP.EXE file in the `Wizards\Pdwizard\Redist\` folder in the VB folder with the new file. The package and deployment wizard then integrates the new version into your package's setup version when it produces a setup version.

Unfortunately the current documentation is not set up using the "typical" MDAC setup (MDAC_TYP.EXE). You will find this in the *MDAC SDK*[3], which you have to download and install separately. Unfortunately the MDAC SDK is part of the *SDK Platform*. Installation of the extensive SDK platform is perhaps a little too complicated if you only require the MDAC documentation. You should of course only ever use up-to-date documentation. Copy all documentation files into the `Help` folder in the Windows folder, then you will have the Visual Basic Help at your disposal.

When you have updated to MDAC 2.5, you should still take care that you make reference to the "Microsoft ActiveX Data Objects Library 2.5" in your projects. You probably still have versions 2.0 and 2.1 installed on your computer. Your projects can still use the old ADO versions.

10.3 The different variants to access data

With ADO you can access data sources using different VB 6 technologies. In the following list you will find the fundamental options:

---

3. Software development kit

1   In the source code you produce an ADO recordset and work directly with this object without binding the recordset to the controls. With this variant you have to see to all the necessary display and update actions yourself which can make a lot of work. For a pure database editing application this variant takes a lot of time but is very flexible for the job. Mostly the direct creation of an ADO recordset is however used for internal program search and update actions (without displaying the data to be edited). This most flexible variant is described in some detail in this book.

2   In the source code you produce an ADO recordset and bind different controls that match the data fields such as text boxes and checkboxes to the recordset. When you change the current recordset with the recordset move methods, all changes made in the controls in the current recordset are *automatically* written to the data source and the new recordset likewise automatically displayed in the binding controls. You can check and control the response of the recordset via different recordset object events. You also have great flexibility using this variant, without however having to spend a lot of time programming the display of the current recordset fields. From page 338 onwards you will find information on how to use this variant.

3   As an alternative to the recordset produced in the source code you can develop a class in VB 6, which can serve as a data source for producing ADO recordsets or binding controls. The class implements access to the fundamental source code (either yourself again using ADO or directly). Data source classes mainly serve as a medium layer in multilayer application models. Data source classes are not described in this book because of their very special application.

4   Another variant works with the Data Environment. A Data Environment is a designer which allows you at design time to connect to data sources and visually produce lists of records with the help of dialogs and wizards. A Data Environment is shown in a window in the development environment and displays in a hierarchy the connections to data sources and recordsets that have been produced. Recordsets produced in this way can be used in exactly the same way as recordsets produced in the source code. In addition you can connect controls on forms with recordsets even at the design stage which have been produced in the Data Environment. The advantage of the Data Environment is the really simple visual arrangement of the connection to the data source and the recordsets. It is also an advantage to be able to use Drag&Drop to place complete recordsets or individual fields onto a form or a report (whereby the development environment automatically produces binding controls).

Unfortunately with the Data Environment you lose some control of your database connection. For this reason and also because of space restrictions I am not describing the Data Environment in this book.

5　The last variant is the use of the ADODC control instead of a recordset object that has been produced yourself. You can initialize this control as early as design time using properties. When opening the form that contains the ADODC control, the underlying recordset automatically opens. As with an ADO recordset produced yourself, you bind different controls to the ADODC control in order to give the user a surface for processing data. The (negligible) advantage of using the ADODC control is that you do not need to program anything in order to enable the user movement in the recordset, because the control already contains corresponding buttons. A serious disadvantage of the ADODC controls is its unprofessional programming. As with the old (DAO) data control you will establish in time when working with the ADODC control that it cannot be used for professional programming. In addition this control only really offers the buttons for moving in the recordset that you yourself can produce with very little effort (or have produced using the add-in *VB 6 data form wizard*. For this reason you will not find a description of this control in the book.

10.4 The ADO object model

ADO consists of several classes structured in a hierarchy. The most important classes are firstly the `Connection` class, the `Recordset` class and the `Command` class. Out of these classes you produce the objects you will work with in the source code. Most of the objects that are subordinate to these classes can be reached via lists, which are properties of objects higher in the hierarchy. The `Field` object that represents a field in a recordset can be reached for example via the `Fields` list of a `Recordset` object.

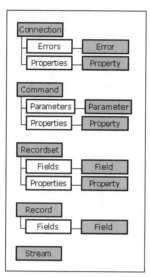

Figure 10.3 *The ADO object model*
(Source: Microsoft MDAC 2.5 documentation)

The ADO classes

You will find the most important ADO classes in Table 10.1. You usually only use *directly* the classes `Connection`, `Recordset` and `Command`. All other classes are the data types of properties of these classes.

Class	Meaning
Connection	An object of the `Connection` class represents a connection to a data source. Since you always need a connection to a data source when you want to query or edit data, a `Connection` object is offered whenever you need this connection more than once (a `Recordset` object can itself build a connection). Likewise direct transactions must be programmed via a `Connection` object.

Class	Meaning
Recordset	A `Recordset` object represents a recordset source resulting from an SQL query and the associated cursor. A recordset can be opened without `Connection` object. An opened connection however enables the production of several recordsets without the connection always having to be remade.
Command	A `Command` object represents an SQL statement that is carried out by the database server whenever you call the `Execute` method of the object. `Command` objects are mainly needed for carrying out stored procedures.
Field	The `Field` object represents an individual field within a data set. You reach the individual field objects of a data set `Fields` listing of a recordset object.

Table 10.1 *The most important ADO classes*

10.5 Basics for working with ADO

Producing ADO objects

To work with ADO in Visual Basic you ideally need a reference to the ADO object library ("Microsoft ActiveX Data Objects 2.5 Object Library"). I have already described how you structure a reference in Section 3.8.1 on page 112. Using this you can directly declare and instantiate using the New operator the object variables and their corresponding class as data type (whereby IntelliSense is available to you).

The ADO class library is shortened incidentally in the Object catalog and in the source code as *ADODB*.

> **Tip** When declaring object variables and instantiating objects you should always specify this library. Possibly your project makes reference to other libraries that contain classes with the same name. If you do not specify the components, the compiler does not know which class you want to use and might use the wrong one. For example, you produce a Connection object in the following way:
>
> ```
> Dim con As ADODB.Connection
> Set con = New ADODB.Connection
> ```

You then still have to open the connection. I describe how it works for the individual data sources from page 311 onwards. This is just a brief example here:

```
con.Open "Provider=Microsoft.Jet.OLEDB.4.0;" & _
        "Data Source=" & App.Path & "\Address.mdb"
```

Working with data

If you want to work with data you use the objects of the `Recordset` class (for querying and editing data) and the `Command` class (for executing SQL statements). You can produce these objects separately without having to make a connection to the database. In this case you specify the necessary information for connection as soon as you create the object. For example, creating a recordset with the Jet provider looks like this:

```
Dim rst As ADODB.Recordset
Set rst = New ADODB.Recordset
rst.Open "SELECT * FROM TITLES", _
        "PROVIDER=Microsoft.Jet.OLEDB.4.0;" & _
        "Data Source=" & App.Path & "\Address.mdb", _
        adOpenStatic, adLockOptimistic
```

This option available in principle should only rarely be used. The disadvantage is firstly that for several recordsets opened at the same time several connections are also made to the database server. Apart from the fact that this reduces the memory and performance, modern database systems are licensed for a fixed maximum number of connections. If your application is based on five opened recordsets and five connections, the licenses are soon used up. For another thing you cannot use this variant for transactions, and transactions – even if you do not know yet what these are – very quickly become important when it comes to professional programming. Therefore you should always open a connection beforehand in a `Connection` object and use this for creating recordset lists for executing commands:

```
Dim con As ADODB.Connection
Set con = New ADODB.Connection
con.Open "Provider=Microsoft.Jet.OLEDB.4.0;" & _
        "Data Source=" & App.Path & "\Address.mdb"
Dim rst As ADODB.Recordset
Set rst = New ADODB.Recordset
rst.Open "SELECT * FROM TITLES", con, _
        adOpenStatic, adLockOptimistic
```

Transferring arguments

In ADO you can often define as argument all arguments needed to carry out an action on executing the method or they may also be defined in separate properties. You can for example instead of

```
rst.Open "SELECT * FROM TITLES", conPubs
```

also write

```
rst.Source = "SELECT * FROM TITLES"
Set rst.ActiveConnection = conPubs
rst.Open
```

The corresponding properties have the same name as the corresponding arguments of the method. You have to decide which procedure is the better one. I actually always use the first variant because it requires less effort.

10.6 The connection object

As I have already said above, opening a connection to the data source using an object of the `Connection` class is considerably better than if every `recordset` and every `command` object builds its own connection. Therefore create an object of this class and open the connection with the `Open` method:

connection.Open [*ConnectionString*] [, *UserID*] [, *Password*]

Except for making up the connection string in the argument *ConnectionString* opening the connection is really unproblematic. The *ConnectionString* consists of several arguments, which are separated from each other by a semicolon. As every provider uses different arguments the *ConnectionString* for every provider looks quite different. The only argument that always appears is the *Provider* argument (where you specify the provider you are going to use, but that already tells you the name of the argument). If you omit the connection string argument *Provider*, ADO always uses the ODBC provider.

In the arguments *UserId* and *Password* of the `Open` method you specify for protected databases the user name and password that is going to be used for the database operation. Alternatively you can also specify this information in the arguments *UID* and *PWD* in the connection string but who knows whether all providers support these connection string arguments. For a connection to an SQL server database you have to specify the User ID and password, for example:

```
con.Open "Provider=SQLOLEDB;Data Source=Zaphod;" & _
         "Initial catalog=Pubs", "sa", "bandit"
```

Because of the different connection strings I will dispense at this point with a list of all the possible arguments. You will find the most important arguments for the individual providers from page 312 onwards where I show you how to make a connection to the individual database systems. As I do not describe all the providers, you will find a list of the providers supplied with MDAC 2.5 in Table 10.2.

Provider	Meaning
MSDASQL	Providers for all databases, for which an OBDC driver is installed on the system. Access is via the ODBC driver.
Microsoft.Jet.OLEDB.4.0	Providers for all Microsoft Jet databases (Access, DBase, Fox-Pro, Excel, HTML, Text etc.).
SQLOLEDB	Providers for SQL server databases.
MSDAORA	Providers for all Oracle 7.3 and 8.0 databases (unfortunately only read-only access, as described but also resolved on page 314).
MS Remote	Providers for remote access to databases (e.g. via the Internet).
MS Data Shape	Special providers for hierarchical recordsets. Hierarchical recordsets are recordsets that "contain" another, subordinate recordset in a field. So, for example, a *customer* recordset could contain a recordset in an *orders* field, which contains all orders for the particular customer. The MS Data Shape provider uses one of the other providers in the background.
MSDAOSP	You use the "Simple Provider" when you want to use data source classes you have written yourself as the provider, when these are not registered in their own provider (please don't ask me how it works!).

Table 10.2 *Providers supplied with MDAC 2.5*

Provider	Meaning
MSIDXS	This provider allows reading access to the index catalog created by the Microsoft index server. The Microsoft index server is part of the *Windows NT Option Pack* that is available and is mainly used for indexing webs (in the intranet or Internet). With the MSIDXS provider you can really easily program a full text search via the web.
ADSDSO Object	This provider allows access to the *Microsoft Active Directory Service* (ADS). ADS is a part of Windows 2000 and can be installed subsequently on Windows NT or 9x.
MSDAIPP.DSO	The "Provider for Internet Publishing" enables access to resources that are managed by the Internet Information Server or by Frontpage with which you can very easily (also via the Internet) read, edit and store web files and folders (like HTML files) on the web server.

Table 10.3 *Other providers by Microsoft available for ADO*

Because of space restrictions I can only describe the most important providers in this book. For the others I would refer you to the MDAC documentation (`Microsoft ADO Programmer's Reference | Using Providers with ADO`) and the Microsoft search page (search.microsoft.com/us/dev/default.asp), where you can easily search for the provider designation.

Closing the connection

You close an opened connection using the `Close` method. In so doing you just have to remember that a run-time error will occur if the connection has not been opened. For this reason I usually turn off the error handling facility again before closing (and of course again after closing):

```
On Error Resume Next
con.Close
On Error Goto ErrHandler
```

Where and when should the connection be opened again?

With classic programs this question was easy to answer: declare the `Connection` variable in a standard module with `Public` and produce and open this in the `Load` event of the start form. In the `Unload` event of the start form close the connection again. In so doing the connection remains closed for as long as your application is running. Today there is often another way you can go – you only open the connection if this is really needed and then close it again immediately. In this way you can achieve ten applications working at virtually the same time with one database, when there are only five licenses available. The *Connection Pooling* integrated in ADO ensures that a connection remains open for about 60 seconds in the background after closing (for this and other clients also). Consequently, reopening this connection is often a speedy process if this is undertaken within these 60 seconds. In Visual Basic you can implement this technology by using global `Connection` variables for every data processing form that is produced and opened in the `Load` event of this form and closed in the `Unload` event.

Tips and tricks

Connection string via the Data Environment

The connection string is really difficult to manage. But you can make the work easier by simply integrating a Data Environment into your project (`Project | Add Data Environment`). Set the provider and the database connection in the Connection properties with the help of the wizard. Just select the connection string afterwards from the `ConnectionSource` property of the Data Environment. Remove the Data Environment if you no longer need it.

Watch for spaces

ADO is very "sensitive" when it comes to spaces in the string. Only add spaces where you see spaces in the examples. Too many or too few spaces often result in misleading error messages. So if you receive an odd error message, check your connection string first.

10.6.1 Connection to an Access database

If you want to produce a connection to an *unprotected* Access database, use the Jet Provider (*Microsoft.Jet.OLEDB.4.0*) and specify in the connection string argument *Data Source* the full file name of the database.

Open the database BIBLIO.MDB, which is anticipated in the application folder:

```
Dim con As ADODB.Connection
Set con = New ADODB.Connection
con.Open "Provider=Microsoft.Jet.OLEDB.4.0;" & _
         "Data Source=" & App.Path & "\BIBLIO.MDB"
```

If the database is protected by a password, then specify this in the connection string argument Jet OLEDB - Database Password. If the database is protected via a work group, you have to specify the system database where the users are listed. This information is given in the *Jet OLEDB - System database* argument. Remember to state the user name and password. The following example opens a connection to an Access database that is protected by a database password and in a work group:

```
con.CursorLocation = adUseClient
con.Open "Provider=Microsoft.Jet.OLEDB.4.0; " & _
    "Data Source=" & App.Path & "\Orders.mdb; " & _
    "Jet OLEDB:Database password=Merlin" & _
    "Jet OLEDB:System database=" & App.Path & _
    "\Orders.MDW"
```

Tip If you use the Jet Provider 4.0, you have to set the property `CursorLocation` of the recordset to be opened later to `adUseClient`. If you set nothing or `adUseServer`, the binding to some controls such as Data Grid will not work. The controls then just display nothing.

Tips and tricks

Avoiding the error "ISAM setup cannot be found"

If you do not correctly specify the necessary arguments, ADO with the Jet provider produces (erroneously) in many cases the error "ISAM setup cannot be found", which normally means for ISAM databases that the driver for the specified database was not found or is not registered. In this case however you usually have to correct your specification.

10.6.2   Connection to an SQL server database

Unlike Oracle, the SQL server does not require any particular precautions to be taken on the client-side. For a native connection to the Microsoft SQL server you specify the *SQLOLEDB* provider. You write the name of the SQL server, which manages the database, to the connection string argument *Data Source*. The name of the database is finally transferred to the provider in the *Initial Catalog* argument (why the *Database* argument is not used has always been unclear to me). You open a connection to the example database *Pubs* on the computer *Zaphod* with the user "sa" and the password "bandit" for example as follows:

```
Dim con As ADODB.Connection
Set con = New ADODB.Connection
con.Open "Provider=SQLOLEDB;" & _
        "Data Source=Zaphod;" & _
        "Initial catalog=Pubs", _
        "sa", "bandit"
```

The SQL server provider supports other optional provider-specific arguments for controlling the connection. The most important are listed in Table 10.4.

Argument	Description
Trusted Connection	If you enter `True` here the SQL server uses a *Trusted Connection* to login, i.e. the Windows login information (User ID and password) is transferred to the SQL server as login. The user is then saved having to log into the SQL server. The login must of course be defined in the SQL server. The presetting is `False`.
Current Language	The language to be used for messages and formatting. The specified language must be installed on the server.
Application Name	The name of the application which makes the connection. The SQL server uses this name for error and other messages.
Workstation ID	A string with which the SQL server can identify the client workstation. The SQL server uses this ID for error and other messages.

Table 10.4   *The most important provider-specific connection arguments of the SQL server provider*

10.6.3 Connection to an Oracle database

For Oracle connections, unlike the SQL server, connection software must be installed on the client-side. For Oracle 8 databases this is at the present time *Net 8*. You will find this connection software on the Oracle CDs. Alternatively you can also install the current Oracle provider. Besides the actual provider the installation also contains Net 8. You will find the current Oracle provider at www.oracle.com (register free of charge at the OTC, made possible using Link Downloads. You will find the provider in the OTC). If Net 8 is installed, you might have to set up a *service* with the *Net 8 Assistant*. Using this service Net 8 later identifies the Oracle instance that is going to be used. The standard setup is the *ORCL* service, which either points to the local Oracle instance or if this is unavailable to a remote instance specified on installation of Net 8. So you have to organize a new service if need be in the *Net 8 Assistant* that indicates the correct Oracle instance. To do this click in the *Net 8 Assistant* and onto the plus sign to set up a new service. You can deal with the rest using the Wizard. You then specify the service you have set up in this way in the argument *Data Source* when you open the connection in the connection string (see the example below).

Connection to an Oracle database using Microsoft tools is unfortunately none too easy and does not work very satisfactorily. The Oracle provider *MSDAORA* supplied with MDAC 2.5 only allows read-only access with no bookmarks (for which reason recordsets cannot be displayed for example in the Data Grid). If you want to try out this provider anyway:

```
con.Open "Provider=MSDAORA;User ID=Scott;" & _
        "Password=Tiger;Data Source=Arthur;"
```

This example opens a connection to the Oracle instance, which is defined by the Net 8 service *Arthur*, and uses the Oracle user example *Scott* with the password *Tiger*.

Possibly a better solution is the use of the ODBC provider with the Microsoft Oracle ODBC driver. It is true this permits writing access, but unfortunately at the present time only Oracle 7 features. All new features (including the new Oracle 8 data types) are not supported:

```
con.Open "Provider=MSDASQL;DRIVER={Microsoft ODBC " & _
        "for Oracle};SERVER=Arthur;UID=Scott;PWD=Tiger"
```

Probably the best solution is to use the current Oracle provider (see above for the prerequisites). This provider must enable all the Oracle 8 features and furthermore is very well documented:

```
con.Open "Provider=OraOLEDB.Oracle;" & _
         "User ID=Scott;Password=Tiger;" & _
         "Data Source=Arthur;
```

> **Tip** The Oracle provider supports queries that can be updated, but if the query contains Joins, as with most other providers, you have to use a cursor on the client-side.

> **Tip** The Oracle provider at the present time still has some problems with ADOX (ADO extensions for DDL and security). It is really easy to produce databases and tables using ADOX and to edit their structure. Up to now though, I have been unable to create a single table using the Oracle provider. To make matters even more difficult the provider unfortunately does not issue any error messages. So far inquiries in various newsgroups and at Oracle support have been fruitless.

10.6.4   Using the ODBC provider

The ODBC provider represents a bridge to ODBC (open database connectivity) and with this allows access to all databases where there is an ODBC driver available.

The data source

To build an ODBC connection various instructions are necessary, which differ for the different ODBC drivers. In order to simplify connection to a database in spite of the wealth of instructions, *ODBC data sources* (DSN)[4] exist that can be identified with an identifier. These can already record most of the necessary details (user name and passwords for login are of course not saved here). You can edit the data sources installed on your system using the ODBC data source administrator (in the system control item Data Sources (ODBC)). Because of space restrictions I am going to omit a diagram at this point and only explain the meaning of the registers in this dialog. User DSN can only be used by the user of the local computer and System DSN by all users having the required access

---

4. Data source names.

rights. `File DSN` are file-based and can be used by all users who have installed the same driver. To date I have not found out what File DSN really are. If you find out, drop me quick e-mail.

You can create new data sources in the `ODBC data source administrator` using the `Add` button. After you have selected the driver, enter the connection options, which differ considerably for the different database systems (which is why I am omitting a diagram). Some data in the data source is optional, such as for example database details for the SQL server. You can then add these details in the connection string when opening the connection.

Opening the connection

If you have pre-defined a DSN, specify this in the *DSN* argument (alternatively you can also open the connection without DSN, then specify the driver and all other necessary data individually, but as a rule this is too complicated):

```
Dim con As ADODB.Connection
Set con = New ADODB.Connection
con.Open "Provider=MSDASQL;DSN=Animals"
```

All details still missing in the DSN can be specified in other arguments (e.g. *DBQ*, *UID* and *PWD*).

10.7 The recordset object

The `recordset` object is the most complex and important ADO object. It allows you access to data. When creating `recordset` objects several options are available at the same time: you can produce a `recordset` object yourself and open using the `Open` method. This variant is the most flexible. If you only require a read-only recordset, which you can go through in sequence once only, you can also just transfer an SQL query to `Execute` method of a `Connection` object and use the recordset that is returned. A third option remains where you use a `Command` object, which using the right command also returns a `Recordset` object.

10.7.1 Opening using the Open method

Opening with the `Open` method is the most flexible variant to produce a list of the recordset. Here for example you have control over the cursor you are using and the locking mechanism (see page 318 onwards):

```
recordset.Open [Source] [,ActiveConnection] _
              [,CursorType] [,LockType] [,Options]
```

In *Source* you transfer an SQL SELECT instruction, the name of a table, a Command object or a Stored Procedure call. I have never understood the point in transferring a Command object, you usually call a Stored Procedure via a separate Command object. So you can reduce the possibilities here to a table name and an SQL-SELECT instruction.

In *ActiveConnection* you can either transfer a Connection variable, if the recordset is to use this connection, or a connection string (which is constructed like the connection string of the Connection object) whenever the recordset is going to construct its own connection.

The *CursorType* argument defines the cursor you are going to use. The argument *LockType* determines the lock setting. You will find a description of these arguments and the possible settings for these below. Note that the default setting of the cursor and the lock setting (adOpenForwardOnly, adLockReadOnly) have the effect that the recordset is read-only and can only be worked through once from front to back.

In *Options* you can specify the type of command. You can normally omit this argument as the presetting (adCmdUnknown) has the effect that ADO itself recognizes whether you have specified a table name or a SELECT instruction.

Value	Description
adCmdText	Determines that the interpretation occurs as text (SQL statement with relational databases, other commands with other data sources).
adCmdTable	Determines that the string transferred in *Source* is interpreted as a table name. ADO then automatically generates an SQL SELECT statement, which contains all table fields.
adCmdStoredProc	Determines that the string transferred in *Source* is interpreted as a Stored Procedure.
adCmdUnknown	Default: The command type is unknown. ADO tries to recognize the command type from the context, something which normally works.
adCmdTableDirect	Determines that the string transferred in *Source* is interpreted as a table name and that the table is opened directly. ADO does not generate an SQL SELECT statement. This option is needed for searching in indexed fields using the Seek method.

Table 10.5 *The constants of the option argument on opening a recordset*

Normally you will open a recordset using a SELECT query and specify a Connection object as a connection. Accordingly a normal example looks as follows:

```
Dim rst As ADODB.Recordset
Set rst = New ADODB.Recordset
rst.Open "SELECT * FROM Titles", mconn, _
        adOpenForwardOnly, adLockReadOnly
```

Note: This example uses a global `Connection` variable and assumes that the connection has been opened in Form_Load of the form.

SQL

Since you usually specify the data source with an SQL statement, you should of course have fundamental SQL knowledge. With cleverly thought out SQL queries you often receive events in the recordset, meaning you do not have to spend much time doing calculations. For this reason at the same stage in many other books you will find a substantial treatise on SQL. This is not the case in this book. I am going to omit a description because I believe that there is no need to repeat this general language again and again in every single book.

10.7.2   The cursor

A cursor is a pointer to a (the current) record of a data record list. If in your application you change to a different recordset (for example with the `MoveNext` method), the cursor is set to this data recordset. ADO or the management program of the database can access this data set using the cursor. Cursors can have different functions. Simple cursors allow you to work through a data record list once only or display only a picture of the data stock at the time of opening, elaborate cursors allow all move operations and always show the updated data stock. The more elaborate a cursor becomes, the slower the processing of a record list becomes. In addition the type of cursor influences the time needed for the production of a data record list.

The type of cursor

In the *CursorType* argument you specify precisely on opening which type of cursor you want to use. Table 10.6 describes the constants available and the related cursor type.

A *forward cursor* (`adOpenForwardOnly`) has the effect that you can only go through the data recordset once record by record. You can update such a forward recordset (all according to the database). Data values are static, i.e. changes by other users do not become visible in the recordset as long as it is opened. A forward cursor is usually more efficient than the other cursor types.

A *static cursor* (adOpenStatic) allows the data record list to be completely managed (with all fields) in the working memory. A static cursor can usually be updated. Changes by other users do not become visible in the recordset as long as this recordset is open (because an image of the data records is managed in the working memory). This cursor is slower when producing the recordset, but there again when it comes to read access to databases possibly faster than a keyset or dynamic cursor (depending on the database, the number of queried records, the lock option and the cursor location). If you want to see amendments to queried data records made by other users in your recordset, you would not use the static cursor.

With a *keyset cursor* (adOpenKeyset) ADO simply stores unambiguous keys (for example the primary key) for individual records in the working memory. When accessing a record, the record is identified and dynamically read in with the help of the key. Updates by other users become visible in the recordset provided data records are not added. Since the number and sequence of data records is certain once the recordset has been created, added records and updates, which affect the data sequence, cannot be seen as long as the recordset is open. A keyset cursor is usually constructed more quickly than a static cursor, but needs somewhat more time for accessing a data record.

A *dynamic cursor* (adOpenDynamic) resembles the keyset cursor, but differs because it does not support a bookmark and the data record sequence is not fixed. Since ADO continually checks whether all data records corresponding to the SQL statement are still available in the data source, this cursor causes the most management time. A dynamic cursor however is built more quickly than a keyset cursor, because on opening the recordset there is no need to create a key set. With this cursor all changes by other users to the queried data are visible. Added data records are dynamically inserted into the recordset and amended data records may possibly cause another sorting of data records within the recordset.

Constants	Description
adOpenForwardOnly	Forward cursor. Presetting. You can only go through the recordset once record by record.
adOpenStatic	Static cursor. The list of data records is managed completely in the working memory (all fields). Amendments made by other users to the data are not visible.
adOpenKeyset	Keyset cursor. ADO only manages key values for data records in the memory. Changes by other users to data are visible.
adOpenDynamic	Dynamic cursor. As with the keyset cursor changes by other users become apparent including new and deleted data records and changes in sorting.

Table 10.6 *Constants for cursor type*

Server-side or client-side cursor?

Besides the type of cursor, *client-side* and *server-side* cursors are different. Before opening the recordset you determine which cursor location you are going to use in the CursorLocation property. If you do not, ADO uses the connection setting in the CursorLocation property. For setting the cursor location you can use the constants in Table 10.7.

Server-side cursors use the original cursor from the data source or the provider. With client/server databases the cursor is managed on the computer where the database system is running. For desktop databases the expression "server-side cursor" should not be taken too literally. Since there is no process running on the computer which takes care of data management on desktop databases that are stored on a remote computer, the cursor is also managed (by the provider) for desktop databases on the client computer. Server-side cursors in many cases give enhanced performance on large quantities of data for client/server databases because opening the recordset does not cause any network loading (only the SQL statement is transferred to the server). With desktop databases a server-side cursor can likewise be an advantage according to the provider. With JetProvider for example because the data, as is the case for client-side cursors, are not cached twice (once in the Jet Engine and once in the Cursor Service).

With *client-side* cursors ADO uses the "Microsoft Cursor Service for OLE DB" for producing the data record list. This cursor service requests the data from the provider and in so doing uses a read-only forward cursor and saves the cursor information in its own cache on the client computer. Whenever you request data, the cursor service by preference fetches the data from its cache. Client-side cursors can give better performance when accessing individual data records (depending on the type of cursor) than server-side cursors. On opening the recordset, however, the cursor information on all data records has to be fully transferred to the client via the network, which depending on the network capacity can take a lot of time.

Constants	Cursor
adUseServer	Server-side cursor.
adUseClient	Client-side cursor.
adUseNone	No cursor is used. This setting is available only for backward compatibility reasons and should not be used.

Table 10.7 *Constants of the cursor location*

Choosing the right cursor

When deciding *where* you are going to manage the cursor, besides performance, the ADO features you want to use are also an important factor. ADO-specific features such as *connectionless recordsets*[5] *or batch updates*[6] are only possible with client-side cursors. But even if you want to use SQL queries that extend beyond more than one table (with Joins for example) as a rule you need a client-side cursor if you want to be able to edit the data record list. Features specifically for the data source on the other hand are only available with server-side cursors. So for example the available option after MDAC 2.1 for searching in the index of a table is linked to a server-side cursor.

When selecting the cursor location you should still remember that server-side cursors handling large quantities of data with many users at the same time can cause a high server loading. However a server-side cursor is mostly more efficient, because it dispenses with the transfer of management information. Because of this network traffic is often considerably reduced depending on the cursor (with a static client-side cursor for example all requested recordsets have to be transferred via the net, which causes a high level of network interaction).

When choosing the cursor type you have to first decide which basic features you need. You then select the cursor which is probably going to give you the best performance. In the book *"ADO 2.1: Programmers Reference"* David Sussmann has tested the different cursor very extensively using different databases. Consult these performance tests if you want to optimize performance.

---

5. Connectionless recordsets are recordsets whose connection is set on Nothing. With such recordsets you can go down the database from time to time while the recordset remains open.
6. Updating batches does not result in data being written to the database as yet. It is only when you call the UpdateBatch method that all amendments are written to the database in one go. Batch updates are mainly required for connectionless recordsets and data updates via the Internet.

Selecting the correct cursor is also problematic because nobody can say for sure whether certain features (e.g. being able to update the recordset or the possibility of managing bookmarks) are available with the individual cursors for certain databases. For example you cannot manage bookmarks in the recordset with Access databases using server-side cursors, but this works very well with client-side cursors. There is usually no way of avoiding experimentation.

10.7.3   The lock options

When you open the recordset, the *LockType* argument defines the lock option. Every database system has to lock a data record when it is going to be updated, at least for the short duration of physical writing, so that at the same time other users or applications do not describe the same data record, which can cause damage. There is no way of avoiding the lock option – just set your lock preferences. Table 10.8 describes the available settings.

Constants	Lock option
adLockReadOnly	Lock Read Only. Default: you can only read your data.
adLockPessimistic	Pessimistic lock: a data record is opened for editing and locked so other users cannot edit.
adLockOptimistic	Optimistic lock: a data record is opened for editing and locked so other users cannot edit only for the moment where Update method is carried out.
adLockBatchOptimistic	Optimistic batch updates are required for updating batches. Updating batches is not described in this book.

Table 10.8 *The lock options when opening a recordset*

If you also want to open the recordset for editing, you have to either use optimistic or pessimistic locking. With optimistic locking an edited data record is only locked for the brief moment when the Update method is implemented. If in doing so it is discovered that the data record has been amended compared with the original data read in, then a run-time error will occur. With pessimistic locking a data record is locked as long as the record is open for editing (i.e. from the first writing of a value to a field in the recordset right up to the Update method).Here a run-time error will occur if another user has already opened the data record (shortly before) for editing. By the way, the concepts "optimistic" and "pessimistic" mean here that you are either optimistic that normally no other user will have simultaneously opened an already opened data record for editing, or you are pessimistic and presume therefore that collisions can occur anyway.

Dealing with locking options and the arising run-time errors in different situations is really complicated. Here unfortunately there is no room for an adequate description.

10.7.4 Opening as a result of the Execute method

The `Execute` method of the `Connection` and the `Command` object returns a `Recordset` object whenever you transfer a query, the name of a Stored Procedure or a table name:

```
Set rst = mconn.Execute("SELECT * FROM Titles")
```

With this variant you have no option to define the cursor type or the lock setting. A read-only forward recordset is always returned. If this read-only forward recordset is sufficient for you, this variant is a fast and efficient solution to the production of a recordset.

10.8 Editing data

10.8.1 Move in the recordset

You can move around in a recordset using the Move methods. You obtain information regarding the position and number of data records via the BOF, EOF, AbsolutePosition and RecordCount properties.

Go through the titles table:

```
Dim rst As ADODB.Recordset
Set rst = New ADODB.Recordset
rst.Open "SELECT * FROM Titles", mcon, _
        adOpenStatic, adLockReadOnly
While Not rst.EOF
    ...
   rst.MoveNext
Wend
```

If you want to memorize the position of a data record, you can save its *bookmark* from the property Bookmark into a Variant variable. Later you can jump back to this data record with an instruction from this bookmark to the Bookmark property. Remember that the cursor and the provider have to support bookmarks (which is not always the case), the variable has to be of the Variant type (even if the bookmark looks like a string) and that bookmarks lose their validity when the recordset is requested again (therefore also filtered or sorted).

The most important methods for moving in the recordset

Method	Description
MoveFirst	Put the cursor on the first data record.
MoveNext	Put the cursor on the next data record.
MovePrevious	Put the cursor on the previous data record.
MoveLast	Put the cursor on the last data record.
Move (*NumRecords*, [*Start*])	Put the cursor on a particular data record. In *NumRecords* you can specify the number of data records that are going to be skipped. Because negative values are possible too, you can also jump backwards. In *Start* you can specify from which data record you are going to jump. If you enter nothing here, the jump will be from the current record.

Table 10.9 *The Move methods of the recordset object*

The most important properties for Move in the recordset

Property	Description
BOF	BOF (Bottom Of File) is True, when the cursor is *in front of* (not *on*!) the first data record. If the cursor is on BOF, you cannot edit the data record (because no record is current) or change to the previous record using MovePrevious. The cursor is on BOF when the MovePrevious method has been applied to the first data record or when the recordset is empty.
EOF	EOF (End Of File) is True whenever the cursor is *behind* (not *on*!) the last record. If the cursor is on EOF, as is the case with BOF, you cannot edit the record or change with MoveNext to the next record. The cursor is on EOF whenever the MoveNext method has been applied to the last data record or when the recordset is empty.
Absolute Position	AbsolutePosition contains the absolute position of the cursor as integer. If for example you are on the tenth data record, then the absolute position has the value 10.
RecordCount	RecordCount has the number of data records in the current record list. Remember that RecordCount is not updated with different cursor types until you have jumped at least once to the last record using MoveLast. Often RecordCount initially has the value 0 after opening a recordset.

Property	Description
Bookmark	This property manages the bookmark of the current data record as Variant. You can read and of course also reset the bookmark in order to jump back to a tagged data record. The cursor and the provider have to support bookmarks, which is not always the case.

Table 10.10 *The most important information properties of the recordset object*

10.8.2 Access to data

You gain access to data using the Fields list, to which you transfer either the integer index or the field name of the data field. This list references individual Field objects, which stand for each field (column) of the data record list. You can receive information on a field via different properties. The most important property is Value. Value contains the datum stored in the field[7]. The following example goes through all data records for the titles table of the library database and writes all titles to a list box:

```
Dim rst As ADODB.Recordset
Set rst = New ADODB.Recordset
rst.Open "SELECT * FROM Titles", mcon
lstTitles.Clear
While Not rst.EOF
  lstTitles.AddItem rst.Fields("Title").Value
  rst.MoveNext
Wend
```

If you want to edit a data record simply write the new values into the Value property of the Field objects concerned and afterwards call the Update method of the recordset object:

```
recordset.Update [Fields, Values]
```

---

7. Datum is used here as the singular of data.

Run through the *Products* table of the *NWind* database and increase the price of the products by 10%:

```
Dim rst As ADODB.Recordset
Set rst = New ADODB.Recordset
rst.Open "SELECT * FROM Products", mcon, _
        adOpenKeyset, adLockPessimistic
While Not rst.EOF
  rst.Fields("UnitPrice").Value = _
        rst.Fields("UnitPrice").Value * 1.1
  rst.Update
  rst.MoveNext
Wend
```

Note: This example is very inefficient. For these types of action it is preferable to use an SQL UPDATE statement:

```
mcon.Execute "UPDATE Products SET " & _
            "UnitPrice = UnitPrice * 1.1"
```

If after editing you want to cancel all the amendments, instead of calling `Update` call the `CancelUpdate` method.

Tip You must remember to open the recordset with the correct cursor type and lock setting. With the default settings (`adOpenForwardOnly`, `adLockReadOnly`) you cannot edit the recordset (and only run through once from front to back).

Properties and methods for editing data in the recordset

Property / method	Meaning
Fields	Via the Fields list you can access the individual fields of the current data record. You use the Value property of the Field objects referenced via Field in order to read or write the saved value.
Update [Fields, Values]	You use the Update method for writing to the database all amendments made to the current data record. As an alternative to writing values via the Fields list mentioned previously you can also transfer the fields and their new values immediately on update (but nobody does this).
CancelUpdate	Using this method you can cancel the update of a data record for example whenever a run-time has occurred when writing to a field.

Table 10.11   *The properties and methods for editing data in the recordset object*

Tips and tricks

Error "Avoid invalid use of zero"

Since database fields can also always contain the value zero (i.e. are empty), you cannot normally use these fields without a statement for zero in expressions or instructions. The statement is too laborious:

```
If IsNull(rst.Fields("Title").Value) = False Then
    strTitle = rst.Fields("Title").Value
Else
    strTitle = ""
End If
```

It is better if you use the concatenation operator &, which automatically converts zero into an empty string:

```
strTitle = rst.Fields("Title").Value & ""
```

10.8.3   Attach and delete data records

With the AddNew method you can produce a new data record:

```
recordset.AddNew [Fields, Values]
```

For *Fields* and *Values* the same applies as for Update. After describing the fields of this data record as when editing you have to call Update or CancelUpdate. The following example produces a new data record in the titles table:

```
Dim rst As ADODB.Recordset
Set rst = New ADODB.Recordset
rst.Open "SELECT * FROM TITLES", mcon, _
        adOpenKeyset, adLockOptimistic
rst.AddNew
rst.Fields("Title").Value = _
    "Nitty Gritty Visual Basic"
rst.Fields("ISBN").Value = _
    "not known yet"
rst.Fields("PubId").Value = 49
rst.Update
rst.Close
```

Using the `Delete` method you can delete individual or several data records:

recordset.Delete [*AffectRecords*]

If you specify nothing in *AffectRecords* or `adAffectCurrent`, the current data record is deleted. Alternatively you can delete a group of data records by setting the `Filter` property of the recordset and transferring the constants `adAffectGroup` to *AffectRecords*. Normally you probably want to delete the current data record and then simply specify nothing in the argument *AffectRecords*. If you want to delete several data records, it is better to do this anyhow using an SQL DELETE statement.

Methods for adding and deleting data records in the recordset

Method	Meaning
AddNew [*Fields, Values*]	AddNew produces a new, empty data record, which you then describe as an already available data record and which you can write to the database using Update.
Delete [*AffectRecords*]	Delete deletes the current data record if you specify nothing in the argument *AffectRecords* or adAffectCurrent. *If you specify here* adAffectGroup, all data records are deleted which match the conditions specified in the Filter property of the recordset.

Table 10.12 *The methods for adding and deleting data records in the recordset object*

10.8.4 Searching data records

You can search in an opened recordset for a particular data record with the Find or the Seek method. Find carries out a sequential search, usually without taking account of any possible index. Seek searches in an index, which of course you need to specify. Seek unfortunately at the present time is supported by only very few providers and for this reason will not be described any further here, but you will find a description on the website.

With Find you can search in almost every type of recordset (except in a Forward recordset):

```
Recordset.Find (Criteria [, SkipRows] _
         [, SearchDirection] [, Start])
```

In *Criteria* you specify the search criteria. To do this you use the syntax that the SQL dialect of the database system prescribes. Usually in the search criteria, the operators >, >=, <, <=, = and Like are permitted. If you compare using LIKE, you can use the wildcards "%" for any characters and "_" for a precise character. Remember that ADO deviates here from the SQL dialect of the database system (which sometimes uses "*" and "?"). If the comparison value is a number, then you normally denote a comma with a dot. A string is put in simple apostrophes (for example "last name = 'Smith'"). For date values the matter becomes more difficult. Most database systems differ considerably from one another. With Access databases you specify a date for example in the American version embedded in hash signs (for example "Date_of_invoice > #7/22/97#").

> **Tip** Incomprehensibly at the present time Find (ADO 2.5) does not allow you to specify several search patterns which are concatenated via logical operators or to use the usual IN operator in SQL. Well, it may be more effective in most cases to produce instead a new recordset with a corresponding SQL statement, but you then have a filtered recordset. If you want to search in a recordset without having to refilter it for good or bad, you have to use the Find method.

In *SkipRows* you can specify an offset. The search then starts at the data record which is situated the stated number of data records either before or after (according to the setting in *SearchDirection*) the current data record or the data record given in *Start*. Normally you probably use *SkipRows* to enable a *Search next*.

In *SearchDirection* you specify whether you want to search forwards (adSearchForward, presetting) or backwards (adSearchBackward).

In the *Start* argument you can specify a bookmark that you saved previously from the `Bookmark` property into a variant variable where the search should start. Unfortunately you cannot specify in Start a logical data record number, only a bookmark.

If you have specified nothing in *Start*, ADO searches from the current data record, and also takes this record into account in the search. Unfortunately since you cannot specify in the *Start* argument the number of the data record from where you want to search (which remains incomprehensible to me), the recordset has to be set beforehand at the first data record with `MoveFirst`, if you want to search for the first matching data record. If you want to search from the current data record you have to specify the value 1 in the `SkipRows`, otherwise search finds the current data record over and over again.

Whenever a data record is found the cursor is placed on this data record. Otherwise the cursor stays on EOF if you search forwards or BOF if you search backwards. Therefore you might have to memorize the current data record using its bookmark in order to be able to set the recordset back to the current data record if ADO cannot find a matching data record.

Unfortunately there is no property that sends a Search result message (similar to `NoMatch` of DAO). You have to check on EOF or BOF in order to determine whether anything has been found. `Find` unfortunately does nothing more than a sequential search through the recordset. But if you think you can do a sequential search yourself then `Find` is considerably faster than your own search.

Search for the *first* data record whose title begins with "Visual":

```
Dim varBookmark As Variant
' If Search is to take place after the first data record,
' the recordset has to initially be set on the
' first data record.
If (mrst.BOF And mrst.EOF) = False Then
   mrst.MoveFirst
Else
    ' If BOF and EOF are True, the recordset is empty,
    ' then no search can take place.
    MsgBox "The recordset is empty", vbExclamation
    Exit Sub
End If
' Memorize the current data record
varBookmark = mrst.Bookmark
' Search
mrst.Find "Title Like 'Visual%'"
```

```
If mrst.EOF = False Then
   ' Found
   MsgBox "Found: " & mrst.Fields("Title").Value
Else
   ' Not found
   MsgBox "Not found", vbInformation
   ' Put back to the current data record
   mrst.Bookmark = varBookmark
End If
```

Note: This and the following example assume that the recordset has been opened in a global variable (mrst) in Form_Load.

Search for the *next* data record,whose title begins with "Visual":

```
Dim varBookmark As Variant
' When you have to search for the next data record,
' only then do you have to set the record on the
' first data record, when it is on EOF or BOF .
If mrst.EOF Or mrst.EOF Then
   If (mrst.BOF And mrst.EOF) = False Then
      mrst.MoveFirst
   Else
      MsgBox "The recordset is empty", vbExclamation
      Exit Sub
   End If
End If
' Memorize current data record
varBookmark = mrst.Bookmark
' Search for  the next data record requires
' specification of 1 in the SkipRecords argument.
mrst.Find "Title Like 'Visual%'", 1
If mrst.EOF = False Then
   ' Found
   MsgBox "Found: " & mrst.Fields("Title").Value
Else
   ' Not found
   MsgBox "Not found", vbInformation
   ' Reset to the current data record
   mrst.Bookmark = varBookmark
End If
```

When you search for the last matching data record, set the recordset to the last data record, search with *SearchDirection*:=adSearchBackward and check at BOF to detect whether anything has been found.

Tip After your own attempts, creating a recordset is often considerably more effective than using the Find method. In addition you have the advantage here that the new recordset contains only the data records affected, so you do not need to search any further, but simply go through the recordset. If however you want to search for a data record using its key, an option would be to use the Seek method to search in the index, which would be considerably easier to program.

10.8.5 Sorting and filtering data records

Sorting

If you want to sort a recordset, you can deal with this ideally immediately on opening using the ORDER BY clause of the SQL query:

```
rst.Open "SELECT * FROM Titles ORDER BY Title", _
    mconn, adOpenKeyset, adLockPessimistic
```

Alternatively before or after opening you can set data sorting in the Sort property of the recordset. If however you do not set any data sorting at this point until after you have opened, the recordset is normally queried again.

Tip Whether setting the Sort property after opening the recordset works depends entirely on the provider and the cursor settings. With the Jet provider for example you have to use a client-side cursor to do this. In order to avoid problems, it is better if you close the recordset yourself when it is being resorted and open it again when the data is going to be sorted afresh (which you can then set in Sort).

Filtering

When you want to filter a recordset, you do this likewise ideally immediately after opening the recordset by using the WHERE clause. If for example you want to select all the titles in the library database that contain "Visual" in the title, you use the following example:

```
rst.Open "SELECT * FROM Titles " & _
         "WHERE Title LIKE '%Visual%'", mconn, _
         adOpenKeyset, adLockPessimistic
```

> **Tip** As you can see from the example, when filtering you use a percent sign as a wildcard for searching in text fields. When searching and querying data ADO uses the percent sign for any character and the underscore for an exact character independent of the provider used. This of course applies only, when the data source is a database queried with SQL.

With a recordset that has already been created you can also use the `Filter` property for filtering. You can enter a complex filtering condition into this property. After setting the `Filter` property, the recordset is filtered accordingly:

```
Dim rst As ADODB.Recordset
Set rst = New ADODB.Recordset
rst.CursorLocation = adUseClient

' Select all books
rst.Open "SELECT * FROM Titles", _
         mcon, adOpenStatic, adLockPessimistic
...

' Subsequent filtering:
' Select all books, that contain 'C++'
' in the title, into another List box
rst.Filter = "Title LIKE '%C++%'"
While Not rst.EOF
  lstTitles(1).AddItem rst.Fields("Title").Value
  rst.MoveNext
Wend
```

All properties and methods then refer to the filtered recordset. So `Recordcount` gives you the number of filtered data records. You can remove the filter again by setting the `Filter` property to an empty string or the constant `adFilterNone`.

Alternatively you can filter by writing an array of bookmarks to the `Filter` property. In this way you can filter the recordset for data records which you have "memorized" previously in this array (for example the ones where the user has pressed the `Memorize` button you prepared). Likewise you still have the option of describing the `Filter` property with special filter constants, which is mainly to find out which data records could not be updated after a batch update.

Properties for sorting and filtering a recordset

Property	Meaning
Filter	You can write a conditional expression to this property that corresponds to the valid query syntax for the data source. If you do this before opening the recordset, the recordset is immediately opened and filtered. Setting the filter for an opened recordset has the effect that this is queried again whenever the cursor and the provider allow this. As an alternative to the filter expression you can also write a `Variant` array with bookmarks to the filter property. The recordset then receives only the data records that are represented by bookmarks. Using an empty string you can remove a filter again that you have set.
Sort	`Sort` defines sorting in the valid syntax for the data source. If you define Sort before opening the recordset, the recordset is immediately opened and sorted. Setting Sort for an opened recordset results in this being queried again. You can remove Sort again with an empty string.

Table 10.13 *Properties for sorting and filtering a recordset*

10.9 Executing (SQL) commands

10.9.1 The Execute method of the Connection object

With the `Execute` method of a Connection object, you can execute commands in the data source. With relational databases, the SQL language comes into play. Since OLE-DB however also supports other data sources such as the Microsoft Index Server or ADSI for example, languages other than SQL may be required.

```
connection.Execute CommandText _
    [,RecordsAffected] [,Options]
```

In the argument *CommandText* you specify the command. In *RecordsAffected* you can transfer a long variable, which contains the number of data records affected by the command once the command has been executed. In *Options* you define how the command is to be interpreted. To do this use the constants that you also use when opening a recordset (Table 10.5).

Tip If you use the presetting for the *Options* argument, ADO needs some computing time to recognize the type of command. For this reason you should always set the type. If the type does not match the command, ADO generates an error.

With selection queries `Execute` always returns a `Recordset` object, which you can allocate to a recordset variable:

```
Dim rst As ADODB.Recordset
Set rst = mconn.Execute("SELECT * FROM Titles")
...
rst.Close
```

Timeout

Since executing commands often takes a lot of time, the presetting of 30 seconds for timeout is often insufficient and ADO generates a run-time error if the command has not been completed in good time. On first accessing a table, a client/server database for example needs a lot of time in comparison to the following access examples, since data has to be loaded first of all into the server cache. You can determine the timeout for the command execution in the `CommandTimeout` property. You will also find this property using the `Command` object.

10.9.2   Calling Stored Procedures using a Command object

A `Command` object serves mainly to execute commands (with databases therefore SQL queries and Stored Procedures). The `Execute` method works as for the `Connection` object, except that here you do not transfer the command as argument but write to the `CommandText` property. You transfer the type of command via the `CommandType` property.

You transfer the name of the Stored Procedure in the `CommandText` property. If you set `CommandType` on `adCmdStoredProc`, this accelerates execution a little. If the Stored Procedure possesses arguments, you have to produce these either using the `CreateParameter` method of the `Command` object and at the same time like the `Parameters` list attach these with their `Append` method. Alternatively you produce a separate `Parameter` object, set its properties and attach this to the `Parameters` list. In both variants you have to make different settings, which are described in the example of the `CreateParameter` method:

```
Set Parameter = command.CreateParameter([Name,] _
    [Type,] [Direction,] [,Size] [,Value])
```

Name is the more unimportant name of the parameter. Later if you want to gain recourse to this parameter using the `Parameters` list (something you do not have to do as a rule), you can use this name in place of the integer index. `Types` specifies the type of argument. Use here the ADO constants fixed for the data type (`adInteger`, `adVarWChar`, `adCurrency`, etc.). You will find the constants used in the MDAC documentation if you search in the index for the `Type` property. The correct selection of the data type is in practice not easy for text and date fields. Here you inevitably have to experiment. The `Direction` argument states whether the argument writes a value to the procedure or the procedure returns a value in the argument or both (Table 10.14).

Constant	Meaning
`adParamInput`	Default: the parameter is written to the Stored Procedure.
`adParamOutput`	The parameter is set by the Stored Procedure.
`adParamInputOutput`	The parameter is written to the Stored Procedure and set by the same.
`adParamReturnValue`	You specify this value for the first parameter of the `Parameters` list when the Stored Procedure is a function which returns a value.

Table 10.14 *The constants of the Direction argument when defining the arguments for a Command object*

You must specify the correct setting defined in the Stored Procedure for *Direction*, otherwise this will not be executed and a run-time error will be produced.

Size determines the maximum size of an argument with variable length data (as a rule these are text fields). If you do not specify the maximum length a run-time error is often produced when attaching the `Parameter` object to the `Parameters` list. The reason lies in the fact that ADO reserves as much memory location for variable length arguments as the data type potentially needs. Often however this is too little.

In the `Prepared` property you determine whether a transferred command should be compiled before the first execution. If `Prepared` is set to `True`, the first access to the query is carried out somewhat more slowly, all the following ones however run somewhat more quickly. If the provider does not support the compilation of a query, an error is generated.

Before you can execute the Stored Procedure, you still have to allocate either a Connection variable (if you have already opened a connection to the database) or a connection string to the `ActiveConnection` property of the `Command` object.

Return values

If a Stored Procedure is a function, i.e. returns a value, you have to produce the first parameter of the parameters list using *Direction*=`adParamReturnValue`. After execution, this parameter contains the return value of the procedure. No need to get confused: a Stored Procedure can have a return value and/or produce a recordset object. The recordset object is returned by the `Execute` method of the `Command` object, the return value in the first parameter.

Executing the procedure

If all parameters are attached, you carry out the procedure with the `Execute` method. For procedures that produce recordsets, the following is valid:

```
[Set Recordset = ] command.Execute( _
        [RecordsAffected] [,Parameters] [,Options])
```

In *RecordsAffected* you can use a long variable in which the number of affected data records is stored after execution. In *Parameters* as an alternative to attaching parameters to the `Parameters` list, you can transfer parameters in a variant array. This variant has however the disadvantage that return values are ignored. *Options* defines the command type and should be set here on `adCmdStoredProc`.

Example

The Stored Procedure `byroyalty` in the Pubs database of the Microsoft SQL server identifies which authors have a share of what proportion of the conferred royalties from their books and:

```
Dim con As ADODB.Connection, cmd As ADODB.Command
Dim rst As ADODB.Recordset

Set con = New ADODB.Connection
Set cmd = New ADODB.Command
con.Open "Provider=SQLOLEDB;Data Source=Zaphod;" & _
        "Initial Catalog=Pubs", "sa", ""

' Set the name of the Stored Procedure
cmd.CommandText = "byroyalty"

' Set the type of command
cmd.CommandType = adCmdStoredProc

' Set connection
Set cmd.ActiveConnection = con

' Produce parameters and attach immediately
' (Identify authors with 50% share)
cmd.Parameters.Append cmd.CreateParameter( _
    "", adInteger, adParamInput, 2, 50)
```

```
' produce recordset with this
' Stored Procedure

Set rst = cmd.Execute
' go through recordset
While Not rst.EOF
    lstAuthors.AddItem rst.Fields(0).Value
    rst.MoveNext
Wend
rst.Close
```

10.10 Binded controls

With ADO it has become in the first instance very simple to bind controls to a data source. The binded controls then automatically display the contents of the current data record. User amendments are likewise automatically written to the data source as soon as the recordset changes to another data record or closed. Because of space restrictions I can only describe here the basic technique for binding controls.

Some criticism

In practice you will notice sooner or later when using binded controls that ADO and the associated controls are not quite so sophisticated. When trying to delete a data record in a DataGrid, errors like "A given HROW referred to a (permanently or temporarily) deleted line", after the previous deletion of a different data record has failed because of an error, speaks for itself. The DataCombo control, which at a first glance seems very helpful, produces an error for example when trying to delete the value in the text field in order to empty the table field[8]. With the help of `DataFormat` objects you can at least now transfer this bug (see page 156). Also, for example, the attempt to make the DataCombo control somewhat more user-friendly by showing the user the matching item in the text field as with Access whenever he has made an input fails because the really simple `ListIndex` property is missing.

Recordsets produced in the source code or the ADODC control?

The ADODC control only provides a surface, via which the user can move in the recordset – nothing more. Unfortunately the underlying recordset is enclosed by the ADODC control, so that for example the error interpretation when moving in the recordset has to take place via the `Error` event of the ADODC control.

---

8. The DataCombo control tries to write an empty string to the table field (instead of the zero value), which of course fails for most fields.

Because of the extremely negative experiences using the old data control I would not recommend using the ADODC control. This mainly affects the difficult error handling for this control. It is easy to bind a self-produced recordset to controls and to provide the user with some buttons, which enables him to move in the recordset. For this reason I am concentrating on linking self-produced recordsets to controls.

Binding a recordset to controls

Most controls are in a position to display individual fields of a recordset. Some, such as for example the DataGrid, can display several fields and several data sets at the same time. Controls which can display fields possess the properties DataSource, DataMember and DataField. DataSource is the data source and can be set on an ADO recordset, an ADO data control, an ADO data source class or a Data Environment object. DataMember distinguishes the Command object to be used when DataSource is set on a Data Environment object. When you bind the control to a normal recordset DataMember remains empty. DataField finally identifies the field that is going to be displayed. Controls that can display several fields (such as for example the DataGrid) are lacking the DataField property of course.

After you have produced the recordset you bind this to the controls, which ideally happens in Form_Load of the editing form:

```
Set mconBiblio = New Connection
mconBiblio.CursorLocation = adUseClient
mconBiblio.Open "Provider=Microsoft.Jet.OLEDB.4.0;" & _
                "Data Source=C:\Biblio.mdb"
Set mrstTitles = New ADODB.Recordset
mrstTitles.Open "SELECT * FROM TITLES Order by Title", _
                mconBiblio, adOpenStatic, _
                adLockBatchOptimistic
' Bind text fields to the data source
txtTitle.DataField = "Title"
Set txtTitle.DataSource = mrstTitles
txtISBN.DataField = "ISBN"
Set txtISBN.DataSource = mrstTitles
```

This is quite sufficient to achieve automatic display of data in the current data record. If you move the recordset with the Move methods, amendments are automatically written to the recordset and likewise the display automatically updated. Of course you can ensure that the controls match the data fields. You can edit the recordset with the usual methods. So for example you can search using Find for a data record and with Update write the current amendments to the data source. If the user or the application changes the data record, `Update` is implicitly called as needed.

The recordset events

In order to be able to influence the response of the recordset object, the recordset has events. As you need these only rarely and only when using ADO recordsets with binded controls, I do not describe the events here because of space restrictions.

Tips and tricks

Avoiding the ZERO problem when saving

There is often a problem when binding controls to a recordset. Whenever a control that previously contained data is emptied, ADO tries to save an empty string in the data field. This of course often goes wrong with non-text fields or fields which do not permit spaces (which in Access databases for example is displayed by the "meaningful" error message "Process cancelled"). You have to ensure yourself that ADO does not save an empty string but saves the value `Null`. To do this use a `StdDataFormat` object, which you declare with `WithEvents` at the module level. Incidentally you can also use an `StdDataFormat` object for user-defined, automatic formatting of data in the controls.

```
Private WithEvents mfmtNullWorkaround As StdDataFormat
```

In Form_Load you produce the object and bind it to all controls that are going to convert empty entries into `Null`:

```
Private Sub Form_Load()
 . . .
 Set mfmtNullWorkaround = New StdDataFormat
 ' Bind DataFormat object for the Null bug
 Set txtPubId.DataFormat = mfmtNullWorkaround
 Set txtTitle.DataFormat = mfmtNullWorkaround
 . . .
```

In the `UnFormat` event of the `StdDataFormat` object you convert an empty entry into a `Null` value:

```
Private Sub mfmtNullWorkaround_UnFormat( _
    ByVal DataValue As StdFormat.StdDataValue)
 ' Transfer the bug when entry empty
 If DataValue.Value & "" = "" Then
    DataValue.Value = Null
 End If
End Sub
```

The deployment of your application

At some time you are finally going to want to pass on your application to happy customers and friends (also enemies depending on what you have programmed). To this end it is possibly appropriate to produce a Help facility before creating an installation version that you will want to integrate into your project. Creating a Help facility is unfortunately not all that easy with the means available. For this reason because of space restrictions you will not find how to do this here. I merely describe in this chapter how you produce an installation version of your application.

Creating an installation version is always necessary for your application if you want to install your package (or have it installed) on another computer. The *Package and Deployment Wizard* by Visual Basic is the tool to help you do this.

11.1 Precautions

Before creating an installation version there are some precautions you should take so that your installation does not become too large and therefore works.

Remove all unnecessary references

In order to avoid any unnecessary files being accepted into the installation version, remove from the project all ActiveX controls, components and references which you do not need. In so doing you can simply proceed to try to remove all ActiveX controls and references in sequence. As a rule Visual Basic will not allow removal if you have used the control or the reference in your project. If you have worked with CreateObject to create objects (which really you should avoid), you then start the application with (F5) and test the functions of your application. By doing this you can check whether some references possibly have to be switched on again.

Increasing the version number

Ensure that your application and all the COM components you have used and programmed yourself receive a higher version number whenever you create a new installation version. The application or component is not overwritten when installation is repeated if it already exists with the same version number. Ideally in the project options you set it so that each compilation automatically increases the revision number. I experienced enormous problems when installing a newer version of an application because I had forgotten to increase the version number of a used, and in the new version changed, COM component. As this was not overwritten in the renewed installation, the application only partially ran, because the older version of the COM component already installed on the target computer did not implement the required interface. Save yourself this trouble.

Update dependency files of components you have developed yourself

If your application uses class libraries you have written yourself (ActiveX code components) or controls, you should still ensure in every case that the dependency file of these components is up to date. This dependency file defines which DLLs and COM components your components depend on. The Package and Deployment Wizard uses this file in order to recognize additional files which have to be installed. So in the first instance produce possibly a new dependency file with the package and deployment wizard for these components. The procedure for creating such a file is the same as for normal installation, only at stage 3 of the wizard you specify that you want to produce a dependency file instead of a package.

Produce an EXE file

Then produce an EXE file in order to be able to smooth out any existing problems. The package and deployment wizard is certainly in a position to compile the EXE file by VB remote control, but the errors that occur if the EXE file cannot be compiled are not particularly meaningful.

Storing the correct MDAC version for applications that use ADO

If your application uses ADO, the package and deployment wizard add the file MDAC_TYPE.EXE to the package from the folder \Wizards\PDWizard\Redist in the VB folder. If you have updated to a newer MDAC version after the installation of Visual Basic, in every case you have to copy the new MDAC_TYPE.EXE into this folder. If you forget to do this, your application will refer for example to the *Microsoft ActiveX Data Objects 2.5 Library*, but on the target computer only the *Microsoft ActiveX Data Objects 2.0 Library* will be installed.

11.2 The Package and Deployment Wizard

You start the Package and Deployment Wizard ideally via the corresponding add-in which you have to initially integrate using the add-in manager. Alternatively you can start the wizard using the entry in the VB file in the Start menu, then however you must specify the project file.

After starting the wizard it nearly always tells you that you have to save the project. So in this dialog therefore click Yes, to save the project.

Stage 1

At the first stage you can choose between three different options (Fig. 11.1).

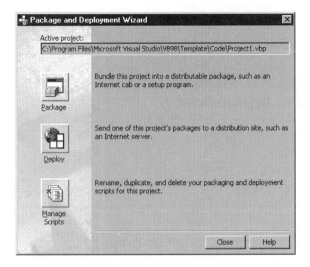

Figure 11.1 *Stage 1 of the Package and Deployment Wizard*

Using the Package button you produce a normal or Internet version[1]. The Deploy button leads into a dialog where you can either copy a previously produced installation version into a directory on the hard disk or in the network or send it to a web server folder (for Internet installation). Via Manage Scripts you can manage previously saved package scripts. All settings are saved in a package script, which you implement when creating the installation version.

---

1. For an Internet installation, you usually install ActiveX components used in HTML files. Reference is made to this component in an OBJECT tag in the HTML file. In addition there is a description in the OBJECT tag of where to find (on which URL) the installation version of the component. The URL stands for a folder that is itemized as a web folder on the web server. You send the installation version of the components to this folder.

Click the Package button. Following this the wizard almost always reports that different project files are newer than the executable file (no wonder when the wizard itself has saved these files previously) and the executable file should be compiled once again. If you have carried out compilation shortly before yourself, you do not need to compile again. If you are unsure, compile once again using the Yes button.

Stage 2

At the second stage you can select from a list a package script that has already been created. (Fig. 11.2).

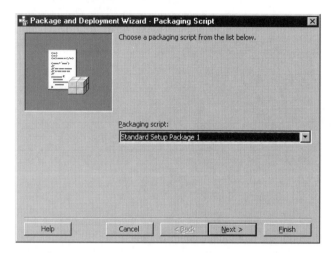

Figure 11.2 *Stage 2 of the Package and Deployment Wizard*

In the last stage of the wizard you can save the settings into an available or new packaging script. If at stage 2 you select this packaging script when you next produce an installation version, you do not have to redo the settings. Management of package scripts is project-related. When you first create an installation version there is still no script at your disposal.

Stage 3

At stage 3 you specify whether you want to produce a normal installation version or a dependency file (Fig. 11.3).

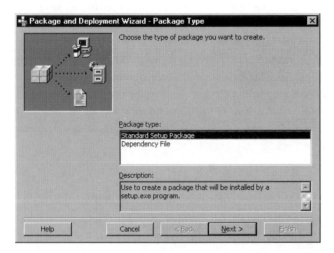

Figure 11.3 *Stage 3 of the Package and Deployment Wizard*

If you bundle a COM component, the `Internet package` option is added to the package types. Normal EXE files cannot be bundled for Internet installation. The package type defines what the wizard produces (Table 11.1).

Package type	Meaning
Standard setup package	This option results in the creation of a normal installation program for normal applications (EXE files), ActiveX controls, ActiveX code components and ActiveX documents.
Internet package	This type of package is used for ActiveX server and ActiveX documents (and for this reason is only available there). It is used to produce a CAB file that can be stored on an Internet server so ActiveX objects can be used on HTML pages. When the HTML page is called, the ActiveX server is automatically installed as required on the client's computer from this CAB file.
Dependency file	This package type results in the production of a dependency file. You will find more information on this below.

Table 11.1 *Package types of the Package and Deployment Wizard*

The dependency file

A dependency file is always required whenever an application is going to be installed as part of another application. This file with the ending DEP (Dependency File) receives the same name as the application. From this file the Package and Deployment Wizard recognizes which files are needed for the secondary application. If for example you write an ActiveX control that uses different references and its own Help file and you use this control in a normal EXE file, with the help of the Package and Deployment Wizard you create a dependency file for the ActiveX control. If you produce an installation version for the EXE application, the Package and Deployment Wizard uses this dependency file and adds to the installation version the additional necessary files (in this example in particular the files required for the references and the Help file).

Stage 4

At stage 4 you specify the folder where you want to produce the package (Fig. 11.4).

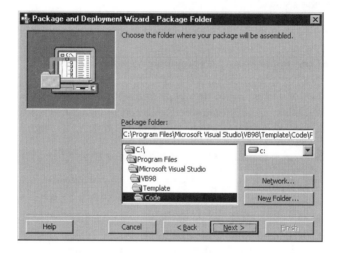

Figure 11.4 *Stage 4 of the Package and Deployment Wizard*

If you click on Next, as shown in Fig. 11.5, a message appears that the folder cannot be found.

Figure 11.5 *The package folder cannot be found*

Click on Yes to create the package folder.

Stage 5

At the next stage the wizard displays the files that will be installed with your application and gives you the opportunity to add files (Fig. 11.6).

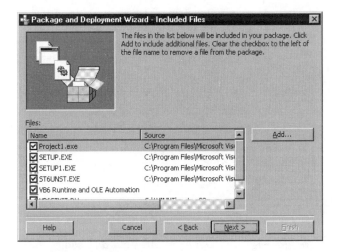

Figure 11.6 *Stage 5 of the Package and Deployment Wizard for adding files*

Even if it is possible you should not deselect any files here otherwise there is a risk that your application will not run on the target computer. Sometimes you have to add your own Help files, Ini files, picture files, etc. Besides this you will possibly have to add the EXE or DLL file of COM components that your application uses. As a rule the wizard automatically finds the COM components your application is referring to and enters these into the list. If however you use a COM component in your application without reference (via CreateObject), you have to add this manually. However, with applications such as Microsoft Word as the COM component for instance, you will have to refrain from doing this as installation will certainly fail and is illegal.

Stage 6

At stage 6 you select whether you want to produce a single CAB file or several. If you produce several CAB files, you can deploy these on disks. For both variants installation by hard disk or CD can follow.

Stage 7

At this stage you can simply specify the installation title. SETUP.EXE announces after the start "Welcome to the *xyz* installation program", where *xyz* is the name of the installation program.

Stage 8

At stage 8 you can specify in the Start menu in which group the application is being initialized (Fig. 11.7).

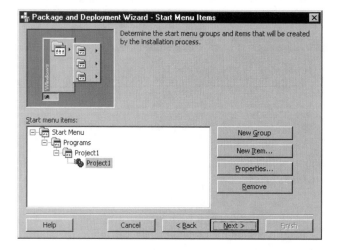

Figure 11.7 *Stage 8 of the Package and Deployment Wizard to select the Start menu items*

Here you can initialize further sub-folders (New Group) and in all these folders set up file references (New Element). So for example you can add to the Start menu references to a Help or Readme file.

Stage 9

At stage 9 you can determine the place of installation for all the files being installed (Fig. 11.8).

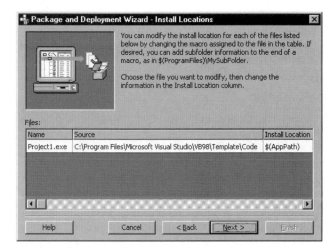

Figure 11.8 *Stage 9 of the Package and Deployment Wizard for selecting the places of installation*

Normally very little should be changed here. You have to possibly change the place of installation for files added subsequently or for some COM components. COM components are normally saved in the system directory (`$(WinSys-Path)`), the wizard however often wants to file them in the application directory (`$(AppPath)`). Since COM components are normally used by several applications there can be problems later with de-installation if the component is saved in the application directory.

Stage 10

At this stage you can select which files are to be installed as *shared files*. The wizard lists here anyway only files that are not being installed as shared files.

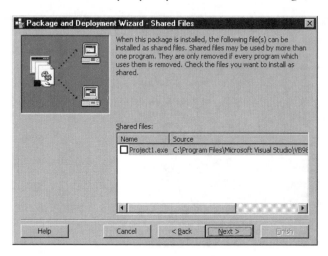

Figure 11.9 *Stage 10 of the Package and Deployment Wizard for the selection of shared files*

You can usually confidently ignore the files listed here. Your application and all associated files (Ini file, Help, etc.) cannot be installed at all as a shared file. The MDAC_Typ.ExEfile that is always associated with installation whenever your application refers to ADO is itself an installation version (of ADO) and for this reason cannot be installed as a shared file either. COM components that appear in the list should simply be marked as shared file.

Stage 11

In the last stage you can save your settings in a package script. Simply enter a new name when you create the first package. When you have selected a package script at the first stage you can select this and overwrite with any possible new settings.

11.3 Problems with Setup

Setup of VB applications unfortunately does not always run smoothly. You should be prepared for some problems and make the user aware of possible problems.

Sometimes it is necessary to restart Windows

The user starts setup by executing the file SETUP.EXE. Setup runs to the known standard. Often Setup reports before installation however that some system files on the target system have not been updated and have to be replaced. The user must confirm with OK after installation of these files to restart Windows and afterwards run SETUP.EXE again. Users often forget to re-run SETUP.EXE after restart. So refer to this in the program documentation. In this case Microsoft could have simply written SETUP.EXE into the key *RunOnce* in the registry, so that Restart Windows call would have taken place automatically.

Setup from a directory with a long name

Whenever setup is started from a directory with a long name (around 200 characters) or from a folder which has several folders higher in the hierarchy, setup often reports that a file has not been found and then aborts. With installation from a sub-folder, which has several folders higher in the hierarchy, Windows will crash completely. So only run setup from folders with a few subordinate folders and with names that are not too long.

Installation of MDAC in Windows 95

If you use ADO in your application for data access, the Microsoft Data Access Components are automatically accepted into Setup in the form of the MDAC_TYPE.EXE file. During installation Setup calls this file and in so doing automatically calls the MDAC Setup as well. Unfortunately the MDAC Setup in Windows 95 requires the previous installation of DCOM 95 or DCOM 98. If DCOM 95/98 is not installed on the computer, the installation of the MDAC components fails *without error message*. You can tell that the installation has been unsuccessful simply because the MDAC Setup is carried out considerably more quickly. You therefore must ensure that before installing your application the target computer has DCOM95 or DCOM98 installed. Unfortunately DCOM 95 is not integrated into the MDAC Setup. You can find DCOM on the Visual Basic CD or you can download the updated version from the Microsoft website. Indicate in the installation instructions that the user has to install DCOM *before* your application. Alternatively you can intercept error 429 "Object creation not possible by ActiveX component" in your project when you first make a connection and inform the user that MDAC in Windows 95 must be installed before DCOM 98, as the following example demonstrates:

```
Private Sub Form_Load
 ' Try to make ADO connection
 On Error Resume Next
 Set mconn = New Connection
```

```
If Err.Number = 429 Then
    ' Error 'object creation not possible by ActiveX
    ' component' produced if
    ' MDAC incorrectly installed
    MsgBox "The Microsoft Data Access Components (MDAC) " & _
            " necessary for the application " & _
            "are incorrectly installed. " & _
            "Install MDAC by " & _
            "calling file MDAC_Typ.exe." & _
            "under Windows 95 you have to" & _
            "install DCOM 98 beforehand.", vbCritical
    End
ElseIf Err.Number <> 0 Then
    ' All other errors are trapped by
    ' normal error handling
    GoTo ErrHandler ' The only! exception for a Goto
End If
```

You should therefore always supply the files MDAC_TYPE.EXE and DCOM98.EXE with your setup. With MDAC_TYPE.EXE you should remember that this has to be located in a separate folder. After decompressing the archive held in the Exe file, the SETUP.EXE file is called automatically. If MDAC_TYPE.EXE is stored in the same folder as the installation version of your application, the wrong setup is called (i.e. the one for your application).

Error "Cannot start Main Setup Program" with repeated installation

This error appears mainly when an older installation has been aborted and therefore the setup files are left on the target computer. Look in the Windows directory for CAB files that belong to your application and delete them. Likewise you should delete the folder MSFTQWS.PDW in the Temp folder, if present. Then you should check again whether the file VB6STKIT.DLL in the system directory and the file ST6UNST.EXE in the Windows directory have a size of 0 bytes. If this is the case, delete these files. Setup should then work.

Other causes for this error can be a defective CAB file or hardware-specific problems. You will find a detailed description of this problem in Knowledgebase article Q216231.

The actual setup is not executed by the SETUP.EXE file. This file simply sees that the necessary files for the file SETUP1.EXE are copied and starts SETUP1.EXE. The actual setup is executed by this application, which is written in VB. This setup is available in the source code as a Visual Basic project in the directory \Wizards\Pdwizard\Setup1\ in the VB folder. If you want to adapt the setup you can use this project. If you simply want adaptations for a particular setup and not for all setups, you should simply copy the complete project, recreate the EXE file after the amendments, compress this with COMPRESS.EXE and copy the folder to your installation. The package and deployment wizard uses the compiled SETUP1.EXE from the \Wizards\Pdwizard\ folder as standard for all new installation versions.

The actual adapting process is not going to be discussed here. You only need to know that installation is carried out mainly in Form_Load of the form *frmSetup1*. You will find information on adapting the SETUP1.EXE on the Microsoft website when you search for "Installation Options".

Tip The Setup project is somewhat "buggy" and does not allow compilation. In my version I forgot to put an inverted comma in front of the ("Do nothing") comment and the End Select was missing from the Select Case instruction.

Appendix

A.1 Important key combinations

General

F5	Start application
F8	Execute single step (in Pause Mode)
(⇑) F8	Execute procedure step (step over procedures; in Pause Mode)
Ctrl Pause	Stop program
(⇑) F5	Restart program
Ctrl L	Calls the call list (only in Pause Mode)
Ctrl G	Calls the Immediate window (only in Pause Mode)

Module window

F2	Displays the Object Browser
(↑) F2	Jumps to the source text of the procedure on whose name the cursor currently stands (if present)
Ctrl Arrow ↓	Shows the next procedure
Ctrl Arrow ↑	Shows the previous procedure
F9	Set/reset breakpoint
F3	Under Edit | Find: find next match
(↑) F3	Under Edit | Find: find previous match

Design window

(¦) Ctrl + *Letter*	Jump into the properties window and onto the first property of the current control that begins with the letter
F7	View code window
Ctrl + *Click*	Add a control to the current selection
Click + Drag	Select several controls at once
F4	Display Properties window (only during design stage)

Properties window

F4	Changes to Properties window
Alt F6	Switches between the Properties window and the Form window
(¦) Ctrl + *Letter*	Jump into the properties window and onto the first property of the current control that begins with the letter
Double-click	Set the next possible value of a property that only allows particular values

A.2 Booklist

Appleman, Dan:
Visual Basic 5.0 Programmers Guide to the Win32 API.
Ziff Davis Press. New York 1997.

Chappel, David:
Understanding ActiveX and OLE
Microsoft Press, Germany. Unterschleißheim 1996.

Füssel, Thomas:
Product discussions: Printing (preview) components. (Produktbesprechung: Druck(Vorschau)-Komponenten.)
In basicpro 5/99. Steingräber Fachverlag. Kiel 1999.

Kofler, Michael:
Visual Basic 6. Programming Techniques, Databases, Internet. (Visual Basic 6. Programmiertechniken, Datenbanken, Internet.)
Addison Wesley-Longman. Bonn 1999.

McKinney, Bruce:
Hardcore Visual Basic 5.0: Secrets, Short-cuts and Solutions for Windows Programming without C.
Microsoft Press. Redmond, Washington 1997.

McKinney, Bruce:
Saying Goodbye to Hardcore Visual Basic.
www.vb-zone.com/upload/free/features/vbpj/1999/mckinneytoc.asp

Mey, Andreas:
The 1x1 of OLE Drag & Drop. (Das 1x1 des OLE Drag & Drop.)
In basicpro 5/99. Steingräber Fachverlag. Kiel 1999.

Pattison, Ted:
COM and MTS Programming with Visual Basic. Programming Distributed Applications with COM and Microsoft Visual Basic.
Microsoft Press, Germany. Unterschleißheim 1999.

Thayer, Rob:
Visual Basic 6 Unleashed.
Sams. 1998.

Index